Ida—
Thanks for everything —

Measurement Issues *and* Assessment *for* Teaching Quality

Measurement Issues
and Assessment *for*
Teaching Quality

DREW H. GITOMER
ETS, Princeton, NJ

EDITOR

Los Angeles • London • New Delhi • Singapore • Washington DC

For information:

Sage Publications, Inc.
2455 Teller Road
Thousand Oaks,
    California 91320
E-mail: order@sagepub.com

Sage Publications Ltd.
1 Oliver's Yard
55 City Road
London, EC1Y 1SP
United Kingdom

Sage Publications India Pvt. Ltd.
B 1/I 1 Mohan Cooperative
    Industrial Area
Mathura Road, New Delhi 110 044
India

Sage Publications
    Asia-Pacific Pte. Ltd.
33 Pekin Street #02–01
Far East Square
Singapore 048763

Printed in the United States of America

Library of Congress Cataloging-in-Publication Data

ETS Invitational Conference (2007 : San Francisco, Calif.)
Measurement issues and assessment for teaching quality/edited by Drew H. Gitomer.
    p. cm.
Includes bibliographical references and index.
ISBN 978-1-4129-6143-1 (cloth)
ISBN 978-1-4129-6144-8 (pbk.)
    1. Teachers—Rating of—United States—Congresses. 2. Teachers—Training of—United States—Congresses. I. Gitomer, Drew H. II. Title.
LB2838.E84 2009
371.14′4—dc22   2008022449

This book is printed on acid-free paper.

08   09   10   11   12   10   9   8   7   6   5   4   3   2   1

Acquisitions Editor:	Steve Wainwright
Editorial Assistant:	Julie McNall
Production Editor:	Kristen Gibson
Copy Editor:	Sarah J. Duffy
Typesetter:	C&M Digitals (P) Ltd.
Proofreader:	Jeff Bryant
Indexer:	Diggs Publication Services
Cover Designer:	Glenn Vogel
Marketing Manager:	Nichole M. Angress

Contents

Acknowledgments   vii
Introduction   1

SECTION I MEASURING TEACHING
QUALITY FOR PROFESSIONAL ENTRY   7

1. Measuring Teacher Quality for Professional Entry   8
   Suzanne M. Wilson

2. Hiring for Teacher Quality at the District Level:
   Lessons From The New Teacher Project   30
   Timothy Daly and David Keeling

3. Professionalizing the Occupation of Teaching
   in a Time of Transition   47
   Alan D. Bersin and Mary Vixie Sandy

   Broadening the Vision of Professional
   Entry—Synthesis of Section I   70
   Ida M. Lawrence and Drew H. Gitomer

SECTION II MEASURING TEACHING QUALITY IN PRACTICE   79

4. Measuring Teacher Quality in Practice   80
   Deborah Loewenberg Ball and Heather C. Hill

5. The Policy Uses and Policy Validity of Value-Added
   and Other Teacher Quality Measures   99
   Douglas N. Harris

6. Approximations of Teacher Quality and Effectiveness:
View From the State Education Agency   **131**
Mitchell D. Chester and Susan Tave Zelman

Measuring Teacher and Teaching Quality:
Considerations and Next Steps—Synthesis of Section II   **150**
Stephen Lazer

SECTION III MEASURING TEACHING QUALITY IN CONTEXT   159

7. Mapping the Terrain of Teacher Quality   **160**
Arturo Pacheco

8. Measuring Instruction for Teacher Learning   **179**
Mary Kay Stein and Lindsay Clare Matsumura

9. Opportunity to Teach: Teacher Quality in Context   **206**
Gloria Ladson-Billings

Crisp Measurement and Messy Context: A Clash of
Assumptions and Metaphors—Synthesis of Section III   **223**
Drew H. Gitomer

Assessment *of* Teaching or Assessment *for* Teaching?
Reflections on the Invitational Conference   **234**
Lee S. Shulman

Author Index   **245**

Subject Index   **250**

About the Contributors   **255**

Acknowledgments

This book is dedicated to the memory of Carla Denise Cooper. Carla was instrumental in organizing the October 2007 ETS Invitational Conference that provided the basis for this volume. More than that, she was a dear friend and colleague who will be missed for her spiritual, intellectual, and administrative gifts. Carla lost a long battle with cancer in June 2008.

My heartfelt thanks to Michael Nettles, for inviting me to organize the conference and providing wise counsel and outstanding support throughout and to Jane Cairns, for providing exceptional administrative and logistical support to all conference participants. I am especially grateful to the staff from Communications and Public Affairs for ensuring that every detail of our conference was attended to. I also sincerely appreciate the steadfast support of the ETS Invitational and related research by ETS President Kurt Landgraf.

Of course, this volume represents the outstanding intellectual contributions from the authors, panelists, and moderators. I thank everyone for making this such a personally rewarding experience. I am also grateful for everyone's patience, promptness, and pleasantness throughout. It has been a joy to work with people of this caliber.

Finally, I am forever grateful to Evelyn Fisch for overseeing the preparation of this volume. Her editorial expertise enabled her to provide support to me and all the authors with equal skill, as well as to effectively communicate with our editorial and production staff at Sage Publications.

Introduction

Why a Conference on Measurement Issues and Teaching Assessment?

T wenty years ago, Educational Testing Service (ETS) held its Invitational Conference and called it "New Directions for Teacher Assessment" (ETS, 1989). If there was a dominant theme, it was that assessment could support the development of the profession of teaching as well as the professional development of teachers. At the time, Lee Shulman, Jim Kelly, and Claire Pelton introduced assessment models that would provide the foundation for the National Board for Professional Teaching Standards (NBPTS). Carol Dwyer described a new generation of teacher assessments for licensure that were based on evolving conceptions of teacher knowledge. Linda Darling-Hammond, David Berliner, Adam Urbanski, and Judith Lanier all considered how assessment practices that engaged discussions of mentors and teachers around teacher performance could support the professional development of both preservice and inservice teachers.

Certainly, the promises made by the contributors to that volume were kept. Teacher licensure tests are now used in virtually every state as a means of ensuring sufficient knowledge to enter into the profession. Over 60,000 teachers have received National Board Certification nationally. Teacher education institutions regularly use assessment practices to inform and improve the practices of their students. Additionally, a number of states have instituted, or are considering the use of, assessment to support the mentoring and development of beginning teachers.

And yet, as prescient as these authors were, they could not have anticipated the impact of the emerging accountability movement in education and the

1

role that teacher assessment would play. Nor did they have much to say about the methodological issues surrounding the use of teacher assessment scores in the evaluation of teachers and policies. The primary focus was on assessment designs and their use in supporting the development of teachers, with only brief consideration of the political context of teacher assessment.

But there was not complete silence. To be sure, Michael Timpane, in his closing remarks, posed the fundamental question that provides a common point of departure for all who are concerned with teacher assessment: Will improving teacher assessment improve the education of children? His answer, "it all depends," was the early warning signal that provided the motivation for the current conference. Timpane cautioned that the ultimate influence of assessments would depend on their place in a larger set of educational policies; their connections to theories of teaching and learning; the content and process of their design, administration, and interpretation; and the actions that are supported or inhibited by their presence. Although the context of teacher assessment has changed dramatically during these two decades, Timpane foreshadowed a set of questions that are as germane today as they were in the 1980s.

In this era of accountability, teacher assessment has a very different place in considerations of educational reform than it did twenty years ago. For one, demonstrations of content knowledge by all teachers, typically through licensure assessments, are now legislated by the federal government through the Highly Qualified Teacher Provision of the No Child Left Behind Act. NBPTS has moved from a thoughtful design to a full-fledged program that has significant presence in a number of states. Finally, assessment components have been embedded as professional development tools for preservice, induction, and inservice stages of the teaching career.

But perhaps the biggest transformation has been the intense focus on educational outcomes, and particularly the political argument that teachers are the primary agent for determining those outcomes. This perspective has had far-reaching implications for how teachers are assessed and how that information is used. Emerging evaluation systems are defining teacher quality, at least to some significant extent, in terms of student learning gains that can be demonstrated on large-scale achievement tests. Increasingly, these definitions of teacher quality are being considered with respect to compensation and pay-for-performance systems.

Policies related to teacher preparation and credentials are being similarly evaluated in terms of student achievement trends. Numerous studies are being conducted that attempt to relate aspects of teacher credentials, program preparation characteristics, and educational practices to student outcomes. These studies are being used to help formulate educational policies at federal, state, and local levels.

Given this range of uses for teacher assessment, Timpane's question—Will improving teacher assessment improve the education of children?—is even more challenging than it appeared to be when first asked. This is because every part of the question is subject to interpretation brought about by differing conceptions of teaching, assessment, education, and their respective improvement.

Take, for example, the idea of teacher assessment. Is the assessment intended to warrant some level of expertise such as that which is used for licensure? Or is it intended to provide evidence that can be used to support professional development efforts? Or is the goal of assessment to assign some relative designation of merit that can be used in an employee evaluation system, including the removal of teachers from the school setting? Given these disparate goals, the criteria differ dramatically in how one might determine what would constitute an improvement in teacher assessment.

Now consider the idea of improving the education of children. Is this to be solely defined by outcome measures on state achievement tests? Are other measures of cognitive development to be considered? What about the development of social and emotional well-being? Once decisions are made about useful outcomes, what is the maturity of our methods to determine the impact of a particular teacher on a group of students?

The heightened attention to teacher assessment, together with the broader set of purposes it was beginning to serve, provided the basis for the 2007 ETS Invitational Conference and this volume. But given the intellectual and political complexity of these issues, it was not a simple task to organize a conference that would be provocative, illuminating, and coherent. As the organizer, it was important for me to ensure that the conference allowed the issues to surface and that practitioners, policymakers, and researchers from different perspectives confronted issues together, rather than talking among themselves in small, like-minded communities of practice. I came up with a few different organizational schemes for the conference, and although I was confident that we could recruit provocative and illuminating contributors, coherence proved to be more of a challenge. This needed to be more than a collection of well-crafted, independent papers. I needed help to find a meaningful direction. In the spirit of searching for direction, I did what so many before me had done. I went to California.

It was at a series of meetings in the Bay Area that the final structure of the conference came together. I had the wonderful fortune to be able to call on Lloyd Bond, Linda Darling-Hammond, and Lee Shulman to help give shape to the conference organization, to avoid the inclination to include too much, and to frame the most important questions. Margaret Gaston was a tremendous help as well in providing a keen sense of the California landscape, where the conference was going to be held.

The goal was to have a conference in which we could address a small set of highly important questions with some degree of depth. We wanted to be sure to include perspectives from researchers and practitioners, and we wanted to have the opportunity for interchange as well. With these considerations in mind, the conference was organized around three central questions.

The first section of this volume addresses measurement challenges that surround assessment of individuals for entry into the profession. Suzanne Wilson sets the stage with a thorough and insightful overview of teacher assessment, challenging both researchers and practitioners to better align our understanding of teacher effectiveness with assessment practices. Timothy Daly and David Keeling describe an ambitious model of assessment used for selection of individuals into The New Teachers Project. This model goes well beyond traditional measures for entry into the profession, giving attention to personal and social dimensions as well as demanding indicators of academic competence. Alan Bersin and Mary Sandy then offer the policymaker's perspective, explaining how a comprehensive model of assessment, grounded in theory, can support the professional development of teachers. Drawing on the designs they contributed to in California, they offer ways in which states and teacher education institutions can use assessment within a coordinated framework to support a coherent vision of effective teaching that begins in preservice education and moves through the early stages of professional entry.

The second section moves from issues of entry into the profession to challenges of measuring teacher quality in practice. What are the challenges to developing assessments of teaching that will contribute to a more effective educational system? What assessment characteristics will support the professional development of practicing teachers? Deborah Ball and Heather Hill present their body of work, which has been instrumental in helping us understand the nature of teaching expertise. They further illustrate how assessments of knowledge and practice can be developed from deep theory of teaching. The next two chapters confront current methods for considering the effectiveness of practicing teachers. Doug Harris provides a detailed, nontechnical, and highly accessible perspective on what has become a tremendous force in the evaluation of teachers: the use of value-added methods. He defines the basic assumptions behind different uses of these models and carefully analyzes a number of their limitations. Mitchell Chester and Susan Zelman then provide another state policy perspective, this time from their work as chief educational officers in Ohio.[1] As with the case of California, Chester and Zelman provide a comprehensive model of teacher evaluation that is grounded in strong theory and has as its ultimate purpose the improvement of educational outcomes through the strengthening of the teacher force in Ohio.

Most models of teacher assessment, whether for entry into the profession or for considerations of quality in practice, consider teacher effectiveness as a construct resulting from a set of attributes that define a particular teacher. On the face of it though, this appears to be a simplistic notion, for teachers' work, like all work, is done within a context. This context includes students, colleagues, school principals and other administrators, and communities. What are the implications for assessment of teacher quality if the conception is broadened to incorporate context? The answer is not obvious, but it provides the basis for the last section of the conference and proceedings.

Arturo Pacheco begins by carefully offering an explication of relevant context to be considered in any claims about teacher effectiveness. He draws on research as well as his own experiences as a teacher and NBPTS board member to build a model of context that begins with interpersonal relationships within a classroom and moves on to those that involve much larger systems, all of which affect the quality and qualities of teaching. Mary Kay Stein and Lindsay Clare Matsumura consider the contextual factors that must be understood to make sense of any assessment of teachers' instruction. Their work is focused on assessment as it supports the professional development of teachers in practice. Gloria Ladson-Billings introduces the concept of *opportunity to teach,* making clear that the observed quality of any teacher's actions only can be interpreted within a framework that attends to the conditions and contexts within which a teacher functions.

Each of the three segments of the conference was enhanced by brief reactions from panels of outstanding colleagues who also have thought about these issues. Some small sense of their contributions is represented in the section summaries that conclude each section of the volume. The volume closes with a wonderful summary and call to action by Lee Shulman.

The title of this volume owes a major debt to a key message that comes through in so many of the chapters and is summarized by Shulman. Originally, the title of the volume was going to be *Measurement Issues and the Assessment of Teacher Quality.* But we are reminded that whether to improve teaching and education through policy or professional development, it is essential to keep at the forefront two principles. First, the goal of educational assessment is not simply to serve an accounting function. It has to satisfy a higher criterion—to improve educational quality. Second, teaching happens within a highly complex social system, to which the teacher brings a set of skills, knowledge, and attributes. The ultimate quality of teaching depends on the interactions of teachers and students within this complex system. Within such a frame, the goal of assessment is not simply to assess the quality of the teacher, but the quality of the *teaching,* with the express purpose of improving teaching and student learning. Thanks to the insights of the contributors to this volume, and particularly Lee Shulman, the title of the volume was changed to *Measurement Issues and Assessment for Teaching Quality.*

Note

1. In 2008, Chester was named the commissioner of elementary and secondary education of the Massachusetts Department of Education.

Reference

Educational Testing Service. (1989). *New directions for teacher assessment: Proceedings of the 1988 ETS Invitational Conference.* Princeton, NJ: Author.

Section I

Measuring Teaching Quality for Professional Entry

1

Measuring Teacher Quality for Professional Entry

Suzanne M. Wilson

Director of the Center for the Scholarship of Teaching and Professor of Teacher Education, Michigan State University

Teacher quality has become a central concern of policymakers and educators alike. This is not new; there is a long history of rhetoric concerning the need for well-prepared teachers and the central role that teachers play in student learning. Nor is the intense interest in the quality and character of teacher preparation new. Discussions of who should be a teacher and how we should determine the character and quality of our nation's teachers have a history almost as long as that of our public school system (e.g., Bestor, 1953; Conant, 1964; Koerner, 1963; Lynd, 1953; Ravitch, 2000; Smith, 1949). Throughout this age-old discussion of how to reform teacher preparation and certification, there have been those inside of the system of teacher preparation attempting to alternatively improve and protect it, and critics attempting to alternatively improve and dismantle it. The content of those discussions has been well documented, both in historical documents and in contemporary analyses of those debates (Cochran-Smith & Fries, 2001; Grossman, 2008; Wilson & Tamir, 2008; Zeichner, 2003).

This chapter focuses on the current landscape of discussions of and research on how we measure teacher quality for purposes of professional entry. The chapter is organized around three questions: What do we currently measure? What are the challenges of such measurements? What would it take to create a different system of measurements for initial entry?

Current Measures of Teacher Quality for Professional Entry

How and what do we currently measure in terms of quality at entry? Before answering that question, I note two issues that complicate how this question can be authoritatively answered. First, decisions about teacher licensure and certification are local decisions, and there is considerable variability. Thus, here I paint a broad-strokes portrait of current practices in an attempt to characterize generally how beginning teachers are assessed when they enter the profession.

Second, what counts as entry also varies. Should we define entry as the moment that a new teacher is given responsibility as a teacher of record? Or should entry be defined as the moment that a new teacher is certified to teach? Given the plethora of structural approaches to teacher preparation—both within and across what some label as "traditional" and "alternative" preparation programs—it is very difficult to pinpoint a clear entry point. Participants in the Teaching Fellows Program or Teach for America become teachers of record while they are completing requirements to obtain certification. Participants in year-long internship programs may have extended opportunities to take responsibility for one or several classes, but they do not become teachers of record until program completion. Prospective teachers in programs that "front load" university-based coursework may have many field experiences in schools, but they are not fully certified to enter the profession until graduation. Thus, professional entry has no clear beginning or end. This presents considerable measurement problems when attempting to assess either a teacher's quality or a program's effectiveness. Rather than stipulate an answer to the "When is entry?" question, here I array the varied measures that are currently used for the purposes of ensuring teacher quality upon entry.

So what do we measure? Many things, for while some might simplify the question by pointing to summative measures that are used at the end of various programs, the reality is that prospective teachers are assessed for their quality at multiple decision points along the way. They are often required to complete some kind of preparation program accredited by state or national entities. Within those programs, prospective teachers must meet embedded state requirements relating to various experiences and subjects. Most states require some sort of field experience prior to professional entry; many also require secondary teachers to learn to teach reading across content areas and elementary teachers to take courses in the teaching of reading. Prospective teachers are also often required to complete relevant college majors or minors in disciplines or in education, which are often associated with some minimum grade point average (GPA). These requirements become checklists of boxes required for the granting of state certification and are, therefore, important components of how we assess entering teacher quality.

Many states also require basic skills tests and subject matter tests. Given the recent rebirth of interest in teacher tests, it is difficult to get stable and up-to-date statistics on the use of such tests (Wilson & Youngs, 2005). In 1998, more states used basic skills tests than any other kind of test; 38 states required teachers to pass such tests for initial licensure. Fourteen states required some test of general knowledge, typically presumed to be an assessment of a liberal arts education. Twenty-one states required tests of subject matter knowledge. ETS's Praxis II tests included 126 subject matter tests, and National Evaluation Systems (NES) has developed more than 360 tests (K. J. Mitchell, Robinson, Plake, & Knowles, 2001). But these data are not representative of changes that have taken place since the passage of No Child Left Behind's requirements for highly qualified teachers. Currently, we know that virtually every state requires content knowledge testing, yet we lack accurate information as to what kinds of tests are used.

As already suggested, measures—in this case, teacher tests—are used at different points in a prospective teacher's journey to licensure (see Table 1.1). For example, basic skills tests are used at both program entry and exit, and subject matter tests can be used before someone is allowed to student teach, or when applying for licensure.

Teacher education programs use other measures as well: background and fingerprint checks; teaching philosophy or goal statements; interviews designed to assess a prospective teacher's commitment or character; and other program-specific program admission or exit instruments, including

Table 1.1   Number of States Using Initial Teacher Licensure Tests, 1998–1999

	Basic skills	Subject matter knowledge	Pedagogical knowledge	Subject-specific pedagogical knowledge
Admission to teacher education	19	3	0	0
Eligibility for student teaching or degree conferral	1	3	2	2
Licensure	18	25	26	5
Total	38	31	28	7

SOURCE: Mitchell, Robinson, Plake, & Knowles, 2001.

portfolios, locally developed tests, interviews, and field observation instruments (see Figure 1.1 for a representative list of such requirements).

In sum, on the way to gaining a credential, a prospective teacher will take one or more standardized tests administered by the state or a testing house; submit written samples of work; be observed and/or interviewed by teachers, university staff, and principals; submit proof of moral character, academic achievement, and—probably most often—seat time in various required classes or exposure to certain kinds of information. If one also considers the measures that are used to actually obtain employment, there are more interviews, observations, and often commercial hiring instruments (Metzger & Wu, in press).

Now let us consider the character of this panoply of measures. First, we might note that the portrait—across the variability of states' and local programs' decisions about what matters in teaching—is an incoherent *non-*system of assessments, measurements, and requirements that are treated as proxies for things that are deemed to matter.

Second, there is no national consensus about the expectations of what new teachers need to know or be able to demonstrate (that is, we do not agree on what matters), as reflected in the considerable variability across preparation programs (see, e.g., Shulman, 2005), assessment and accreditation systems (Wilson & Youngs, 2005), and debates about teacher education more generally (Cochran-Smith & Zeichner, 2005; Darling-Hammond & Bransford, 2005; Wilson & Tamir, 2008; Zeichner, 2003). You can see this both at the local level in arguments about whether university-based programs ought to have a monopoly on the certification and preparation or teachers as well as at the national level (e.g., Abell Foundation, 2001a, 2001b; Darling-Hammond, 2002; Darling-Hammond & Youngs, 2002). Of late, many have called for the careful examination of existing research evidence so as to examine the empirical evidence that might inform this discussion (Allen, 2003; Cochran-Smith & Zeichner, 2005; Darling-Hammond & Bransford, 2005; Wilson, Floden, & Ferrini-Mundy, 2001). But without consensus, the current landscape of measures includes those of subject matter knowledge, pedagogical and other forms of knowledge and skill, teaching experience, moral character, philosophical fit, and the like. Moreover, all of these are operationally defined in different ways, across different measures, in different contexts, using different metrics (norm-referenced tests, checklists, completion or attendance rates, seat time, local rubrics).

A third feature of the landscape is that few measures used have any demonstrated predictive validity. Although there is some evidence that teachers' verbal ability (as measured on a range of incomparable assessments) is associated with higher student achievement (Allen, 2003; U.S. Department of Education, 2002, 2003; Whitehurst, 2002), there is little to no evidence that any of the measures listed previously—GPA (in disciplinary classes or education classes), number of courses taken, scores on

Successful completion of some kind of "program"

College majors/minors in content and/or education (with associated GPA requirements)

Tests given in disciplinary departments

Program interviews for admissions

Application essays for admissions

ACT and SAT scores

Commercial basic skills tests

Norm-referenced, commercial subject matter knowledge tests

Successful field experience

Collaborating teacher or field supervisor rating based on observation scales or holistic scoring

Background checks

Fingerprinting

Teaching philosophy/goal statements

Portfolios

Lesson plans

Sample units

Observation checklists

Commercial hiring instruments

Program-specific admission instruments (e.g., prescreening interviews, tasks)

Figure 1.1   Sample Assessments and Proxies Currently Used

teacher tests, graduation from accredited institutions, successful completion of a commercially produced hiring instrument—predict either teacher performance or student achievement (Wilson & Youngs, 2005).

We can make other observations about the landscape as well. Some measures are generic and used across all teachers, no matter their subject matter or grade level experience; some are grade level—or subject matter—specific. Some measures are locally developed (organically growing out of the contexts in which they are used); others are offered by commercial vendors. Users tend to see the local measures as more meaningful and more aligned with their particular programs; generic measures are often seen as not well tailored to a program's view of what teachers need to know or be able to do.

In addition, measures are used by many stakeholders. Faculty in the disciplines administer their own (most often) locally developed and calibrated subject matter assessments; faculty in teacher education programs use their own assessments as well. States mandate the use of some tests; school districts use their own measures.

Thus, for any one teacher, the expectations for a beginning teacher's knowledge, skill, capacity, and development might be considerably different at different stages of entry into the profession and might be assessed with different instruments. Further, there is considerable blurring of boundaries of when assessments are used. An undergraduate major, for example, can be assessed through tests in disciplinary courses, which can be required for entry into or exit from a teacher education program. Professional education preparation can require basic skills tests at entry or exit, observations of teaching, or portfolios of teaching materials. *When* a prospective teacher encounters these varied assessments is not uniform within one school system or one state, and certainly is not uniform nationally. Blurring the boundaries further is the question of *who* does the assessing, for this also varies across contexts. The states and the testing industry are implicated, as are faculty in the disciplines and in schools/colleges of teacher preparation. K–12 school principals and teachers also can act as assessors for field experiences, teaching performances, portfolios, and the like (see Table 1.2).

Table 1.2   The Blurred Boundaries of Assessment

Assessments	Assessors
Undergraduate major (GPA) • assessments of content knowledge in individual classes • (sometimes) capstone experience **Can overlap with/precede/be concurrent with** Professional preparation, which can start or end with • basic skills tests, "dispositions" or "commitment" assessments • subject matter tests (which can align or not with undergrad major) • field experiences • portfolios **Can overlap with/precede/be concurrent with** Early career support, which can start or end with • field experiences • hiring instruments • portfolios	• Faculty in the disciplines who teach liberal arts and disciplinary content • Faculty in professional preparation programs • K–12 faculty who are mentors and collaborating teachers • Testing industry • The state

If things were not complicated enough, there can be as much variation within a local context as across contexts. For example, in any large urban school district, there can be new teachers entering the profession at different times from across 30 or more programs or pathways (see, e.g., Boyd et al., 2006). Hence, a cacophony of different measures and metrics are being used to assess readiness to enter teaching in one school district alone. Indeed, even in one school, new teachers who are more or less deemed ready for entry might be subjected to the same assessments at different times or different assessments at the same time.

Finally, given the size of the teaching force, many of the instruments used are blunt. Demonstrating that a prospective teacher has a major or minor in a subject area is a problematic proxy for subject matter knowledge. Required courses are considerably different across institutions of higher education, and grading norms and policies are equally varied. As proxies for contested categories of required knowledge and skill, habits and traits, most measures or proxies lack subtlety. Some would point out that some of the examples I offer here are neither assessments nor measures (e.g., seat time in a disciplinary major). But the fact of the matter is that we use many proxies as important placeholders for what we really want to measure, in this case, knowledge of the subject matter. We presume that historians, biologists, English professors, and mathematicians are using appropriate measures to decide whether their students are learning content. And that seat time—and the proxies such as GPA that go along with them—are important assessments experienced by new teachers.

In sum, describing the current landscape of the measures that are used to determine teacher quality upon professional entry is difficult given the extant local, institutional, state, and national variability. The myriad assessments and proxies used have varying degrees of technical sophistication, little predictive validity, and are a mixture of locally and commercially developed tools. They measure different kinds of knowledge, skill, and qualities, including subject matter knowledge, pedagogical knowledge, character, previous educational experience, and instructional behaviors, which are themselves conceptualized and defined by the measures used differently across local contexts. They are used by a range of actors, including but not limited to faculty in the disciplines, teacher educators, practicing teachers, field instructors, principals, and other school district personnel, many (if not most) of whom have no measurement expertise and little sense of the reliability or validity of the instruments they regularly use. Given this carnival of assessment, we face considerable challenges in pursuit of a system that is more rational, more efficient, and more focused on gathering responsible evidence concerning new teacher quality.

Current Challenges of Assessing Teacher Quality at Entry

CONCEPTUAL CHALLENGES

I have already noted one core conceptual problem: There exists little agreement on what exactly we should be assessing in terms of teacher quality; that is, we lack a widely recognized professional knowledge base for teaching. The current measures used tend to focus on three broad domains: content knowledge, other forms of professional knowledge and skill, and character. In terms of content knowledge, whereas everyone agrees that teachers ought to know the content they teach their students—which is a reasonably logical claim—there is no agreement in terms of what they ought to know about subject matter. As the National Research Council (2001) notes, "although studies of teachers' mathematical knowledge have not demonstrated a strong relationship between teachers' mathematical knowledge and their students' achievement, teachers' knowledge is still likely a significant factor in students' achievement. That crude measures of teacher knowledge, such as the number of mathematics courses taken, do not correlate positively with student performance data supports the need to study more closely the nature of the mathematical knowledge needed to teach and to measure it more sensitively" (p. 375).

For some time now, researchers have attempted to explain the differences between the content knowledge necessary to teach and the content knowledge of an academic major or minor (e.g., Ball, Lubienski, & Mewborn, 2001; Dewey, 1902; Grossman, 1990; Ma, 1999; Shulman, 1986, 1987). Most recent and of high visibility are the efforts of Deborah Ball and her colleagues. As Ball, Hill, and Bass (2005) explain, "we derived a practice-based portrait of what we call 'mathematical knowledge for teaching'—a kind of professional knowledge of mathematics different from that demanded by other mathematically intensive occupations, such as engineering, physics, accounting, or carpentry" (p. 17). Efforts like these highlight the fact that educators are perplexed that we have not been able to find stable, consistent, and clear relationships between measures of teacher subject matter knowledge with student achievement or any other indicator of teaching quality (e.g., Darling-Hammond, Berry, & Thoreson, 2001; Fetler, 1999; Floden & Meniketti, 2005; Goldhaber & Brewer, 2000, 2001; Monk, 1994; Wilson et al., 2001).

In terms of professional knowledge, the same is true. Over the years, there have been multiple attempts to argue for a conceptually coherent, comprehensive, plausible view of the knowledge and skills necessary for teaching. Research attempting to link different kinds of teaching knowledge to student learning remains unpersuasive. And although there have been attempts to argue that basic research on learning, children, schools, and the like serves as the appropriate basis for establishing the professional knowledge necessary for new teachers (Darling-Hammond & Bransford, 2005), there has yet to be a groundswell of support for that particular conceptualization. This is, in part, due to disagreements about the basis upon which anyone can make a claim that teachers need a certain kind of knowledge. Cochran-Smith (2004) argues that the difference is in the questions asked; the contributors to the Darling-Hammond and Bransford volume ask about relevant "basic and applied research that ought to serve as the foundation of the professional teacher education curriculum" (p. 115). The logic of this approach is that teachers ought to have basic knowledge in relevant fields, whether or not research has proven that such knowledge makes them better teachers.

Others search for empirical evidence that having basic knowledge leads to greater student achievement. For example, some skeptics of teacher preparation argue that until we have accumulated evidence like that represented in the National Reading Panel report about the effects of different instructional strategies on student achievement (National Institute of Child Health and Human Development, 2000), we ought not legislate professionally agreed–upon but not empirically proven professional knowledge for teachers. Skeptics also argue that teacher preparation programs not teaching that empirically tested knowledge for teachers (think here again of the National Reading Panel report) ought to be closed down (Walsh, Glaser, & Wilcox, 2006).

Differences do not stop there, for we also disagree about the character necessary for teaching. Some argue for background checks; others aver the need to make sure that teachers are disposed to believe that all children can learn and that they do not hold views that would prejudice them along lines of race, ethnicity, culture, gender, religion, language, sexuality, politics, and the like. Indeed, early attempts to assess teacher quality at entry focused almost entirely on character. Sedlak (2008) recounts that,

> like Massachusetts, most colonies authorized a variety of local actors—religious elders, prominent citizens, lay boards—to be responsible for finding and hiring teachers. Typically, these employers used informal approaches when making decisions about potential instructors. They relied on ministerial recommendations. They queried candidates about their beliefs and values. They assessed their physical strength and courage. They hired their relatives, with whom they were intimately familiar (p. 856).

It was not that long ago that school boards were in the business of populating the schools with their relatives. The nepotism that can result when uncles and aunts, friends and neighbors are allowed to decide—with idiosyncratic and personal metrics—who should be a teacher highlights the complexity of assessing teacher character. "Character" is alternatively discussed as rapport, drive, openness, empathy, and mission. And discussions of teacher character remain contentious today, as columnists swap anecdotes about how progressive educators systematically disenfranchise anyone with "conservative" views: "Many education schools discourage, even disqualify, prospective teachers who lack the correct 'disposition,' meaning those who do not embrace today's 'progressive' political catechism. Karen Siegfried had a 3.75 grade-point average at the University of Alaska Fairbanks, but after voicing conservative views, she was told by her education professors that she lacked the 'professional dispositions' teachers need. She is now studying to be an aviation technician" (Will, 2006, p. 98).

The recent controversy over whether the National Council for Accreditation of Teacher Education ought to mandate that teacher education programs teach and assess prospective teachers' "dispositions" is the most recent case of our national differences about requisite teacher character boiling over into the policy domain (Borko, Liston, & Whitcomb, 2007; Burant, Chubbuck, & Whipp, 2007; Wilkerson, 2006).

In sum, whether we consider the literature on necessary subject matter knowledge, professional knowledge and skill, or teacher dispositions and character, we suffer from a lack of conceptual clarity and agreement on what we ought to be assessing with the measures we use. Yet every measure used represents a view of good teaching or teacher, and so we operate within a system in which the measures used often do not and, given the lack of agreement about the domains described previously, cannot align with a coherent and collective normative view of the qualities necessary for entry into teaching.

A second conceptual challenge concerns the appropriate expectations for professional entry, that is, we lack agreement—either logical or empirically based—on the knowledge, skill, and character of *new* teachers. Although many might agree that much teaching wisdom is acquired through practice, we have a fairly vague sense of how to differentiate expectations for beginning teachers or well-launched beginners (Feinman-Nemser, 2001) and their more experienced colleagues. Typically, policymakers take standards for all practicing teachers and simply scale them back some, softening the language of expectations. The Interstate New Teacher Assessment and Support Consortium standards, for example, were developed by "backward mapping" from the standards for the National Board for Professional Teaching Standards. Danielson (n.d.) offers another example, proposing that there are four levels of teaching practice: unsatisfactory, basic, proficient, and distinguished. Thus, those assessing new teachers often presume that new teachers will be at basic and proficient levels, for it ought to take them a while to reach the distinguished level. Despite claims that these leveled conceptions of new teacher quality are based on research, they are more often based on logical assumptions that new teachers are simply less mature versions of their accomplished, more experienced colleagues.

But should our expectations of new teachers be understood as lesser versions of those we have for accomplished teachers? That is, are new and experienced teachers best understood as different points on a single continuum? Or are new teachers profoundly different than experienced teachers and thus the connections between them discontinuous? Consider some relevant questions: Should beginning teachers start their careers with deep knowledge of a limited number of things or shallow knowledge of many? Are beginners better off teaching in more traditional, less "adventurous" (Cohen, 1988) ways? Should we focus on the development of a few carefully selected components of teaching practice in the early stages of teachers' development and reserve work on more advanced pedagogies, understanding, or knowledge until later stages of their careers? We do not have definitive answers to these, and related, questions.

In other fields, it is not unusual to conceptualize development as discontinuous. A colleague of mine who is an artist was quite accomplished for much of her career: She had showings, sold art, and won prizes at juried displays. But when she wanted to progress to a new level of expertise and entered a master's of fine art program, the first thing she needed to do was "unlearn" that which had made her successful to that point. This phenomenon is well known in the performing and fine arts, athletics, technology (see, e.g., Starbuck, 1996), and organizational theory (see, e.g., Hedberg, 1981). We presume that learning to teach is a continuous function and that new teachers are less mature versions of their more accomplished peers. But learning to teach might be discontinuous, and it might require the unlearning of some knowledge and skill at critical junctures.

One final conceptual challenge concerns the issue of "connecting the dots." What are the appropriate outcomes by which we should all judge the quality of teachers and teacher preparation? Clearly, there is a press to connect teachers to student outcomes (McCaffrey, Lockwood, Koretz, & Hamilton, 2003), so much so that some value-added models of teacher quality insist that the sole measure of teacher quality ought to be student learning. That "value-added" discussion has recently been applied to the topic of teacher preparation. The question then becomes: Can we assess the effectiveness of teacher preparation by assessing the achievement of the K–12 students taught by program graduates? (See Figure 1.2.) Using value added models to assess the quality of teacher education programs has proven to be quite difficult, and we are some distance away from mastering the technical difficulties posed by such modeling.

For some, this press to connect the dots—even if the technical problems were solved—is not conceptually sound: Teacher preparation is too distant,

Figure 1.2   Connecting the Dots

both in time and across contexts, from student outcomes, and the intervening variables (e.g., experience, school contexts, student and community factors) are too many and too powerful. Hume (1896), in arguing that cause is an act of the mind (not an empirical "fact"), claims that causal inference requires both succession and contiguity:

> Since therefore 'tis possible for all objects to become causes or effects of each other, it may be proper to fix some general rules, by which we may know when they really are so.
>
> 1. The cause and effect must be contiguous in space and time.
>
> 2. The cause must be prior to the effect.
>
> 3. There must be a constant union betwixt the cause and effect. 'Tis chiefly this quality, that constitutes the relation.
>
> 4. The same cause always produces the same effect, and the same effect never arises but from the same cause. (p. 173)

Thus, for some educators, the lack of tight contiguity in space and time between teacher preparation and student outcomes, combined with the lack of consistent effect solely attributable to the teacher education program, makes efforts to connect the dots in Figure 1.2 suspect.

Further complicating this issue is the question: Should the quality of teachers at the beginning of their careers be tied to student outcomes? Much of teaching is learned on the job, and the literature on teacher quality suggests that experience contributes to more effective teaching (Allen, 2003; Wilson et al., 2001). Should new teachers be held to a standard of K–12 student learning outcomes before they have had sufficient experience?

What might be alternative outcomes of teacher quality for beginning teachers and the programs that prepare them? One argument might insert more "dots" (see Figure 1.3).

In this logic, paths into teaching would equip teachers with certain qualities, including the capacity to use research-based instructional practices that lead to student learning (recall here the National Reading Panel report). However, this would not guarantee that new teachers would use their knowledge and skill successfully in the schools and classrooms in which they teach. Ascertaining that individuals have certain qualities does not guarantee their appropriate use, for as Cohen,

Figure 1.3   Connecting Other Dots

Raudenbush, and Ball (2003) explain, "resource effects depend both on their availability and their use" (p. 133). Thus, although new teachers might not know how and when to use their knowledge and skills until they have had substantial experience in schools, we could hold teacher education programs accountable for demonstrating that teachers mastered basic knowledge and skills that have been proven to be associated with higher student achievement.

MEASUREMENT CHALLENGES

In addition to these three conceptual challenges (no agreed-upon knowledge base, no clearly stipulated or empirically based conception of expectations for well-launched beginners, and little clarity about how and which dots should be connected), the field also suffers from measurement challenges. There is the problem of measuring complexity. Instruction, as a performance, is a complex act that is not readily decomposed into a set of demonstrable understandings. There are at least two aspects of the problem to consider.

First is the matter of scale. We have thousands of teachers whose quality needs to be assessed, thus the need for efficient proxies for requisite knowledge and skill. But the current measures used are deeply problematic. Consider subject matter knowledge. Whether someone has majored in a content domain has little meaning; what constitutes a major varies wildly across higher education. Demonstrating seat time in a set of courses is another unsatisfying measure of how much someone knows. GPAs are equally problematic, especially given reported trends in grade inflation (Kuh & Hu, 1999; McSpirit & Jones, 1999). The content knowledge tests published by various testing houses generally have not been released for content analysis by experts, although there have been a few promising exceptions to this practice recently, including ETS working with the National Mathematics Panel. One modest analysis of a handful of tests suggests that the content of teacher subject matter knowledge tests might be more related to high school curriculum than to college majors (R. Mitchell & Barth, 1999).

Obviously, the measurement problems are related to conceptual ones. With no agreed-upon conceptualization of content knowledge for teaching, either through expert consensus or empirical evidence, it is very difficult to develop scalable, efficient measures. However, the work of the Study of Instructional Improvement suggests that, with sufficient conceptual clarity and resource investment, it is possible to develop tests that differentiate the knowledge of teachers in ways that predict student achievement in mathematics and literacy (Ball et al., 2005; Hill, Rowan, & Ball, 2005). Thus, it might be possible to develop better measures of teacher knowledge and skill that can be used on a large scale, but it would take significant conceptual work, time, and money to create the items.

In addition to the issue of scale, there is also the issue of professional judgment in the prudent use of teacher knowledge and skill. Much has been written about the situated, contextualized, uncertain nature of teaching (e.g., Brown, Collins, & Duguid, 1989; Jackson, 1986; Lampert, 2001; for a synthesis of the literature, see Helsing, 2007), which includes judgments concerning the integrity and responsibility of the choices that are made. Thus, assessing a teacher's readiness at professional entry might require assessments of her or his ability to apply whatever knowledge and skill has been acquired in and through various opportunities to learn. Ball (this volume) points to the difference between discussions of teacher quality and teaching quality, which is apt here. Teachers might have quite a lot of capacity—knowledge or skill, habits or character—that are empirically, logically, or normatively determined to be related to quality. But those capacities might not be displayed in classrooms where one would hope to observe teaching quality (recall the earlier discussion of connecting the dots).

To put the problem bluntly, without assessments that determine whether teachers are capable of using their capacities and talents in the service of quality teaching, assessments at entry might do little in terms of improving practice. It is not surprising, then, that the practice-oriented aspect of what one needs to measure has attracted considerable attention in discussions of performance assessments across the professions and increased insight into the complexities of those measurement systems (Kane & Mitchell, 1996; Linn, Baker, & Dunbar, 1991). One observation about the current system is that as one gets closer to practice and to assessing new teachers' ability to apply their knowledge and skill in uncertain circumstances that they encounter in their classrooms, the field's reliance on locally developed measures increases. Thus, although most states use commercially developed assessments of teacher knowledge of basic skills, subject matter, or pedagogy, the charge to assess a teacher's ability to use those resources in appropriate ways rests with supervising teachers, field instructors, mentors, collaborating teachers, and coaches who use locally developed measures and metrics. The closer we get to what matters (i.e., whether new teachers are acting in ways that enable children's learning), the more we rely on assessments that are neither widely shared nor validated (consider, for instance, how few states use Praxis III).

INSTITUTIONAL CHALLENGES

We also confront formidable institutional challenges, at all levels of the system, when setting out to both document and possibly improve the measurement of teacher (or teaching) quality at entry. In teacher education, one institutional challenge concerns the lack of consistency in both what is taught and how learning is assessed. This is equally true in disciplinary departments, where common high-quality local examinations are not always used. One response to this challenge would involve developing a collective understanding of why good measures matter and why they ought to be used across the board, and investing in the development of assessments that teachers in higher education would agree are challenging and align with the curriculum of teacher education and disciplinary majors and minors.

But even if we had such agreement and such assessments, there would still be other challenges. Managing the administration of such assessments and the data generated from them is no small feat. Currently, the teacher education program at my university is attempting to put in place a large-scale assessment system for the more than 1,500 prospective teachers who are in the system at any one time. Because individual courses have multiple sections, and those sections are taught by faculty, adjuncts, and doctoral students, we have to invest significant resources in persuading everyone that such assessments are necessary, fitting them into an already crowded curriculum, coordinating with faculty in the disciplines who also need to be persuaded that such assessments matter, and creating a database that will record scores for individual students across multiple years. Although our university data management systems can keep track of grades, we have to build our own instructional system to keep track of assessment scores.

Finally, there is the challenge of the necessary institutional and political will. Education reforms are vulnerable to shifting political winds, which makes it hard to create any longitudinal program of aligned assessments and practices. My university regularly gets bombarded with new standards for teachers and requirements for teacher preparation, all of which threaten the creation of a stable system of experiences and assessments. These new requirements are seldom informed by research and are more often informed by a politician's beliefs about quality teachers or teaching. Building a system to measure teacher quality upon entry would require policymakers, state departments of education, disciplinary departments, teacher education programs, and K–12 schools and teachers (who regularly oversee teacher education and induction experiences) to collectively commit to a set of yet-to-be-developed measures that require collective agreement on the reasonable expectations for new teachers. That is, indeed, a tall order. More depressing still is that, whenever one aims for such large-scale agreement, the measures that everyone can or will agree on tend to lose precision in the name of consensus.

Toward a Better System of Assessing Quality for Entry

Given the typically American local character of most assessment of teacher quality for entry, there may be little that we can do to change the national landscape. It would take considerable political, institutional, and professional will—as well as human and material resources—to move toward a more coherent, theory-driven, research-informed system of assessment. It may be that kind of investment is not really necessary; clearly, the extant system has its own mechanisms for vetting new teachers considering that at least 50% of new teachers are gone within 5 years.

But the teachers who leave might not be the right ones, and the parents of children who have those new teachers would like some guarantee that their children receive a quality education. So I propose one strategy for making progress in the next ten years.

The current nonsystem squanders local resources on a panoply of measures, many of which are likely neither reliable nor valid. People are very busy administering assessments right and left. Perhaps we—the various stakeholders invested in beginning teacher quality—could agree on a small set of hypotheses that we want to test through large-scale investments in research that would be embedded within teacher preparation systems. That is, faculty from disciplinary departments and schools of education in universities, school systems in which new teachers have internships and student teaching experiences, and state departments of education might work together with researchers to embed promising assessments in teacher preparation pathways and, over time, test the capacity of a set of assessments to predict a new teacher's success in the classroom. The image here is not unlike Ohio's Teacher Quality Partnership or what Teachers for a New Era might have enabled had research been seen as a core aspect of its agenda.

This system experiment would also require—at least within the teacher preparation system in question—collective commitment to test a small set of strategically selected hypotheses that would inform both current practice and policies of teacher preparation and theory about professional preparation and learning. These hypotheses would need to be based on a coherent theory of teacher learning, the development of teacher quality, and the content and character of teacher quality. We would need agreement on conceptual grounds. This would make such an experiment quite different than either the Ohio Partnership, whose programs continue to be quite different in what they assume about the nature of teacher/teaching quality, or Teachers for a New Era, which did not include any investment in collective measures to be used across institutions. The measures used in such an experiment would need to be both economical and nuanced enough to assess the knowledge and skill that really matters. They would need to be publicly credible, theoretically sound, and well aligned with a clear sense of which qualities matter in new teachers.

Such an undertaking would require interdisciplinary work by educators and researchers who equally understand the conceptual and measurement challenges discussed previously. The experiences of several research teams that have explored complex data systems for assessing the value-added model of teacher education have already laid important foundations for this work in programs in Florida, Louisiana's Value-Added Teacher Preparation Assessment Model (Noell, 2006), and the Pathways Project in New York City (see, e.g., Boyd et al., 2006). In neither the Florida nor New York project (or others under way), however, are actors across the system committing to the repeated use of parallel assessments. Instead, researchers are largely limited to existing measures, many of which are at a level of abstraction too high to measure important differences (the Pathways Project is an exception here). Just as scholars concerned with subject matter knowledge have yet to develop the appropriate measures to capture important differences in teacher knowledge, so, too, have researchers concerned with understanding the assessment of teacher and teaching quality yet to develop a set of appropriate measures. That would be an important investment of such an experiment. Of course, this kind of professional investment by teacher educators, faculty in the disciplines, and educational researchers would need to be supported by the political will to allow the development of the experiment and the material resources necessary to create and use measures, construct good databases, and conduct the appropriate analyses.

Conclusion

Ours is an age of accountability. The public demands—of teachers, teacher educators, and of many professions—guarantees of quality and value-added. Our current system of assessing teacher quality is undertheorized, conceptually incoherent, technically unsophisticated, and uneven. Calls for making more defensible decisions with better evidence should allow us to improve our practices and policies concerning teacher quality in state departments of education, universities, school districts, and teacher education programs. If, however, calls for accountability and evidence are being used to cloak other agendas (e.g., the wholesale dismantling of teacher preparation programs), we must be wary. The history of measurement in this country is full of negative intended and unintended consequences of unrestrained enthusiasm to believe that measures cloaked in "science" are accurate and helpful in making high-stakes decisions. We humans tend to quickly forget that the measures we use are more often convenient than valid.

In his work exploring value-added models in business, the economist Luis Garicano is quick to note that "a lot of reform . . . is about measuring output, but you should only measure output if it makes sense" (quoted in Bradshaw, 2007, p. 9). Especially important are the metrics we use. When those metrics are not sufficiently related to performance, it may be counterproductive to use high-powered incentives. In describing the time he spent working in the U.S. intelligence services, Garicano says that the evaluation and promotions of CIA field agents were based on the number of informants each agent signed up, whereas with analysts it depended on the number and length of reports they produced. In each case, the impact of these incentives was to induce the wrong kind of performance, as the actual value of the intelligence was unlikely to be related to these metrics.

It is fair to say that the current measures used to assess teacher quality at entry and the quality of teacher education programs are problematic—technically, empirically, and conceptually. Attracting and keeping better teachers is too important a goal to compromise with assessments used because they are readily available or easily recorded. Without more conceptually sound, technically reliable, publicly credible, and professionally responsible assessments, we should be wary of the clarion call to legislate the widespread use of any measure of teacher quality at entry into the profession.

References

Abell Foundation. (2001a). *Teacher certification reconsidered: Stumbling for quality.* Retrieved May 2, 2008, from http://www.abell.org/pubsitems/ed_cert_1101.pdf

Abell Foundation. (2001b, November). *Teacher certification reconsidered: Stumbling for quality: A rejoinder.* Retrieved May 2, 2008, from http://www.abell.org/pubsitems/ed_cert_rejoinder_1101.pdf

Allen, M. (2003). *Eight questions on teacher preparation: What does the research say?* Denver, CO: Education Commission of the States.

Ball, D. L., Hill, H. C., & Bass, H. (2005, Fall). Knowing mathematics for teaching: Who knows mathematics well enough to teach third grade, and how can we decide? *American Educator, 14*–22, 43–46.

Ball, D. L., Lubienski, S., & Mewborn, D. (2001). Research on teaching mathematics: The unsolved problem of teachers' mathematical knowledge. In V. Richardson (Ed.), *Handbook of research on teaching* (4th ed., pp. 433–456). New York: Macmillan.

Bestor, A. E. (1953). *Educational wastelands: The retreat from learning in our public schools.* Urbana: University of Illinois Press.

Borko, H., Liston, D., & Whitcomb, J. A. (2007). Apples and fishes: The debate over dispositions in teacher education. *Journal of Teacher Education, 58,* 359–364.

Boyd, D. J., Grossman, P., Lankford, H., Loeb, S., Michelli, N. M., & Wyckoff, J. (2006). Complex by design: Investigating pathways into teaching in New York City schools. *Journal of Teacher Education, 57,* 155–166.

Bradshaw, D. (2007, September 17). Professor to watch—Luis Garicano: Trendy subject taught with aplomb. *Financial Times.* Retrieved May 2, 2008, from http://us.ft.com/ftgateway/superpage.ft?news_id=fto091720070529273622

Brown, J. S., Collins, A., & Duguid, P. (1989). Situated cognition and the culture of learning. *Educational Researcher, 18*(1), 32–42.

Burant, T. J., Chubbuck, S. M., & Whipp, J. L. (2007). Reclaiming the moral in the dispositions debate. *Journal of Teacher Education, 58,* 397–411.

Cochran-Smith, M. (2004). Ask a different question, get a different answer: The research base for teacher education. *Journal of Teacher Education, 55,* 111–115.

Cochran-Smith, M., & Fries, M. K. (2001). Sticks, stones, and ideology: The discourse of reform in teacher education. *Educational Researcher, 30*(8), 3–15.

Cochran-Smith, M., & Zeichner, K. (Eds.). (2005). *Studying teacher education: The report of the American Educational Research Association panel on research and teacher education.* Mahwah, NJ: Lawrence Erlbaum.

Cohen, D. K. (1988). *Teaching practice: Plus ca change* (Issue Paper 88–3). East Lansing: Michigan State University, College of Education, Institute for Research on Teaching.

Cohen, D. K., Raudenbush, S. W., & Ball, D. B. (2003). Resources, instruction, and research. *Educational Evaluation and Policy Analysis, 25,* 119–142.

Conant, J. B. (1964). *The education of American teachers.* New York: McGraw-Hill.

Danielson, C. (n.d.). *The framework for teaching.* Retrieved May 2, 2008, from http://www.danielsongroup.org/theframeteach.htm

Darling-Hammond, L. (2002). Research and rhetoric on teacher certification: A response to "Teacher certification reconsidered." *Education Policy Analysis Archives, 10*(36), 1–54.

Darling-Hammond, L., Berry, B., & Thoreson, A. (2001). Does teacher certification matter? Evaluating the evidence. *Educational Evaluation and Policy Analysis, 23,* 57–77.

Darling-Hammond, L., & Bransford, J. (with LePage, P., Hammerness, K., & Duffy, H.) (Eds.). (2005). *Preparing teachers for a changing world: What teachers should learn and be able to do.* San Francisco: Jossey-Bass.

Darling-Hammond, L., & Youngs, P. (2002). Defining "highly qualified teachers": What does the "scientifically-based research" actually tell us? *Educational Researcher, 31*(9), 13–25.

Dewey, J. (1902). The child and the curriculum. In *The child and the curriculum: The school and society* (pp. 3–31). Chicago: University of Chicago Press.

Feinman-Nemser, S. (2001). From preparation to practice: Designing a continuum to strengthen and sustain practice. *Teachers College Record, 103,* 1013–1055.

Fetler, M. (1999). High school staff characteristics and mathematics test results. *Education Policy Analysis Archives, 7.* Retrieved May 2, 2008, from http://epaa .asu.edu/epaa/v7n9.html

Floden, R., & Meniketti, M. (2005). Research on the effects of coursework in the arts and sciences and in the foundations of education. In M. Cochran-Smith & K. Zeichner (Eds.), *Studying teacher education: The report of the American Educational Research Association panel on research and teacher education* (pp. 261–308). Mahwah, NJ: Lawrence Erlbaum.

Goldhaber, D. D., & Brewer, D. J. (2000). Does teacher certification matter? High school teacher certification status and student achievement. *Educational Evaluation and Policy Analysis, 22,* 129–145.

Goldhaber, D. D., & Brewer, D. J. (2001). Evaluating the evidence on teacher certification: A rejoinder. *Educational Evaluation and Policy Analysis, 23,* 79–86.

Grossman, P. L. (1990). *The making of a teacher: Teacher knowledge and teacher education.* New York: Teachers College Press.

Grossman, P. L. (2008). Responding to our critics: From crisis to opportunity in research on teacher education. *Journal of Teacher Education, 59,* 10–23.

Hedberg, B. (1981). How organizations learn and unlearn. In P. C. Nystrom & W. H. Starbuck (Eds.), *Handbook of organizational design* (Vol. 1, pp. 3–27). New York: Oxford University Press.

Helsing, D. (2007). Regarding uncertainty in teachers and teaching. *Teaching and Teacher Education, 23,* 1317–1333

Hill, H., Rowan, B., & Ball, D. L. (2005). Effects of teachers' mathematical knowledge for teaching on student achievement. *American Education Research Journal, 42,* 371–406.

Hume, D. (1896). *A treatise of human nature.* Oxford, UK: Clarendon Press.

Jackson, P. (1986). *The practice of teaching.* New York: Teachers College Press.

Kane, M. B., & Mitchell, R. (Eds.). (1996). *Implementing performance assessment: Promises, problems and challenges.* Mahwah, NJ: Lawrence Erlbaum.

Koerner, J. S. (1963). *The miseducation of American teachers.* Boston: Houghton Mifflin.

Kuh, G., & Hu, S. (1999). Unraveling the complexity of the increase in college grades from the mid-1980s to the mid-1990s. *Educational Evaluation and Policy Analysis, 21,* 297–320.

Lampert, M. (2001). *Teaching problems and the problems of teaching.* New Haven, CT: Yale University Press.

Linn, R. L., Baker, E. L., & Dunbar, S. B. (1991). Complex, performance-based assessment: Expectations and validation criteria. *Educational Researcher, 20*(8), 15–21.

Lynd, A. (1953). *Quackery in the public schools.* Boston: Little, Brown.

Ma, L. (1999). *Knowing and teaching elementary mathematics: Teachers' understanding of fundamental mathematics in China and the United States.* Mahwah, NJ: Lawrence Erlbaum.

McCaffrey, D. F., Lockwood, J. R., Koretz, D. M., & Hamilton, L. S. (2003). *Evaluating value-added models for teacher accountability.* Santa Monica, CA: RAND.

McSpirit, S., & Jones, K. E. (1999). Grade inflation rates among different ability students, controlling for other factors. *Education Policy Analysis Archives, 7*(30). Retrieved May 2, 2008, from http://epaa.asu.edu/epaa/v7n30.html

Metzger, S., & Wu, M. (in press). Commercial teacher selection instruments: The validity of selecting teachers through beliefs, attitudes, and values. *Review of Educational Research.*

Mitchell, K. J., Robinson, D. Z., Plake, B. S., & Knowles, K. T. (Eds.). (2001). *Testing teacher candidates: The role of licensure tests in improving teacher quality.* Washington, DC: National Academy Press.

Mitchell, R., & Barth, P. (1999). How teacher licensing tests fall short. *Thinking K–16, 3*(1), 3–23.

Monk, D. H. (1994). Subject area preparation of secondary mathematics and science teachers and student achievement. *Economics of Education Review, 13,* 125–145.

National Institute of Child Health and Human Development. (2000). *Report of the National Reading Panel. Teaching children to read: An evidence-based assessment of the scientific research literature on reading and its implications for reading instruction* (NIH Publication No. 00–4769). Washington, DC: U.S. Government Printing Office.

National Research Council. (2001). *Adding it up: Helping children learn mathematics.* J. Kilpatrick, J. Swafford, & B. Findell (Eds.). Mathematics Learning

Study Committee, Center for Education, Division of Behavioral and Social Sciences and Education. Washington, DC: National Academy Press.

Noell, G. H. (2006). *Annual report of value added assessment of teacher preparation.* Baton Rouge: Louisiana State University, Department of Psychology.

Ravitch, D. (2000). *Left back: A century of battles over school reform.* New York: Simon & Schuster.

Sedlak, M. (2008). Competing visions of purpose, practice, and policy: The history of teacher certification in the United States. In M. Cochran-Smith, S. Feinman-Nemser, J. D. McIntyre, & Demers, K. (Eds.), *Handbook for teacher educators: Enduring questions and changing contexts* (3rd ed., pp. 855–887). New York: Routledge, Taylor, and Francis Group and the Association of Teacher Educators.

Shulman, L. S. (1986). Those who understand: Knowledge growth in teaching. *Educational Researcher, 15*(2), 4–14.

Shulman, L. S. (1987). Knowledge and teaching: Foundations of the new reform. *Harvard Educational Review, 57,* 1–22.

Shulman, L. S. (2005, Fall). Teacher education does not exist. *Stanford Educator, 7.*

Smith, M. (1949). *And madly teach: A layman looks at public education.* Chicago: Henry Regnery.

Starbuck, W. H. (1996). Unlearning ineffective or obsolete technologies. *International Journal of Technology Management, 11,* 725–737.

U.S. Department of Education. (2002). *Meeting the highly qualified teachers challenge: The secretary's annual report on teacher quality.* Washington, DC: Author.

U.S. Department of Education. (2003). *Meeting the highly qualified teachers challenge: The secretary's second annual report on teacher quality.* Washington, DC: Author.

Walsh, K., Glaser, D., & Wilcox, D. D. (2006). *What education schools aren't teaching about reading and what elementary teachers aren't learning.* Washington, DC: National Council on Teacher Quality.

Whitehurst, G. J. (2002, March). *Scientifically based research on teacher quality: Research on teacher preparation and professional development.* Paper presented at the White House Conference on Preparing Tomorrow's Teachers, Washington, DC.

Wilkerson, J. R. (2006, April 20). Measuring teacher dispositions: Standards-based or morality-based? *Teachers College Record.* Retrieved on August 13, 2007 from http://www.tcrecord.org/Content.asp?ContentID=12493

Will, G. (2006, January 16). Ed schools versus education. *Newsweek, 98.*

Wilson, S. M., Floden, R. F., & Ferrini-Mundy, J. (2001). *Teacher preparation research: Current knowledge, recommendations, and priorities for the future.* Seattle: University of Washington, Center for the Study of Teaching Policy.

Wilson, S. M., & Tamir, E. (2008). The evolving field of teacher education: How understanding the challenge(r)s might improve the preparation of teachers. In M. Cochran-Smith, S. Feinman-Nemser, J. D. McIntyre, & Demers, K. (Eds.), *Handbook for teacher educators: Enduring questions and changing contexts* (3rd ed., pp. 908–936). New York: Routledge, Taylor, and Francis Group and the Association of Teacher Educators.

Wilson, S. M., & Youngs, P. (2005). Accountability processes in teacher education. In M. Cochran-Smith & K. Zeichner (Eds.), *Studying teacher education: The report of the American Educational Research Association panel on research and teacher education* (pp. 591–643). Mahwah, NJ: Lawrence Erlbaum.

Zeichner, K. M. (2003). The adequacies and inadequacies of three current strategies to recruit, prepare, and retain the best teachers for all students. *Teachers College Record, 105,* 490–519.

2 Hiring for Teacher Quality at the District Level

Lessons From The New Teacher Project

Timothy Daly

President, The New Teacher Project

David Keeling

Director of Communications, The New Teacher Project

E ducational inequality is the great social injustice of our time. America's public schools should function as equalizers, mitigating the disparities linked to skin color and socioeconomic class while preparing every child to learn and succeed. Yet in cities across the country, our schools have done little more than systematize failure. In urban school districts, where poor and minority students tend to be concentrated, the average high school graduation rate is only 60%—a rate 10% lower than the national average and almost 15% lower than the suburban average (Edwards, 2006). On average, young adults who attend urban and high-poverty schools have much higher poverty and unemployment rates later in life than those who attend other schools (Lippman, Burns, & McArthur, 1996), and numerous studies have shown that those who drop out of school, in particular, are far more likely to commit crimes, rely on public assistance, and use publicly financed medical care in the future.

The implications are especially critical to the nation's minority students, 62% of whom attend urban schools (Hoffman, Sable, Naum & Gray, 2005). In urban areas, dropout rates of African American (12.8%), Hispanic (25.5%), and American Indian (16.3%) youth far exceed dropout rates of white (6.5%) and Asian (4.3%) youth (Provasnik et al., 2007[1]). Today, nearly half (46%) of all African American students and over a third (39%) of all Hispanic students attend schools in which graduation is not the norm (Balfanz & Legters, 2004).

In seeking a solution to this challenge, researchers have consistently proven what parents, school principals, and students have long understood intuitively: High-quality teachers are essential. Recent studies have shown teacher quality to be the single most important school-based factor influencing student achievement, surpassing school quality and other factors (Hanushek, Kain, & Rivkin, 1998). Importantly, other research has illustrated that urban students can succeed if they are taught by high-quality teachers. A recent study by the Education Trust, for example, shows that Illinois students in high-poverty schools who had high-quality teachers were twice as likely to meet state standards as students in similarly high-poverty schools who had low-quality teachers (Peske & Haycock, 2006). Bringing qualified teachers into classrooms as efficiently as possible is therefore key to helping urban students succeed.

But how do we know which teachers will be top performers, and how can we ensure that all school districts, including those facing the greatest challenges, can staff all classrooms with high-quality teachers? That is the work of The New Teacher Project (TNTP). We are a national nonprofit organization dedicated to improving teacher quality in high-need schools across America. Since our inception in 1997, we have trained or hired approximately 28,000 new teachers in partnership with more than 200 school districts in 26 states. We have worked with many of the nation's largest public school systems, including those in Baltimore, Chicago, Denver, Miami, New Orleans, New York, Oakland, and Philadelphia.

TNTP's mission is twofold: to increase the number of outstanding individuals who become public school teachers and to create environments for all educators that maximize their impact on student achievement. We strive to achieve these two overriding goals through a multipronged approach that includes the following:

- creating innovative programs that bring high-quality teachers into hard-to-staff schools

- identifying the systemic policy and practice barriers that school districts face in hiring the best teachers possible and advocating for necessary reforms

- working hand-in-hand with school districts to optimize their teacher hiring and school staffing functions
- developing new and better ways to prepare, develop, and certify effective teachers

In its ten years of existence, TNTP has become especially well known for its trademarked Teaching Fellows programs. Now operating in 19 cities nationwide, these high-quality programs recruit and train accomplished career changers and recent college graduates to become teachers for low-performing schools through alternate routes to teacher certification. In 2007 alone, these programs attracted more than 37,000 applicants and had an average acceptance rate of only 15%—comparable to the nation's most prestigious universities. The 3,000 Teaching Fellows hired by schools in 2007 boast an average undergraduate GPA of 3.33, and 84% are eligible to teach high-need subjects such as math, science, and special education. They are also ethnically diverse: 34% are people of color. And virtually all teach in low-income communities, with 82% teaching in Title I schools.

Creating a pipeline of excellent teachers for challenging schools requires the kind of high-touch campaign usually associated with competitive private-sector industries. TNTP's Teaching Fellows programs share several common components, which together comprise a formula for a high-quality alternate route to teacher certification. These components span the new teacher hiring continuum and include the following:

- *Aggressive recruitment:* High-impact marketing strategies and straightforward, compelling messages pique the interest of talented, high-achieving individuals and build a diverse applicant pool.

- *Rigorous selection:* A standardized three-phase selection process enables the program to assess each candidate comprehensively against pre-defined criteria and to ensure that only the most promising applicants are accepted.

- *Intensive preservice training:* All candidates must complete a manda-tory six-week training program prior to beginning teaching. During this time they internalize TNTP's strategies for effective teaching by teaching in a summer school, observing experienced teachers, and engaging in intensive professional development sessions with their colleagues. Candidates complete preservice in the districts where they will eventually teach.

- *Cultivation and placement:* Throughout the application, enrollment, and training process, program staff members identify high-priority candi-dates (e.g., those who are eligible to teach high-need subjects) and use spe-cial events and outreach efforts to keep these individuals engaged in the program. Program staff also establish a placement process that efficiently matches candidates and schools through technology, individualized assistance, and large-scale interview opportunities.

• *Certification and program administration:* Working in partnership with local certification providers, program staff enroll Teaching Fellows in state-required education coursework and ensure that they make progress toward full state certification. In many cases, the cost of this coursework is subsidized by the school district.

One of the factors that differentiates TNTP from other organizations and consulting groups is its unique partnership approach. We maintain an intense focus on the needs of urban schools and design programmatic and policy solutions that specifically target their most acute challenges. Our Teaching Fellows programs exemplify this approach, establishing and expanding new streams of qualified teachers based on the most immediate needs of urban schools. By increasing the teacher supply pipeline, we have been able to help districts alleviate their most urgent needs (e.g., staffing their classrooms) and focus on other facets of the teacher quality challenge. For example, we began researching the policy and process barriers to effective teacher hiring when we realized that, in many districts, our programs were readily building large teacher applicant pools but losing quality candidates as a result of bureaucratic delays and convoluted school staffing rules. We have since released two national studies on teacher hiring issues in urban districts, *Missed Opportunities* (Levin & Quinn, 2003) and *Unintended Consequences* (Levin, Mulhern, & Schunck, 2005), and embarked on a growing national initiative to illuminate and reform the systemic obstacles that keep urban schools from hiring and keeping the best possible teachers.

In this chapter, we describe how TNTP has attempted to measure and maximize teacher quality for school districts through its programs and initiatives, the results we have been able to produce, and some of the obstacles we have encountered in our work. As a case study, we draw heavily on our New York City Teaching Fellows program, one of our most widely studied programs. Our experiences with some of the nation's most troubled school districts have convinced us that great progress on issues of teacher quality and educational equity are within reach, but realizing that progress will require dramatic changes across the continuum of teacher recruitment, hiring, preparation, and development.

Identifying the Problem

When we began working with urban school systems, we assumed that the lack of high-quality teachers was essentially a supply problem to be solved through deliberate recruiting for high-need schools and subject areas. Through early experiences working in close coordination with the human resource (HR) departments of urban school districts, we learned that these districts typically suffered from an inadequate pipeline of certified teachers and were thus forced to hire unlicensed teachers on an ad hoc basis. In some districts, it had become standard practice to hire hundreds of uncertified or emergency-licensed teachers immediately prior to the start of a school year with only minimal quality screening. Annual news coverage documenting the number of vacancies on the first day of school cemented the impression in the public mind that a systemic shortage of teachers led directly to a lack of certified teachers in urban districts.

Unfortunately, insufficient supply was only one of several chronic problems. In fact, as *Missed Opportunities* (Levin & Quinn, 2003) reveals, supply challenges were among the easiest to overcome. We soon learned through our district partnerships that HR departments often obstructed, rather than facilitated, effective teacher hiring. Department directors tended to view themselves as responsible for *transactions,* such as placing teachers on payroll, processing salary steps, and ensuring delivery of health benefits, rather than *outcomes* in the recruitment and management of a high-quality workforce. Rarely was anyone assigned to or accountable for the task of ensuring that all school-level vacancies were filled by the start of the school year. The notion of using sophisticated screening practices to measure the relative strength of applicants for teaching positions was almost universally absent from large urban districts. The prevailing sentiment tended to be that teachers were interchangeable: Any certified teacher was good enough for any vacancy.

Compounding the problem was a relationship between school districts and teacher preparation institutions (primarily universities) that consistently failed to meet the needs of urban districts. Put simply, there was a chasm between district demand and university supply. Though districts had vacancies in all content areas and all grade levels, they had the greatest difficulty filling positions at the secondary level in critical subjects such as math, science, bilingual education, and special education. Teacher preparation institutions did not have robust or large-scale recruitment efforts for those subjects, leading to relatively few graduates possessing much-needed credentials. Moreover, a considerable number of teacher preparation programs provided coursework that teachers in uniquely challenging urban classroom environments found to be irrelevant and disconnected from their daily experiences.

Though there are plenty of exceptions to the rule, on the whole, universities were not responsive to the pressing challenges of urban school districts, with funding streams, regulatory policies, institutional culture, and personnel all colluding to inhibit reforms within the institutions themselves. Schools of education tended to offer programs that their full-time faculty members were qualified to teach, but shifts in faculty rarely kept pace with the evolving needs of school districts. We were told time and again by prospective university partners that they lacked the faculty infrastructure to offer a program in special education or to expand the slots available for math teachers.

Universities also tended to respond to the demands of prospective students rather than those of nearby urban districts. For example, despite a surplus of elementary teachers and pronounced deficits of teachers in secondary-level subject areas, elementary education has long been among the most popular courses of study for new teachers and continues to be the most common certification area at many schools of education, even when local districts have a surplus of elementary teachers. This is in part due to the attractiveness of these programs to incoming students, but also because entry requirements are extremely general (e.g., subject-specific content prerequisites are broad and general) and these programs are typically cheaper for the institution to offer.

Finally, teacher education students interested in pursuing courses of study that lead to certification in high-need areas such as special education sometimes face disincentives; specialized degrees require additional seat time and credits to earn, but most students' primary interest is in completing their degree and entering the workforce as quickly and as cheaply as possible. The fact that many districts still do not compensate teachers who work in high-need subject areas any differently than teachers of other, low-need subjects further discourages teacher candidates from pursuing these more lengthy and costly options.

If universities were aligned to district needs, the intake of students would be more focused on producing teachers capable of filling vacancies in high-need subjects and attracting teachers interested in working with middle and high school students from low-income communities. Unfortunately, this is not the case, and state funding streams serve to reinforce the status quo. State universities that work to respond to the needs of urban schools receive no greater funding than other institutions, and those that reliably produce mostly elementary teachers receive no less. Neither are they evaluated or accredited any differently.

In light of these issues, TNTP concluded that a fundamentally different approach to teacher hiring and teacher quality was required if school districts were to make good on their commitments to students and families. That approach had to be rooted in rigorous, relentless pursuit of teacher quality throughout the teacher recruitment, preparation, and hiring continuum. Through our Teaching Fellows programs, we were able to help urban school districts respond to two of their chief concerns: (1) the inadequate supply of qualified teachers produced by schools of education for the full range of subject areas in which districts had chronic vacancies and (2) the simmering reputation of alternate-route programs as back-door entrances to the classroom for low-quality candidates. Our Teaching Fellows programs address these challenges by opening the teaching profession to a broader spectrum of people, urging them to make a difference for their communities by teaching, and establishing a sophisticated selection methodology to winnow the pool down to the highest-quality individuals. The remainder of this chapter describes some of the major lessons we have learned from this work and our experiences to date.

1. We must stop using the teacher shortage as an excuse for inadequate screening of teacher candidates.

As teacher vacancies proliferated in urban schools in the 1990s, districts recognized the need to respond but too often did so by simply lowering their standards. Emergency, temporary, and provisional licensure emerged as an especially easy way to enable teachers of dubious qualifications to teach, and many of these teachers ended up in schools serving high-poverty urban communities, where vacancies were most persistent. A "warm body" was a primary screening criterion used—only half jokingly—by HR staffs as they struggled to match teachers with classrooms. Districts began looking to alternate routes to certification as a way of dealing with these challenges, but many of these programs lacked rigor and accomplished little more than to open state-sanctioned back doors into schools for low-quality teachers. The poor reputation of alternate-route programs led to complaints from university preparation programs—some of which were justified.

Although we continue to face shortages of teachers in specific content areas and although teacher quality is not evenly distributed across districts or schools, TNTP has demonstrated time and again that large numbers of talented individuals are willing to enter the teaching profession and to teach in our neediest schools. It is insufficient, irresponsible, and incorrect to suggest that students must accept mediocre or poor-quality teachers because no better options exist.

In 2007 alone, TNTP's teacher recruitment and training programs and staffing initiatives received more than 37,000 applicants and helped supply more than 4,800 new teachers to schools nationwide. More than 80% of these teachers were eligible to teach shortage subject areas such as math, science, and special education. Their impact on our nation's urban and high-poverty schools is exponential, affecting tens of thousands of children, classroom by classroom, year after year.

TNTP's Teaching Fellows programs demonstrate that the right strategies can ensure an excellent applicant pool for districts that are not typically portrayed as attractive for teachers. For example, our Chicago Teaching Fellows program received 2,074 applicants for only 119 positions in its most recent cohort. Similarly, our Philadelphia Teaching Fellows program attracted 2,142 applicants for 113 openings. Even on a larger scale, the data suggest that candidates are eager to enter the teaching profession: In 2007, our New York City Teaching Fellows program, which has provided over 13,000 new teachers to date, received 19,846 applicants for 1,790 positions.

Overall, TNTP's programs receive approximately 12 applications per vacancy. We have found that emphasizing the selective nature of these programs only increases interest in them, especially among high-achieving individuals who seek out challenges—precisely the types of people whom urban districts must attract if they are to succeed.

2. It is possible to recruit significant numbers of teachers for shortage areas.

Districts desperately need teachers who increase the diversity of the local workforce and who have the background to teach high-need subjects. On both counts, the data are encouraging. In 2007, over one third of new Teaching Fellows across all TNTP programs were people of color, including 40% of those in New York City and 60% of those in Miami. We are especially encouraged that such selective programs have been able to attract minority candidates who meet the competitive admission criteria, leading to a local workforce that more closely mirrors the student population.

Just as importantly, 84% of new Teaching Fellows in 2007 were eligible to teach subjects designated by local districts as high need. In recent years, TNTP has dramatically decreased its recruitment of teachers for subjects such as elementary and social studies to focus on filling district needs that are not being met through other avenues. For example, 71% of TNTP's Baltimore City Teaching Residents and 90% of Chicago Teaching Fellows teach high-need subjects. In many other cities, including Philadelphia, Miami, Memphis, and Oakland, all Teaching Fellows teach such subjects. In 2008, we are opening new programs in Saint Paul, Denver, and Phoenix that also will focus exclusively on filling high-need subjects.

The diversity and subject matter knowledge of these teachers undermines the conventional wisdom that districts must use emergency credentials and workarounds to staff important teaching positions. Qualified candidates are available, they are interested in teaching subjects for which chronic shortages of teachers exist, and they are willing to work in inner-city schools. What they need is a clear pathway into these schools, training to ensure that they can be as prepared as possible, and a sense that they are making a difference for their communities.

3. A rigorous selection process for all teachers is essential to ensure quality.

(a) Allocate resources wisely when measuring teacher quality.

Though TNTP receives many applications for each vacancy, not all applicants are cut out to be teachers. Interviewing every eligible candidate would be an enormous and ultimately unwarranted investment of time, given that most will not receive offers. Instead, TNTP divides its application process into three phases.

i. **Prescreening:** Prescreening involves an initial review of each candidate's written application, including resume, cover letter, personal statement, academic transcripts, and any other required materials. During this phase, trained screeners look for evidence that a candidate meets general program criteria and has the potential to succeed in a more intensive selection process. Reasons for not advancing a candidate to the next phase of selection might include poor writing skills, weak job history, inadequate academic preparation, or poor fit with the teaching profession. Though results vary significantly by program, approximately 60% to 70% of applicants are advanced to the interview stage. By eliminating a significant percentage of candidates based on the written application, TNTP is able to begin formulating a detailed picture of promising candidates while reducing the resources consumed in the subsequent steps.

ii. **In-person interview:** TNTP is unique among teacher hiring organizations in requiring an extensive in-person interview lasting several hours before making an offer of admission to a candidate. Interviews are conducted by trained selectors who are currently working as teachers or administrators in the school district and who know the local context intimately. They are trained for at least 16 hours and required to pass an assessment of their selection skills prior to reviewing candidates. The interview itself consists of several components, each of which is designed to give selectors a window into candidates' individual skills and qualities. Throughout the interview, selectors measure candidates' abilities in defined areas of competency with the aid of a rubric:

- *Teaching sample:* In a group of approximately ten candidates, each applicant conducts a five-minute sample lesson on the topic of his or her choice, with the other applicants serving as "students" at the appropriate grade level.

- *Discussion group:* In small groups, candidates discuss a challenging classroom situation without facilitation by TNTP's selectors.

- *Writing sample:* Each candidate independently completes a written response to a prompt that asks the candidate to assume the role of classroom teacher in a difficult urban school.

- *Personal interview:* A selector follows up on issues raised on the candidate's written application or during the course of the interview event during a 20-minute interview.

- *Recommendation:* Following the interview event, selectors make a preliminary recommendation to accept or not accept a candidate into the program. Less than half of all candidates are typically recommended for acceptance by selectors. Program staff members conduct periodic norming sessions to ensure that experienced selectors' ratings and recommendations remain consistent.

iii. **File review:** Each selector's recommendations are reviewed by program staff to ensure that adequate evidence exists to support the decision. Selectors are required to make objective ratings based on clear criteria and present documented evidence to support their assertions. Between 10% and 20% of decisions are reversed by the review committee.

(b) Use consistent, rigorous criteria.

TNTP believes that the most important determinant of teachers' success is the nature of their fundamental personality and character traits. We have developed a specific, manageable list of selection criteria that identify and define as comprehensively as possible the qualities that, regardless of the individual's experience or training in education, TNTP has found its most successful teachers to have. These criteria are based in part on indicators of teacher effectiveness established through research (e.g., an applicant's verbal ability, the selectivity of his or her college, his or her undergraduate performance) and in part on our experience recruiting thousands of new teachers and tracking their progress after entering the classroom. Though TNTP does not publish its selection model in its entirety, these are some of the qualities that are considered crucial in successful candidates:

- achievement in past endeavors
- ability to analyze situations thoroughly and generate effective strategies
- effective written and oral skills
- evidence of constant learning
- respect for norms of interaction in different situations
- commitment to raising academic achievement in high-needs schools
- accountability for reaching outcomes despite obstacles

TNTP's experience has shown that a strong performance during the selection process is predictive of strong performance during the preservice training all new TNTP teachers must complete (especially the classroom practicum component) and in the classroom (as measured by the principal's assessment of each teacher's performance). Our selection process is constructed in a way that requires applicants to display desired characteristics and behaviors repeatedly rather than only at one particular juncture, which decreases false readings and assessments. Evaluation of competencies is not based on numeric formulas or absolutes; instead, each piece of evidence gathered from each component is relevant in establishing patterns of performance and in making a final decision about which of the candidates will receive offers to become program participants. Additionally, candidates are asked to assume roles and to make decisions that are quite similar to those they will encounter as classroom teachers.

(c)   When necessary, counsel struggling candidates to leave the program before they enter the classroom as full-time teachers.

Not everyone is meant to be a teacher, but this is not always immediately apparent. Some candidates appear promising through their written applications and in-person interviews but do not perform effectively during preservice training. In these cases, which are relatively rare, TNTP program staff members do not hesitate to have direct conversations with candidates to help them make the best decision regarding their future as a teacher. In some cases, the individuals decide to pursue employment in a different industry. Although this entails an immediate cost (the loss of a teacher), which may seem especially painful in the context of teacher shortages, it precludes the far worse possibility that the teacher's withdrawal occurs only after a year or more of disservice to students.

What Lessons From TNTP Might Be Applicable Elsewhere?

LESSON 1: SUBJECT-AREA PROFICIENCY SHOULD NOT BE MEASURED EXCLUSIVELY IN TERMS OF ACADEMIC CREDITS OR MAJORS

States seeking to maintain a high bar for teacher quality typically measure content knowledge through postsecondary coursework credits or academic majors. In many states, candidates seeking teacher certification must possess a full major in a specific subject to be licensed to teach that subject. Although well intentioned, this structure is not always effective. Consider the following scenarios:

- Candidates who successfully completed a premedical program as undergraduates—consisting of multiple lab courses in biology, physics, and chemistry—frequently do not have enough courses in any one science discipline to teach science even at the middle school level.

- Candidates who majored in disciplines requiring exceptional mathematics competency, such as engineering or physics, but who did not actually major in mathematics, are typically not permitted to be certified as math teachers.

The problem with this approach is the use of an academic major or credits as the sole proxy for content knowledge. Although possession of a major in a subject is generally a reliable and useful measure of an individual's knowledge of that subject, this type of requirement assumes that it is the only such measure. Moreover, it reduces the assessment of candidate qualifications to a binary question in which a candidate is either entirely qualified or entirely not, ignoring significant variations even among holders of the same degree, some of whom may have received middling marks, attended an uncompetitive institution, or passed courses only with substantial support or tutoring. Meanwhile, other individuals who are truly proficient may be prevented from teaching the subject due to overly rigid credit or major requirements. The result is a system that disallows an engineer with years of experience in the industry from teaching seventh-grade geometry.

It is not unreasonable to suggest that districts and states can permit greater flexibility in teacher certification requirements without lowering quality standards. New York State took an aggressive approach to this issue by creating a "math immersion" option for alternatively certified candidates wishing to become math teachers. Candidates must have substantial undergraduate coursework in mathematics (including at least one calculus course) with a grade of B– or better, must have career experience using math, and must pass the state's standardized Content Specialty Test in Mathematics prior to entering the classroom. In addition, all candidates must complete a master's degree in mathematics instruction prior to earning full certification. The results of this program, which was designed and piloted by staff members of the New York City Department of Education in conjunction with TNTP, have been astounding. By permitting nonmajors to seek math certification, New York inadvertently created an opportunity to test whether having a math major ensured greater math proficiency on the state's math exam. Although math majors performed quite well, it is clear that math majors are not the only candidates who are capable of doing so. Table 2.1 reports scores for New York City Teaching Fellows tested during summer 2006. A passing score on the exam is 220, and a perfect score is 300.

It is noteworthy that only 23 math majors took the exam. If New York did not have the math immersion program, none of the other candidates captured in the table would have been permitted to teach math. Fortunately, 32 engineering majors were accepted into the program, and collectively they outscored their colleagues who majored in math. The more interesting aspect of the data, however, is that 15 history majors with a strong math background scored the highest of all. Indeed, many nonmath majors did well on the exam.

Table 2.1   Average Teaching Fellow Scores on New York State Math Content Specialty Test by Undergraduate Major, Summer 2006

Undergraduate major	Average score	Number of scores
History	270	15
Engineering	267	32
Mathematics	264	23
English	253	19
Biology	248	9
Computer science	247	16
Economics	243	16
Political science	240	15
Psychology	238	41
Management	235	9
Communications	235	13
Accounting	231	23
Business	229	15
Marketing	226	12
Finance	223	18
Information systems	219	7

To date, the math immersion program in New York has provided the city with approximately 1,500 new math teachers, or about a quarter of all math teachers working in city schools. The success of this program has shown that states must be more innovative in seeking solutions to teacher quality and that content knowledge must be measured by more than academic credits if we are going to ensure that the best candidates enter the classroom. New York City has dramatically expanded its pool of math candidates through the math immersion program and has been able to open schools for several consecutive years without math vacancies. This is a far cry from the situation that existed just 10 years ago, when the State of New York was aggressively pushing the city to eliminate thousands of uncertified teachers from its rolls. Today, all New York City math teachers carry state certification.

Although the impact of these teachers has not been fully assessed, preliminary indications suggest that they are making a difference. In fact, New York City students are now outperforming students in peer districts on standardized math exams. In a *New York Times* article, Medina (2007) noted, "Math scores for students across New York State improved significantly in every grade tested this year, powered by sizable gains in New York City.... The city's increases were larger than those in any of the other big-city school districts except Syracuse and showed the city nearing the statewide performance average. In every grade tested—third through eighth—New York City had jumps, in most cases in the double digits, in the proportion of students performing at grade level or above" (p. 1–2).

LESSON 2: RECRUITING AGGRESSIVELY AND SELECTING FOR QUALITY CAN YIELD RESULTS

One of the questions consistently asked of TNTP is: How can your teachers make a difference in schools where students have had very little success for a long time? Our answer is that they can and do make an enormous difference. Our programs are strategically calibrated to identify and secure individuals who exhibit the skills and qualities most likely to lead them to success despite challenging assignments, and we expect them to be immediately effective in the classroom. That is not to say that they do not struggle—like most novice teachers, many find their first year extremely difficult—but they develop rapidly and often become dynamic educators.

Several studies of the effectiveness of TNTP's teachers have been completed in recent years. In general, they conclude that Teaching Fellows perform quite well relative to their colleagues from other certification pathways and programs. In terms of the value they add to student performance, two studies conducted in 2005 concluded that Fellows start out slightly behind traditionally certified teachers, but that by their third year in the classroom, they generate gains that are equal to or larger than those of traditionally certified teachers (Boyd, Grossman, Lankford, Loeb, & Wyckoff, 2005; Kane, Rockoff, & Staiger, 2006). The same studies found that the retention rate of Teaching Fellows was no different than that of traditionally certified teachers. A study released by the Urban Institute's National Center for Analysis of Longitudinal Data in Education Research finds that the hiring of Teaching Fellows in New York City between 2000 and 2005 led to a dramatic shrinking of the gap in teacher credentials between the highest- and lowest-poverty schools in the city and that the reduction in this gap contributed to a shrinking student achievement gap (Boyd, Lankford, Loeb, Rockoff, & Wyckoff, 2007). Boyd, Lankford, et al. note that "the dramatic reductions in the teacher-qualifications gap have been driven primarily by changes in the qualifications of newly hired teachers and the ways in which they vary with the poverty status of schools" (p. 9) and that, "in particular, these changes can be attributed to the New York State policy that eliminated uncertified teachers and the New York City policy that established the Teaching Fellows program and, to a lesser extent, employed Teach for America [TFA] teachers" (p. 18).

In 2000, before New York City had significant numbers of Fellows and TFA teachers, 63% of newly hired teachers in the highest-poverty quartile were temporarily licensed teachers. The hiring of Fellows and TFA teachers into high-poverty schools, instead of temporarily licensed teachers, has been responsible for much of the narrowing of the gap in teacher qualifications between high-poverty and low-poverty schools (Boyd, Lankford, et al., 2007).

We believe these data suggest that teacher quality can be positively affected by substantially increasing the supply of well-qualified, carefully screened candidates to high-need schools, even if those candidates do not have prior teaching experience. We are seeing evidence that if TNTP's programs and others like them are brought to scale, we can simultaneously close the achievement gap while reducing or ending the teacher shortage.

LESSON 3: THERE ARE NO SHORTCUTS TO TEACHER QUALITY

Too often, districts seek the equivalent of get-rich-quick schemes in addressing their teacher quality challenges. Faced with budgetary and political constraints, superintendents choose interventions that promise quick gains for little cost and with minimal disruption to existing systems. We are unaware of any large-scale solutions to the teacher quality challenge that meet these criteria.

Instead, improving teacher quality requires long-term investment in people and systems. An excellent example is New York City and its aforementioned Teaching Fellows program. Operated as a partnership between the city's Department of Education and TNTP since 2000, the endeavor has placed more than 13,000 teachers in over 1,100 schools across all five city boroughs. Fellows comprise about 10% of all active teachers in New York and tend to make up at least half of all new hires annually in the shortage-area subjects of math, science, and special education.

The program's success has not happened overnight, and it has required considerable financial resources from the district. In addition to contracting with TNTP for the operation of the program, the district pays selectors to interview candidates, provides living stipends to Fellows during training, assigns mentors to new Fellows during their initial years in the classroom, and subsidizes state-mandated master's degree coursework for all Fellows. Given the competing budgetary needs of any district, it would have been understandable if Chancellor Joel Klein and his leadership team viewed the Fellows program merely as a vehicle for providing alternatively certified teachers that allowed the district to release its thousands of uncertified teachers. However, Chancellor Klein fundamentally regarded the Fellows program as a source of new talent for high-need schools, and he continued to invest in it. Now seven years old, the program has become a foundational element of New York's human capital strategy.

Conclusion

As this chapter illustrates, TNTP's experience working with urban school districts over the past 10 years suggests that districts must address several priorities, including the following, if they are to put in place a sustainable, high-quality human capital strategy:

- Expand the pool of prospective teachers by aggressively recruiting top-tier candidates.

- Select candidates using a rigorous model that calls on applicants to repeatedly display desired characteristics.

- Advocate for reasonable flexibility in teacher licensing regulations, especially for teachers in high-need subject areas.

- Devise a long-term, holistic approach to improving teacher quality, and give it the time and resources necessary to succeed.

In this effort, New York City provides a compelling model. By creating and rapidly scaling the Teaching Fellows program, the New York City Department of Education and TNTP established a foundation from which to recruit aggressively, select for quality, and pursue practical innovations that target both immediate and anticipated needs. The effects of the program are increasingly clear: a surge in teacher quality in historically low-performing schools and a corresponding narrowing of the student achievement gap in these schools. Other districts and states would do well to follow New York's lead.

Note

1. Dropout rates indicate the percentage of 16- through 24-year-olds who are not enrolled in high school and who lack a high school diploma or equivalent credential such as a General Educational Development (GED). The proportions of students who do not graduate high school in four years are substantially higher than the dropout rates reported.

References

Balfanz, R., & Legters, N. (2004). *Locating the dropout crisis* (Report 70). Baltimore: Johns Hopkins University, Center for Social Organization of Schools.

Boyd, D., Grossman, P., Lankford, H., Loeb, S., & Wyckoff, J. (2005). *How reduced barriers to entry into teaching changes the teacher workforce and affects student achievement* (NBER Working Paper No. 11844). Cambridge, MA: National Bureau of Economic Research.

Boyd, D., Lankford, H., Loeb, S., Rockoff, J., & Wyckoff, J. (2007). *The narrowing gap in New York City teacher qualifications and its implications for student achievement in high-poverty schools* (Working Paper 10). Washington, DC: Urban Institute.

Edwards, V. B. (Ed.). (2006, June 22). Diplomas count: An essential guide to graduation policy and rates. *Education Week,* pp. 5–30.

Hanushek, E. A., Kain, J. F., & Rivkin, S. G. (1998). *Teachers, schools and academic achievement* (NBER Working Paper No. 6691). Cambridge, MA: National Bureau of Economic Research.

Hoffman, L., Sable, J., Naum, J., & Gray, D. (2005). *Public elementary and secondary students, staff, schools, and school districts: School year 2002–03* (NCES 2005–314). Washington, DC: U.S. Department of Education, National Center for Education Statistics.

Kane, T., Rockoff, J., & Staiger, D. (2006). *What does certification tell us about teacher effectiveness? Evidence from New York City* (NBER Working Paper 12155). Cambridge, MA: National Bureau of Economic Research.

Levin, J., Mulhern, J., & Schunck, J. (2005). *Unintended consequences: The case for reforming the staffing rules in urban teachers union contracts.* New York: The New Teacher Project.

Levin, J., & Quinn, M. (2003). *Missed opportunities: How we keep high-quality teachers out of urban classrooms.* New York: The New Teacher Project.

Lippman, L., Burns, S., & McArthur, E. (1996). *Urban schools: The challenge of location and poverty* (NCES 96184). Washington, DC: U.S. Department of Education, National Center for Education Statistics.

Medina, J. (2007, June 13). City students lead big rise on math tests. *The New York Times.* Retrieved February 29, 2007, from http://www.nytimes.com/ 2007/06/13/education/13math.html?pagewanted=1&_r=1&ref=education

Peske, H. G., & Haycock, K. (2006). *Teaching inequality: How poor and minority students are shortchanged on teacher quality.* Washington, DC: Education Trust.

Provasnik, S., KewalRamani, A., Coleman, M. M., Gilbertson, L., Herring, W., & Xie, Q. (2007). *Status of education in rural America* (NCES 2007–040). Washington, DC: U.S. Department of Education, National Center for Education Statistics.

Professionalizing the Occupation of Teaching in a Time of Transition

3

Alan D. Bersin

California State Board of Education

Mary Vixie Sandy

*Center for Cooperative Research and
Extension Services for Schools,
University of California, Davis*

In California, prospective elementary school teachers are required to take and pass four separate tests prior to entry into the profession, measuring basic skills competency, knowledge of the subject matter, ability to teach reading, and overall pedagogical knowledge and skill. Although these are unquestionably important areas of expertise for teachers, the system appears overzealous, even overreaching, in its multiple efforts very early on to measure the quality of teacher candidates. The California credentialing system is not alone in its enthusiasm for teacher testing: A study conducted by the National Research Council (NRC; 2001) counted more than 600 distinct tests administered to teachers across the 50 United States. California accounted for 30 of these assessments (California Commission on Teacher Credentialing, 2006).

In the face of these statistics, one is entitled to wonder whether the system is appropriately balanced in its insistence on measuring teacher quality at the occupational threshold. Indeed, the intense interest in quality assurance we purport to demonstrate at the beginning of a teacher's career is not matched, even remotely in California or elsewhere, by a comparable concern over the course of the teacher's career. This seeming paradox certainly raises a number of pivotal issues regarding teacher support, professional development, and evaluation. However, it poses a series of even more uncomfortable questions concerning the matter directly at hand: What is it that we are seeking to measure through entry-level examinations? What are the notions of teacher quality that underlie this process and structure of assessment? Are they really so diverse and disparate as to warrant the plethora of approaches that are taken across the country? The timeliness of these questions is highlighted by Loeb and Miller's (2006) finding that most states have not in any systematic fashion whatsoever evaluated their policies governing teacher preparation, certification, and tenure.

In this chapter, we place these questions in the context of exploring current barriers to a genuine profession of teaching. We place the issue of quality at entry into a larger continuum of teacher professionalism. We trace the lack of common ground—and confidence—in defining teacher quality to the absence of a professional culture in pre-K–12 education that recognizes expertise and embodies the essential knowledge, skills, and performance levels necessary for entry and advancement in the profession. We understand quality in terms of professional standards that define the knowledge base and identify effective practice and performance. We propose that core matters of instruction, encompassing both pedagogy and content knowledge, compose and anchor a singular focus in developing measures of teacher quality, and that these measures be differentiated for application at different points along a *learning to teach* continuum. Finally, we turn to the case of California, describe its initial efforts to institute a more satisfactory method of assessing readiness to teach, and suggest next steps along the way to professionalizing the occupation of teaching in a standards-based system.

The Hallmarks of a Profession and Their Relevance to Education

A profession is defined, in traditional sociological terms, as a formal social organization that controls entry to the organization through reference to a specified knowledge base and its implementation in practice. Professions qualify members and control entry based on knowledge and demonstrated competence in practice. Members are empowered by reason of their state-delegated political authority and because of their social status to set the parameters of acceptable professional practice. Central to this power is the predicate that there is an agreed-upon body of knowledge and effective practice, and that members of the profession subscribe to, augment, critique, and build this base collectively and in relationship with one another (Elmore, 2007). There is a strong connection between theory and practice, and the profession takes as its central function the cultivation of both, in accordance with ethical norms, to more effectively solve problems and thereby serve the needs of its consumers, be they patients, clients, or customers. We now discuss five distinguishing characteristics of a profession.

VALIDATED FRAMEWORK OF KNOWLEDGE AND SKILL AND A DISTINCTIVE WAY OF SEEING

There is a particular perspective, a specific way of viewing a situational set of facts, which defines a profession. The core is a validated set of skills and a body of knowledge around which professional training, practice, and experience are organized; these are then applied by the practitioner, as a matter of discretionary judgment, to the facts of a concrete case. There are important differences within variations across professions, but the measure and mark of professional success is matching a satisfactory solution to a problem presented. In the world of education, we often seek the solution for a particular case in a specific answer that we believe must be discovered rather than applied creatively by the practitioner. A lawyer analyzes the facts of a case and construes them according to governing principles in an effort to predict what a judge might conclude at the end of a similar process. What does it mean to think and act like an educator and to be trained and developed as an expert in teaching and learning? What is distinctive about the way we as educators see our world, approach its problems, and generate hypotheses about satisfying particular needs and demands? That there is little agreement on these matters should give pause to the claim of professional status (Burney, 2004; Hiebert, Gallimore, & Stigler, 2002; Stigler & Hiebert, 1999).

AUTHORITATIVE NORMS AND PROTOCOLS

David Garvin (2007) describes the sequence of professional steps through which problems are approached and solved. The first step involves analyzing the situation and precisely identifying the problem presented. The design step encompasses developing options and alternatives and formulating plans for their application to the individual circumstances at hand. Then comes the decision to proceed, which is followed by acts of implementation, including mobilizing resources and communicating direction. When a patient visits a physician to have a broken arm treated, the treatment is not unique to the individual doctor. The doctor uses professional skill in viewing the broken arm through an educated lens and then selecting techniques from a tool kit of knowledge for application to the facts of the case. There are documented protocols of medical procedure, much as there are rules of evidence in the practice of law. Similar guides and methodologies in education to facilitate a teacher's access to useful information are made conspicuous by their absence (Burney, 2004; Day, 2005).

Moreover, such progress appears contingent on significant changes in the nature and extent of educational research, the preparation and training of teachers, and the labor market for them. Each of the following changes in and of itself embodies an enormous challenge to the field of education.

THE NATURE OF RESEARCH IN EDUCATION AND THE SCALE OF EDUCATIONAL RESEARCH

The undeveloped state of the knowledge base in the education occupation, our would-be profession, involves both research and craft knowledge regarding how to obtain desired professional outcomes (Burney, 2004; Day, 2005; Hiebert et al., 2002; Stigler & Hiebert, 1999). There is painfully little documented knowledge in education about how to diagnose learning issues and what we should do instructionally to improve student achievement. This is both a function of the complexities of the cognitive/emotional nature of the teaching and learning process and the predictable result of an investment deficit in building a research infrastructure adequate to the task. The resulting knowledge deficit handicaps us severely in solving problems both at the microlevel of the individual teacher and learner in the classroom and at the macrolevel of large-scale school districts. How can it be that we have no National Institute of Education that might produce in our field remarkable accomplishments similar to those of our National Institutes of Health? It should be a national embarrassment that we have so underfunded the research necessary to make the knowledge and develop the protocols that are so badly needed in education. Again, we in the education world should step up to shoulder our considerable share of responsibility for this situation as a prelude to remedying it.

In 2003, ETS centered its Invitational Conference around the issue of educational research. Ellen Lagemann (2005), historian and former dean of the Harvard Graduate School of Education, presented a paper titled "Toward a More Adequate Science of Education." She articulated, clearly and concisely, the issues that retard the education research enterprise in terms of methodology, rigor, purpose, and presentation. Deborah Stipek (2005), dean of the Stanford Graduate School of Education, has addressed with equal force the requirements of a more satisfactory standard for educational research. Absent the considerable effort required to make research meeting those standards the rule rather than the exception, we are likely to wait in vain for the dollar investment it will take to provide practitioners with the knowledge they need for their students and themselves to be successful.

THE REINVENTION OF SCHOOLS OF EDUCATION

Making the knowledge that will enable communities, in Bill Clinton's words, to "replicate excellence" in the educational context is the paramount challenge confronting schools of education in the United States today. The task early on in the process is fundamentally intellectual: We have much knowledge to create and then make useful and useable by teachers. There are three dimensions to the work: (1) making new and useable knowledge by tightly coupling practice with research; (2) designing, developing, and implementing an infrastructure for educational leadership that will recruit, train, and support the next generation of education professionals on whose minds and shoulders rest the redemption, or not, of our global competitive position in education; and (3) reallocating resources to the nontraditional, cross-disciplinary collaborations on which the first two dimensions of the work almost certainly depend. As David Garvin (2007), quoting Derek Bok, noted in a presentation to the Harvard University Committee on Resources, "in the end, the most valuable contribution that any professional school can offer students is . . . to convey a systematic way of breaking down the characteristic problems of the profession so that they can be thought through in an effective, orderly, and comprehensive fashion" (p. 2).

The tough, hard work of figuring out all of this, and more, is at hand. We are at a turning point with schools of education in this country. Much like medical schools in the aftermath of Flexner's (1910) report and business schools following the Graham-Simpson review in the 1950s, we are in the midst of a period of significant transition for schools of education. Institutionally speaking, inflection points like this one provide opportunities but also pose dangers. At such turning points, history is unforgiving to those who do not turn to meet the demands placed upon them.

THE CONDITION OF THE LABOR MARKET
AND THE PREVALENCE OF INDUSTRIAL UNIONISM

There are deeply ingrained habits of mind in the field of education that have been deposited by history but that no longer are warranted by the circumstances that exist today. Each of them significantly affects the quality of teaching and learning, but none of them is shaped by that consideration so much as the labor market in which they unfold. There is an unacceptable tolerance of unskilled and unsuccessful practitioners in our field. The concept of an "emergency credential," for example, is unheard of elsewhere. Unqualified individuals, once identified, are not permitted to begin or continue practicing either in the operating room or in court, but this happens regularly in public schools. Our willingness to let this occur creates substantial barriers to increasing the rate of compensation for educators based on straightforward principles of labor supply and demand. Nor is there evidence of high levels of compensation in other professional fields in which the compensation is not linked, directly or indirectly, to significant productivity and successful outcomes for consumers such as students and their families.

Richard Kahlenberg's (2007) biography of Albert Shanker brilliantly details how important collective bargaining was to the public sector beginning in the

1960s; it also suggests that Shanker knew even then how increasingly inconsistent industrial unionism would be with a genuine profession of teaching. The requirement that obliges unions to defend the least effective of its members, single salary schedules that preclude differentiated compensation in almost every instance, a rigid seniority system that produces so many dysfunctional school district practices, and the chasm that exists between teaching and administration are all examples of how progressive innovations of one era are converted over time into a series of unanticipated consequences.

What Is to Be Done?

We are caught on the horns of a dilemma. An autonomous institutional capacity to create the required conditions for professionalism in teaching and education is necessary. However, society and government have not granted authority to educators adequate to the mission but rather have assigned to the state itself the functions and power situated elsewhere in the case of traditional professions. This has led some observers to argue that relief resides in a complete deregulation of teacher training and preparation and of teacher licensing. "Leave it to the market" are the watchwords of this point of view. We see the situation differently. To be sure, reforms that reduce the consequences of bureaucratization—delay, inefficiency, and nonresponsiveness—are always in order. However, the state holds the potential for jumpstarting the larger change required here through a process of resource allocation and legislative and administrative judgments. This is particularly true because the market in education remains nascent and immature. To realize this potential through harmonizing official judgments and actions in pursuit of the professional grail requires focus that must be supplied at the outset by purposeful regulation. We argue in the following section that there is evidence of this direction to be found in California, although we hasten to add that it should not be overstated.

California's Credentialing System: An Attempt at Coherence

California is one of a minority of states with a professional standards board that oversees educator licensure. The oldest professional standards board for teachers in the country, the California Commission on Teacher Credentialing (CCTC) is a 19-member board with 15 voting members appointed by the governor, representing education stakeholders and members of the public. Following a decade and a half of reform work shaped by three key pieces of legislation,[1] the CCTC implemented major changes in the system of standards, assessments, and requirements governing teacher licensure. The prior "system" of credentialing requirements and procedures was considered cumbersome and lacking in coherence for candidates, preparation programs, and policymakers. Requirements for preparation in reading, health, technology, and other areas were mandated by the state legislature, incorporated in a piecemeal fashion over a period of several years, and treated independently rather than as part of an overall strategy for teacher development. In 1998, the CCTC and the California legislature enacted a comprehensive reform intended to bring coherence to this troubled area of state policy. The new system was developmental in nature, following what were considered to be the natural stages and phases of learning to teach, and included the following elements (Sandy, 2006).

SUBJECT MATTER PREPARATION

Prospective teachers begin their preparation to teach with an intensive development of subject matter knowledge. They complete a baccalaureate degree in a major that meets state standards or pass a test demonstrating their mastery of subject matter content. Individuals seeking a credential to teach elementary grades are required to pass a test of content knowledge, pursuant to No Child Left Behind. All candidates are also required to pass a basic skills proficiency test prior to earning their first teaching credential.

PROFESSIONAL PREPARATION

Pedagogical training is built on a subject matter foundation and focuses on effective teaching of content. Just under 100 colleges, universities, and school districts in California are accredited by the CCTC and offer student teaching–based ("traditional") preparation programs or alternative certification programs. Close to 20,000 multiple subject, single subject, and special education teachers are credentialed in California each year (CCTC, 2007a). As teachers move into the profession, their second phase of preparation is grounded in mentored practice.

STANDARDS

All phases of learning to teach (subject matter preparation, professional preparation, induction, assessment) are governed by standards developed and informed by the profession, and maintained and enforced by the CCTC. Subject matter and professional preparation standards for teachers are explicitly aligned with the standards and frameworks that govern the K–12 public school curriculum, textbooks, and assessments. All routes into teaching are held to the same standard.

ASSESSMENT OF TEACHING COMPETENCE

Formal assessment of teaching performance is conducted in valid and reliable ways prior to a teacher beginning professional practice. The 1998 reform package added a Teaching Performance Assessment (TPA) to the array of required licensure tests, which include the California Basic Educational Skills Test, the California Subject Examination for Teachers, the Reading Instruction Competence Test (RICA), and formative assessments such as the California Formative Assessment and Support System for Teachers, which are used during induction. TPAs are embedded in professional preparation programs, administered by sponsors of preparation programs, and governed through accreditation procedures based on standards adopted by the CCTC.

LICENSE TO BEGIN TEACHING

Teachers who complete subject matter preparation and professional preparation, pass all required tests, and demonstrate through a TPA their readiness to begin teaching earn a preliminary (Level 1) credential. This authorizes the holder to serve as a teacher of record while completing a required induction program.

INDUCTION INTO TEACHING

A professional (Level 2) credential is conferred once a teacher has served for two years as a teacher of record and completed a program of beginning teacher induction. Induction in California is built on the Beginning Teacher Support and Assessment Program, established as a voluntary professional development program by the state in 1992, and includes structured mentoring and formative assessment of teaching practice.

ONGOING PROFESSIONAL DEVELOPMENT

In 2006, the California legislature removed specific programmatic renewal requirements for the teaching credential from statute. There is an expectation that the California Standards for the Teaching Profession

Table 3.1 California's Teacher Preparation and Credentialing System

	Preparation	Credential issued	Assessments	Ongoing professional development
Level 1	• Baccalaureate degree • Verification of subject matter competence (program or test) • Multiple program routes into teaching: traditional student teaching program, internship/alternative certification program • All programs held to the same standards, aligned with the California Standards for the Teaching Profession (CSTP) and K–12 student content standards • All teacher education programs include a valid teaching performance assessment	Preliminary Teaching Credential Authorizes service as a teacher of record during required induction program	• California Basic Educational Skills Test or approved alternative • California Subject Examination for Teachers • Reading Instruction Competence Assessment • Teaching Performance Assessment	No programmatic requirements for licensure renewal Expectation that the CSTP will guide ongoing professional development
Level 2	Induction program of one- or two-year duration that includes the following: • advanced curriculum preparation • formative assessment and support • frequent reflections on practice • individualized induction plan • application of prior learning Based on the CSTP	Professional Teaching Credential Authorizes unrestricted service as a teacher of record	Formative assessment instruments approved by the state • California Formative Assessment and Support System for Teachers • The New Teacher Center Formative Assessment System	

(CCTC, 1997) will guide professional development over the course of a teacher's career and that specific areas of need for professional development will be determined by individual teachers and their employers.

Elements of the new system that distinguished it from prior state practice include the introduction of valid and reliable performance assessments, new teacher induction, a two-tiered credential structure with required preliminary (Level 1) and professional (Level 2) credentials, and use of a single set of standards to guide all facets of preparation and routes into teaching. All aspects of the system are keyed to the California Standards for the Teaching Profession (CCTC, 1997), which align to various national standards, including the National Board for Professional Teaching Standards, as well as the state-adopted curriculum standards for students (Sandy, 2006). Standards and assessments developed as a result of this reform effort represent the first steps toward orienting one state's credentialing system to the elements of the *instructional core* (Cohen, Raudenbush, & Loewenberg Ball, 2003; Elmore, 2007). We argue in the next sections of this chapter that this orientation is essential to the professionalization of teaching and that through its credentialing system California has taken fundamental steps in this direction.

Focus on the Instructional Core

If one of the challenges to measuring teacher quality at the point of entry into the profession is the absence of a truly professional culture, another is the absence of clarity about what constitutes effective teaching. States have approached this question from a variety of starting points spanning a continuum that runs from professional consensus on one end to student performance on the other. The professional consensus end of the continuum defines teacher quality based on agreements among practicing teachers and researchers about the domains of knowledge and skill thought to be important to the job of teaching. This approach is rooted in a mixture of theory and practice, and the notion that if sufficient numbers of experienced practitioners and education researchers reach agreement about a definition of quality and effectiveness, then that definition has some level of validity. At the other end of the continuum, teacher quality is defined in terms of student performance. This approach is grounded not in consensus or perception about the quality or effectiveness of teachers, but in the outcomes of teaching as defined by student learning gains (NRC, 2001). Neither approach enjoys the universal support of the research or broader teaching community, in part because neither adequately accounts for the complexity of teaching and learning. Cohen et al. (2003) articulate a theory of instruction that begins to capture this complexity:

> Instruction consists of interactions among teachers and students around content, in environments. . . . "Interaction" refers to no particular form of discourse but to teachers' and students' connected work, extending through days, weeks, and months. . . . Instruction is a stream, not an event, and it flows in and draws on environments, including other teachers and students, school leaders, parents, professions, local districts, state agencies, and test and text publishers. . . . [T]eaching is not what teachers do, say or think. . . . Teaching is what teachers do, say and think with learners, concerning content, in particular organizations and other environments, in time. (pp. 122, 124)

Elmore (2004) expands on this framework in what he defines as the core of educational practice: "How teachers understand the nature of knowledge and the student's role in learning, . . . how these ideas . . . are manifested in teaching and class work. The 'core' also includes structural arrangements of schools . . . student grouping practices, teachers' responsibilities for groups of students, as well as processes for assessing student learning and communicating it to students, teachers, parents" (p. 8).

Ultimately, our understanding of teacher effectiveness must take into account the wisdom of practice and research as well as impact on student growth. If we accept Cohen et al.'s (2003) definition of instruction as interaction, the implications for measurement of teaching quality are significant and profound. Paper-and-pencil tests of content and pedagogical knowledge cannot effectively examine a prospective teacher's management of instruction thus defined. A careful examination of teaching performance focusing on the instructional core is essential. Measurement of teaching quality that supports teaching as a professional endeavor must recognize and adequately account for this complexity. The TPA systems that have been developed in California hold great promise in their ability to measure teacher facility with the instructional core and establish norms for instructional practice that are fundamentally professional in their orientation.

California's Teaching Performance Assessments

One of the most ambitious and innovative aspects of California's recent credentialing reform effort is the requirement that all institutions that prepare teachers in the state embed within their programs a state-approved TPA that meets standards of validity and reliability. Sponsors of teacher preparation programs may implement a state-designed assessment or design their own system and submit it for review and approval by the CCTC. Two systems have been developed and adopted for this purpose: the California Teaching Performance Assessment (CA TPA), designed for the CCTC by ETS, and the Performance Assessment for California Teachers (PACT), designed by a consortium of California colleges and universities, including all campuses of the University of California, Stanford University, and several campuses of the California State University. Both systems evaluate evidence from intern or student teaching practice to obtain a measure of teacher quality for licensure. Although both systems are designed to inform a decision about candidate readiness to begin teaching, the PACT system is scored in a manner that provides a diagnostic score report to candidates as well as aggregated data that sheds light on the strengths and weaknesses of preparation programs.

The PACT consists of a Teaching Event (TE), which is administered by all PACT users, and Embedded Signature Assessments (ESAs), which are assignments or sets of related curriculum-embedded and standards-based assessments customized within individual programs. For the TE, candidates respond to a series of queries organized around a unit of instruction or a learning segment that occurs during student teaching. Candidates provide the following:

- a description of their teaching context
- a planning overview and a rationale for a focused, multilesson learning segment
- one or two videotapes of instruction from these lessons, with commentary describing the instruction that took place each day and in these videotaped excerpts
- an assessment plan and an analysis of samples of student work from one assessment given during the learning segment
- written reflections on instruction and student learning

This collection of teacher and student artifacts is based on a Planning, Instruction, Assessment, Reflection, and Academic Language model in which candidates use knowledge of students' skills and abilities—as well as knowledge of content and how best to teach it—in planning, implementing, and assessing instruction (Pecheone & Chung, 2006).

The CA TPA is structured differently than the PACT system and includes four distinct tasks that are completed by candidates over a period of several months during their teacher education programs:

- Task 1 requires candidates to write short constructed responses to a number of scenarios that relate to content-specific and developmentally appropriate pedagogy.
- Task 2 requires candidates to connect instructional planning to student characteristics for academic learning.

- Task 3 relates to classroom assessment. Candidates are provided a set of prompts to guide the selection and planning of an assessment, the implementation of the assessment, and an analysis of evidence of student learning collected with the assessment.

- Task 4 focuses on academic lesson design, implementation, and reflection after instruction. Candidates are provided a six-step set of prompts to guide the planning, implementation, and analysis of a lesson. Candidates submit information on a class and two focus students, information on classroom environment and an instructional plan, adaptations to the plan for the focus students, a videotape of teaching, an analysis of the lesson and student learning, and reflection on the lesson (CCTC, 2003; Sandy, 2005).

Both systems treat teaching as a complex, multi-layered endeavor and require prospective teachers to attend to the content and the students they are teaching. In this attention to complexity, California's TPAs embody an approach to measuring teacher quality at the point of entry into teaching that is fundamentally consistent with the instructional core. Further, the TPA, in the context of California's credentialing system, addresses in some way most of the hallmarks of a profession set forth at the beginning of this chapter.

VALIDATED FRAMEWORK OF KNOWLEDGE AND SKILL AND A DISTINCTIVE WAY OF SEEING

One of the early steps taken by the CCTC in building the framework for the TPA was to conduct a job analysis and construct Teaching Performance Expectations (TPEs) that represent the knowledge and skill deemed by educators, researchers, and stakeholders to be essential for effective teaching (CCTC, 2001). TPEs were built and validated through this process and became the essential knowledge and skill base assessed on TPAs. The validation process involved representative samples of credentialed teachers contributing to and evaluating the TPEs. Although the TPEs did not percolate up from teachers in an organic way, they did have to meet the consensus of professional educators in order to be adopted by the state for assessment purposes. In addition, they incorporate the CSTP as a framework, adding detail for assessment purposes while maintaining a link to standards that were generated by the California teaching profession.

AUTHORITATIVE NORMS AND PROTOCOLS

Both the PACT and the CA TPA follow a pattern that incorporates planning, analyzing the context of teaching, adapting instruction based on learning needs, assessing students, reflection, and application. This process

Table 3.2　　Performance Assessment for California Teachers

Purpose	To evaluate a candidate's teaching based on teaching practice and to provide evidence for a credential recommendation.
Structure	Includes two assessment strategies designed to capture both the formative development of a candidate's knowledge and skills throughout the year and a summative assessment during student teaching.
Embedded Signature Assessments	Each institution using the PACT system develops signature assessments to complement the Teaching Event and to provide evidence of candidate readiness to begin teaching.
Teaching Event	The Teaching Event addresses four categories of teaching: planning, instruction, assessment, and reflection. Candidates plan and teach a three- to five-lesson learning segment; videotape and analyze student learning; and reflect on their practice, organized around the following five tasks:
1. Context for learning	• Provides evidence of candidate's knowledge of students • Assesses ability to identify and summarize important factors related to candidate's students' learning and the school environment
2. Planning instruction and assessment	• Assesses candidate's ability to organize curriculum, instruction, and assessment to help students meet the standards for the curriculum content and to develop academic language related to that content • Provides evidence of candidate's ability to select, adapt, or design learning tasks and materials that offer students equitable access to curriculum
3. Instructing students and supporting learning	• Illustrates how candidate works with students to improve their content skills and strategies during instruction • Provides evidence of candidate's ability to engage students in meaningful content-specific tasks and monitor their understanding
4. Assessing student learning	• Assesses candidate's ability to select an assessment tool and criteria that are aligned with his or her central instructional focus, student standards, and learning objectives • Assesses candidate's ability to analyze student performance on an assessment in relation to student needs and the identified learning objectives • Assesses candidate's ability to use this analysis to identify next steps in instruction for the whole class and for individual students
5. Reflecting on teaching and learning	• Provides evidence of candidate's ability to analyze his or her teaching and students' learning to improve teaching practice
Scoring	The Teaching Event is scored by trained assessors using multiple rubrics. Assessors may be faculty, K–12 teachers, administrators, mentors, supervisors, induction support providers, or other education professionals.

SOURCE: PACT Consortium, 2007.

Table 3.3   California Teaching Performance Assessment

Purpose	To assure that teacher candidates have the knowledge, skills, and abilities required of a beginning teacher in California public schools.
Structure	Four increasingly complex performance tasks embedded in teacher education coursework and supervised field experience, administered and scored by program sponsors.
Task 1: Subject-specific pedagogy	• Assesses candidate's ability to understand how information about students is used to (1) prepare instruction in particular content areas and (2) develop and adapt student assessment plans based on the content being taught • Candidate responds to case studies rather than actual students.

Task 2: Designing instruction	• Assesses ability to
	  o identify and analyze student characteristics and plan instruction based on student learning needs
	  o develop and adapt instruction for English learners and students with other special needs
	• Candidate works with students in field placements to complete this task.

Task 3: Assessing learning	• Assesses candidate's ability to
	  o plan student assessments based on learning goals
	  o administer assessments and evaluate student learning
	  o adapt assessment for English learners and special needs students
	  o reflect on assessment
	• Candidate works with students in field placements to complete this task.

Task 4: Culminating teaching experience	• Assesses candidate's ability to integrate strands of the previous three tasks, focusing on
	  o planning instruction and assessment based on the learning needs of students and the content to be taught
	  o adapting instruction and assessment for English learners and special needs students
	  o teaching and administering assessment, analyzing instruction and assessment results to plan further instruction
	  o reflecting on the lesson, instruction, learning results, and his or her effectiveness as a teacher
	• Candidate works with students in field placements to complete this task and submits a video recording of the classroom instruction.

Scoring	Assessors are trained in the use of rubrics. Each task is scored on its own rubric, and scores range from a high of 4 to a low of 1. Candidates must score at least 12 across all tasks and no lower than 2 on any task. Assessors may be teacher education faculty, K–12 teachers, administrators, mentors, supervisors, induction support providers, or other education professionals.

SOURCE: California Commission on Teacher Credentialing, 2007b.

represents a set of norms or protocols that organize a teacher's approach to—
or way of viewing—teaching and learning in a consistent manner. What is
consistent is the analytical framework. What is dynamic and ever changing is
the situation in which this framework, and ultimately teaching expertise,
is applied. Teaching differs from other professions in this dimension. In the
professions of law, accounting, and medicine there are often strongly recommended steps to take in practice, and others not to take. Although this is true
in education at a macrolevel, the nature of instruction as interaction offers
teachers greater latitude than is available in other professions.

AUTONOMOUS INSTITUTIONAL AUTHORITY TO DEFINE CORE ELEMENTS OF THE PROFESSION

California is ahead of many other states with regard to this aspect of
professionalism. The licensing function has been delegated to a professional standards board (the CCTC) rather than to the lay members of the
State Board of Education. The standards board enjoys a majority of practitioners (teachers and administrators) in voting seats, alongside represen-
tatives from the school boards and the public. The members are appointed
by the governor, however, and the board operates as an agency of state government. Unfortunately, this political orientation reduces the commission's independence and autonomy as a professional standards board. The
governing board for the State Bar, in contrast, is made up of representa-
tives elected by its members. Politics are present in any organization, but
the ability of the members to select their representation and the ability of
a representative board to operate without undue deference to political or
governmental authority are critical aspects of professionalization.

CONTINUUM OF PRACTICE, EXPERIENCE, AND SPECIALIZATION WITHIN SYSTEMS OF SUSTAINED MENTORING, COACHING, AND PEER REVIEW

California's credentialing system is organized in such a manner that
each phase of preparation leads into the next and builds on the former.
With fine tuning and intensive focus on transitions, the system has the
potential to provide an effective continuum of mentored practice for
entering teachers. The TPA is expected to yield diagnostic information
that new teachers can use to tailor and focus the mentoring they receive as
they begin practice. The use of seasoned teachers as mentors and coaches
for the incoming workforce has the potential to alter the dominant culture
of isolation. What is still much needed in California, however, is a radical
departure from the practice of assigning the newest teachers to the most

challenging classrooms as well as ongoing support and professional development of teachers over the life of their careers.

MARKETPLACE JUDGMENTS REGARDING QUALITY

We argue earlier in this chapter that if teaching were a true profession, then the outcomes of teaching (student achievement) would be a critical variable in determining teacher quality. California currently lacks data systems that enable it to match teachers to their students and examine "value-added" in any systematic way. Such data systems are under construction and may well enable policymakers, parents, teachers, and administrators (i.e., the market) to examine the outcomes of teaching in ways that inform our collective understanding (judgments) of teacher quality in the future. As these data systems come online, we will have the opportunity to examine the predictive validity of TPAs as indicators of a prospective teacher's potential to positively impact student learning. If a positive relationship between performance on a TPA and performance in the classroom (student outcomes) can be established, then TPAs will provide a sound basis for evaluating teacher quality at the point of entry into the profession and will frame the dimensions of teacher quality that should be fostered over the course of a teacher's career.

California's credentialing reforms have been in implementation for only a few years. TPAs have been developed and piloted and will be required for licensure beginning in 2008, and it is too early to tell what impact these assessments will have on teacher quality and effectiveness. The implementation of TPAs at scale in California, where approximately 20,000 novice teachers are licensed annually, will enable a whole new generation of research to emerge. The predictive validity of TPAs with respect to student learning gains is one area of research that will be critical to develop.

What Might a More Coherent System Look Like?

Early indicators regarding the success of California's reform efforts suggest that the system could be further streamlined. First, there continue to be too many tests required at the point of entry into teaching. We argue that with the California High School Exit Examination, the SAT and ACT series, and college placement tests in reading and mathematics, the rest of the education system incorporates enough testing of basic reading and writing skills to support removal of the basic skills test from the testing program for teachers. Further, California led the nation in the late 1990s in establishing a freestanding test of teachers' ability to teach reading, a reform that brought needed attention to a critical area of teacher competence. Currently 98% of the teachers who take the RICA pass the test, suggesting that the test does not serve as a screen of any kind (CCTC, 2007b). This could be a result of a low passing standard, though the CCTC and its testing contractor conduct standard-setting studies in a manner consistent with industry norms. High pass rates could also be a direct result of preparation for the test, insofar as all candidates are required to take coursework and pass the test. We argue that the TPAs could (and already do) include a particular focus on a prospective teacher's ability to teach reading and that RICA could be eliminated as a required, stand-alone test. The state should focus its testing program for teachers on subject matter and pedagogy, and reduce the costs and burdens of an overbuilt testing program on teachers.

Second, there are needless redundancies in the system, particularly in the new teacher induction program, that need to be tightened. The state should rely more on instructional performance and effectiveness than highly structured requirements and paper-driven accountability systems. A shift to performance, however, will require longitudinal data systems and further development and use of value-added instruments to assist in judgments of teacher quality and effectiveness. These data systems are currently under development and expected to be online within the next three to five years.

Third, for all of its innovation in establishing and linking licensure to a *learning to teach* continuum, California's licensing system does not recognize or support teacher development beyond the early years of teaching. Indeed, there are critical aspects of teacher professionalism and professional development that fall outside the scope of the state licensing board and should fall instead to the emerging "profession." The state can serve as a proxy, in the absence of an independent and autonomous body with the authority of the profession, and use its regulatory and legislative authority to establish conditions that support the emergence of teaching as a profession. How might the licensing system be structured such that teacher competence is recognized and teacher authority is expanded over time? We propose for consideration and dialogue a career ladder for teachers that includes levels of certification driven by a single standard, or vision of teacher competence, and incorporates and moves beyond early preparation and practice. Levels of credentialing within this structure might include the following:

Level 1: An Intern Credential is issued based on completion of a baccalaureate degree and demonstrated knowledge of the subject matter to be taught, authorizing service as an intern[2] for candidates who choose this route into teaching. Interns should be required to do sheltered teaching, paired with a master teacher in the classroom, with a developmental plan for increasing classroom responsibilities.

Level 2: An Associate Teaching Credential is issued based on completion of a teacher preparation program and passage of a teaching performance assessment, authorizing service as a teacher of record during a two- or three-year induction period.

Level 3: A Professional Teaching Credential is issued based on completion of an induction program, passage of an advanced teaching performance assessment, and student performance results based on multiple measures, authorizing service as a teacher of record with no restrictions. This credential should inform the district-based tenure decision.

Level 4: A Teacher Leader Credential is issued based on specialized training and assessment of leadership knowledge and skill (e.g., National Board for Professional Teaching Standards certification), authorizing service in a recognized coaching or mentoring capacity (e.g., induction support provider, subject matter pedagogy coach).

Level 5: A Master Teacher Credential is issued based on nomination, selection, and training for role, authorizing service in a recognized or new supervisory or leadership capacity (e.g., department or grade level chair, staff developer, and instructional leader).

Such a structure would help move toward professionalization by recognizing higher levels of teacher competence and providing recognized opportunities for teachers to serve in leadership capacities in schools. Currently, these roles do not exist in formal ways. Although teachers currently serve as induction support providers and master teachers, the credential structure remains essentially flat, and advanced levels of performance are neither recognized nor privileged.

Actions that lawmakers could take, which fall outside the scope of the teacher standards board but which, if implemented, would represent additional milestones toward establishing a professional culture in teaching, include conducting annual evaluation of teachers, including measures based on student performance and administrator/mentor/peer review; lengthening the teacher tenure track beyond two years; undertaking compensation reform with a link to professional and instructional effectiveness results; embracing a rational approach to teacher assignment; and increasing interstate portability of teaching credentials. One of the most significant steps the state could take would be to delegate authority for teacher licensure to a fully independent and autonomous standards board. The state should move in this direction in concert with implementing the other changes called for here to ensure adequate, professional accountability for student success in the system.

Conclusion

We have endeavored here to place teacher quality in the context of a larger transformation of professional practice and the struggle of an occupation to become a profession. We submit that both are necessary to meet the central challenges of public education in our country. Professionalizing the occupation of teaching, we believe, is calculated to improve the quality of instruction and accelerate student achievement in ways that the perennial search for a "silver bullet of educational reform" will never match. Assuring informed professional judgment in our classrooms through teachers capable of diagnosing and solving the instructional problems presented by their students is the aim. Structuring the process to assess teacher quality and to assign novice teachers appropriately at entry is a crucial step in the professional direction. We have argued that the California licensing system, imperfect as it is, has taken an important stride with the Teaching Performance Assessment that creates a glide path, built on previous reforms, for accelerated progress in the direction we seek. If this proves the case, then managing the quality issue effectively at entry could precipitate other changes critical to the overall enterprise of professionalizing the occupation of teaching. In doing so, it could provide the decisive momentum we need to develop capacity at scale to implement an effective standards based system of education for all of our students.

Notes

1. Senate Bill 1422 (Chapter 1245, Statutes of 1992, Bergeson), Senate Bill 2042 (Chapter 548, Statutes of 1998, Alpert and Mazzoni), and Senate Bill 1209 (Chapter 517, Statutes of 2006, Scott).

2. In California, and under the provisions of No Child Left Behind, an intern may serve as the teacher of record while he or she completes preparation for a full credential. Interns hold a baccalaureate degree, have met the state's basic skills and subject matter requirements, and are supervised and mentored while in these programs.

References

Burney, D. (2004). Craft knowledge: The road to transforming schools. *Phi Delta Kappan, 85,* 526–531.

California Commission on Teacher Credentialing. (1997). *California's future: Highly qualified teachers for all students.* Sacramento, CA: Author.

California Commission on Teacher Credentialing. (2001). *Standards of quality and effectiveness for teacher preparation programs for preliminary multiple subject and single subject teaching credentials.* Sacramento, CA: Author.

California Commission on Teacher Credentialing. (2003). *Update on development and implementation of California's Teaching Performance Assessment.* Retrieved June 23, 2007, from http://www.ctc.ca.gov/commission/agendas/ 2003–04/April_2003_PERF-2.pdf

California Commission on Teacher Credentialing. (2006). *Report on passing rates of Commission approved examinations 2001–2004.* Sacramento, CA: Author.

California Commission on Teacher Credentialing. (2007a). *Annual report card on California teacher preparation programs, 2005–06*. Sacramento, CA: Author.

California Commission on Teacher Credentialing. (2007b). *CalTPA: California Teaching Performance Assessment*. Sacramento, CA: Author. Retrieved May 12, 2008, from http://www.ctc.ca.gov/educator-prep/TPA-files/CalTPA-general-info.pdf

Cohen, D. K., Raudenbush, S. W., & Loewenberg Ball, D. (2003). Resources, instruction and research. *Educational Evaluation and Policy Analysis, 25*, 119–142.

Day, T. (2005). Teachers' craft knowledge: A constant in times of change? *Irish Educational Studies, 24*, 21–30.

Elmore, R. F. (2004). *School reform from the inside out: Policy, practice and performance*. Cambridge, MA: Harvard Education Press.

Elmore, R. F. (2007). Education: A "profession" in search of a practice. *Teaching in Educational Administration SIG, 15*(1), 1–4.

Flexner, A. (1910). *Medical education in the United States and Canada: A report to the Carnegie Foundation for the Advancement of Teaching* (Bulletin No. 4). Boston: Merrymount Press.

Garvin, D. A. (2007, March). *Educating professionals one case at a time: Lessons from the business, law and medical schools*. Presentation to the Committee on University Resources, Harvard University Business School, Boston.

Hiebert, J., Gallimore, R., & Stigler, J. W. (2002). A knowledge base for the teaching profession: What would it look like and how would we get one? *Educational Researcher, 31*(5), 3–15.

Kahlenberg, R. D. (2007). *Tough liberal: Albert Shanker and the battles over schools, unions, race and democracy*. New York: Columbia University Press.

Lagemann, E. C. (2005). Toward a more adequate science of education. In C. A. Dwyer (Ed.), *Measurement and research in the accountability era* (pp. 7–19). Mahwah, NJ: Lawrence Erlbaum.

Loeb, S., & Miller, L. (2006). *State teacher policies: What are they, what are their effects, and what are their implications for school finance?* Stanford, CA: Stanford University.

National Research Council. (2001). *Testing teacher candidates: The role of licensure tests in improving teacher quality*. Washington, DC: National Academy Press.

PACT Consortium. (2007). *Elementary literacy teaching event candidate handbook 2007–08*. Stanford, CA: Stanford University.

Pecheone, R. L., & Chung, R. R. (2006). Evidence in teacher education: The Performance Assessment for California Teachers (PACT). *Journal of Teacher Education, 57*, 22–36.

Sandy, M. V. (2005). *Teacher licensure assessment in California: A case study*. Davis: University of California.

Sandy, M. V. (2006). Timing is everything: Building state policy on teacher credentialing in an era of multiple, competing, and rapid education reforms. *Issues in Teacher Education, 15*(1), 7–19.

Stigler, J. W., & Hiebert, J. (1999). *The teaching gap: Best ideas from the world's teachers for improving education in the classroom*. New York: Free Press.

Stipek, D. (2005, March 23). Scientifically based practice. *Education Week*, pp. 33, 44.

Broadening the Vision of Professional Entry

Synthesis of Section I

Ida M. Lawrence and Drew H. Gitomer

ETS

The session from which the preceding chapters emanated was titled "Challenges to Measuring Teacher Quality for Professional Entry." After listening to the talks, participating in the panel discussion, and reading the chapters, the nature of those challenges are much clearer, but no less daunting. For these chapters collectively challenge traditional conceptions of measuring, teacher quality, and professional entry.

What are those traditional conceptions? Well, let us take a very basic model that still characterizes much of what is meant by measuring teacher quality for professional entry. In this model, professional entry means achieving a teaching license that certifies that a person has met some basic requirements to teach. Those basic requirements typically involve the demonstration of some level of understanding of content and pedagogy through performance on one or more standardized tests. In this model,

---

Following the papers presented by Suzanne M. Wilson, Timothy Daly and David Keeling, and Alan D. Bersin and Mary Vixie Sandy, an interactive panel discussion was held. Panelists were Linda Darling-Hammond, Charles E. Ducommun Professor of Education and co-executive director of the School Redesign Network, Stanford University; Henry L. Johnson, senior advisor, B & D Consulting; Jay Mathews, education reporter and columnist; and Mari Pearlman, education consultant. This chapter represents an attempt to synthesize selected ideas that were brought forth through the papers and subsequent discussion.

teaching quality is defined as adequate performance on the required tests. Measurement challenges revolve around ensuring the psychometric quality of the test.

This model embraces the legal perspective of licensure—to "do no harm." Here, the state warrants that a teacher entering the profession has sufficient demonstrations of knowledge that he or she will, at the very least, do no harm (see, e.g., Diez, 2002). Yet Linda Darling-Hammond, in her panel comments, highlighted the very real conflict between the interests of a regulatory environment and the more ambitious view of teacher quality that characterizes current discourse:

> We can't underestimate the importance of the regulatory environment. The regulators are actually governing the gate. And the law says that it will decide the definition of *good enough* or *sufficient*. And the definition of sufficient in many cases is what lots of education professionals would consider not good enough.

So what would a new conception mean—one that moved beyond the regulatory definition? The kernels of that conception have been sown in the preceding chapters and the conference commentary. We begin here by summarizing changing conceptions of professional entry and then discuss the implications for what is meant by teacher quality. Only then will we consider the measurement issues that derive from these evolving conceptions.

WHAT IS PROFESSIONAL ENTRY?

The traditional model treats entry as a discrete event. By satisfying a set of educational and statutory requirements, one enters the profession by becoming certified. Bersin and Sandy, building on their practical experience in California, make very clear that this perspective is extremely impoverished.

Bersin and Sandy view professional entry through the lens of professionalism of the teaching occupation. In their chapter, they reflect the consensus view of the session's speakers that entry is a long-term process rather than a single event in time. As they see it, the current situation surrounding entry is characterized by a lack of professional culture in the teaching occupation. This is evidenced by the absence of an explicit trajectory for developing from a novice teacher at entry to a more experienced teacher, with essential knowledge, skills, and performance indicators (standards) explicit at each level.

Jay Mathews argued that the most important entry decisions are ones made around employment itself, not only to hire individuals, but also to retain them:

> A lot of people . . . think the most important assessment point is when a prospective teacher comes into their school. . . . The mention of tenure I

think is interesting. We are talking about a way to perfect the system so that the people we get are the best people possible, but that we can catch them early. I don't think we can expect to be perfect, and I think it is wrong to expect to be perfect. Strong principals in the most effective schools are usually in situations where they can hire a teacher and, if that teacher is not working out, within months after lots of help and assistance, they can let that person go.

Daly and Keeling's discussion of The New Teacher Project also emphasizes the critical nature of decision making required during recruitment, selection, and placement of new teachers. They come at the issue of teacher quality by asking the question: How do we identify those teachers who will be top performers, and how can we ensure that the supply of talent is available to staff all classrooms with high-quality teachers? Their view is that the current reliance on measuring content knowledge via completion of postsecondary coursework credits or major requirements may not link up to proficiency as a teacher and, due to overly rigid requirements for credits or major requirements, may in fact miss individuals who are truly proficient as teachers. For example, they provide interesting data indicating that, with the right infrastructure, it is not unreasonable to allow non-majors to seek certification for teaching.

Taken together, we come to see that using assessment to satisfy the traditional regulatory role fails to address the range of needs associated with entry into the profession. If entry is reconsidered as a legitimately long-term process that includes recruitment, selection, hiring, professional growth, and tenure, then the question turns to how assessment of teacher quality can best support a range of needs.

WHAT IS TEACHER QUALITY?

Given the inherent complexity of teaching, it is not surprising that the participants believed the current operational definitions of quality to be woefully simplistic and incoherent. On the one hand, there is universal dissatisfaction with traditional metrics such as coursework, degrees, background checks, and job interviews. On the other hand, there is significant skepticism that definitions in terms of student achievement outcomes will be satisfactory either.

Henry Johnson was perhaps the most favorably disposed to considering student outcomes as a proxy for teacher quality:

> Once the teacher demonstrates a sufficient content knowledge base, there needs to be a chance for that teacher to demonstrate the facility of actually doing the act and having that act relate to improved learning outcomes for kids. Because after all is said and done, if the knowledge base and the skill set that the individual brings to the learning environment [are] not highly related to learning outcomes for kids, then we've not had successful teaching.

But even as an advocate for this general approach, Johnson also recognized that such measures are only attainable after the teacher has engaged in practice for several years:

> If you accept the premise that schooling is about teaching and learning, and that teaching makes a difference, one only truly knows if the teaching is effective after the fact.

Darling-Hammond represented the more skeptical perspective:

> I think that everyone would acknowledge that we don't have a very good way of measuring what student learning actually means. It's an extraordinarily impoverished view of student learning to use student standardized test scores. Not because they're nothing, but because they're not nearly enough. And certainly teachers are after much bigger gains than students' test scores on standardized achievement tests.

One may reasonably ask: Why is the definition of quality so elusive? Wilson identifies a key conceptual challenge as the lack of agreement on exactly what should be assessed to ensure teacher quality. She argues that there appears to be little agreement on what it means to think and behave like a teacher and what it means to be developed as an expert teacher. The absence of a validated and agreed-upon framework for thinking about these things makes knowing what to measure a significant challenge for implementing a meaningful assessment system. Based on Wilson's chapter, we learn that the body of research linking different kinds of teacher knowledge (e.g., pedagogy, subject matter) to student learning is weak. Furthermore, there is also disagreement about the nature of teacher dispositions and character necessary for good teaching. So a major conceptual challenge is that the field suffers from lack of agreement on what ought to be assessed, and this disagreement on theory is a problem for both the cognitive and noncognitive measures that are currently being used to measure quality for teachers entering the profession.

And yet, throughout the talks and the commentary, there are recurring themes, including focus on teacher knowledge, dispositions, and contextual fit. Teacher knowledge goes beyond simple knowledge of content to a concern about how to teach that content to students of particular ages. Valued knowledge is not only about content but also about child and language development; the social, physical, and emotional needs of different students; and the social contexts within which students develop outside of school. Although the political discourse has occasionally treated the idea of teacher dispositions as a source of controversy when referring to the political stances that a teacher may hold, there appears to be agreement that there are personal dispositions that make an individual more or less likely to successfully engage with students on a daily basis. Finally, a challenge was made to the notion of characterizing the quality of a teacher as an inherent property of an individual. Rather, we see models like The New Teachers Project giving prominent attention to the fit between the background and attitudes of a potential teacher and the students in the classrooms in which they will teach. Teachers will not be equally competent in all contexts, and rather than trying to designate a general level of quality for a teacher, it seems as if an effective teacher entry system is one that maximizes the goodness of fit between a given teacher and a particular school.

Whether in California, New York, or the Midwest, the message of these chapters is that teacher quality is not a characteristic that is captured by any single metric or even array of metrics. Quality involves certain inherent characteristics of the teacher, such as depth of content knowledge. But these sophisticated models of professional entry conceptualize quality as being bound to contexts as well as to time. Bersin and Sandy, for example, make explicit the expectation that quality will change through the professional development of teachers. This much more nuanced approach to conceptualizing teacher quality has profound implications for how it ought to be measured.

WHAT ARE THE MEASUREMENT ISSUES FOR PROFESSIONAL ENTRY?

Wilson describes two technical challenges that result from her analysis: (1) the need for efficient measures of requisite knowledge and skill for successfully entering the teaching profession and (2) the further need for measures of professional judgment in the appropriate use of teacher knowledge and skill.

Wilson points out that what is needed is a new system for gathering evidence concerning the quality of new teachers. She believes that this new system must be more principled and more efficient than the current one. To create a different system for measuring initial entry into teaching, many of the challenges that she poses need to be addressed through a comprehensive research program that, by definition, must be understood as a long-term investment, one from which answers will not come readily. Clearly, if we had the answers we would not have the system we have today. The initiative Wilson envisions would be set up to test various hypotheses about what kinds of assessments could be used to predict a new teacher's success in the classroom. This is an excellent idea, provided that the various conceptual, technical, and institutional challenges delineated by Wilson are addressed. Paramount among the challenges is figuring out what is to be measured and why. In other words, a framework for validating these new assessments needs to be developed and agreed upon by the professional stakeholders. Also, the technical requirements for doing this well must be addressed by defining appropriate outcome measures against which to validate the assessments. This kind of effort would go a long way toward tackling many of the issues raised in the preceding chapters.

But Wilson and the other speakers all recognize that the assessment enterprise is not simply about prediction. It needs to be an active part of the development process, beginning with providing models of good teaching practice. Mari Pearlman reviewed a number of the more ambitious teacher assessment projects that are intended to not only measure, but also illuminate the most important aspects of teaching:

> I want to emphasize the teacher performance assessment that is being developed in California and was described by Alan Bersin. It is a lever for redesign, and it provides what Daly said we often don't have, which is a way to see teachers before they get hired, although some schools do that. The teacher performance assessment in California asks the question: Can a teacher who is graduating from a program, or entering the profession through another route, demonstrate that she can actually plan a unit of instruction and teach it? They videotape teaching, they reflect on the lesson, they evaluate the effect of their instruction on learning, and then they plan for how they will change that.

Pearlman went on to point out that this is not a wholly new approach and builds on work that has been done for the National Board for Professional Teaching Standards as well as in Connecticut. She also suggested that assessments of actual teaching skill help put aside the issue of whether one model of teacher preparation ought to be privileged over another:

> If you have an assessment that says this is what teaching is, if you can do it, it doesn't really matter what pathway you've gone through to get there. It matters that you can demonstrate that you can do the work that kids expect of you. And we build into the assessment the capacity to organize lessons that are responsive to English language learners that work with kids all across the achievement continuum, that are culturally responsive, and that are attendant to the needs of special needs students. All of those things need to be part of the process.

The New Teacher Project includes teaching samples, but also postulates a set of other aspects of the new teacher that ought to be assessed. They address the critical and practical question of how to improve recruitment and selection to ensure that high-quality teachers enter the system (and stay there). Daly and Keeling provide data to demonstrate that certain strategies can be successful at ensuring a high-caliber pool of teacher applicants even in districts not typically viewed as attractive to such applicants. The success of this program would suggest that we perhaps do know a fair amount about what needs to be measured and how to measure it to predict teacher quality at entry. Daly and Keeling believe that a rigorous process for screening all teachers is a critical component of ensuring quality. This screening is very labor intensive, and it involves prescreening and an interview that includes a teaching sample, a discussion group, a writing sample, and a personal interview. The responses are subjected to consistent and rigorous criteria. The rubric is very specific and appears to be informed by research. The process relies on multiple opportunities for evaluation, which is good measurement practice. The process is authentic and mimics behavior that would be needed in the classroom. Many of these measures are mentioned in Wilson's list of components of an incoherent system. But The New Teacher Project addresses many of the concerns raised by Wilson because the design of the measures begins with a set of principles regarding what ought to be measured and then deals with technical issues related to scale and grain size.

The New Teacher Project may be an example of where the field needs to be going to ensure teacher quality at entry, but the experiences of this project are also instructive in outlining what would need to be done and how large a task it is to implement on a wide scale. The use of industry practice and the focus on the problem as one of supply and demand is a useful approach and one that ought to be scrutinized with research and evaluation of the outputs from this kind of selection system. The goal is to have more flexibility and not lower standards. At the same time, Wilson has pointed out that there is no real agreement on what the standards need to be. The program described by Daly and Keeling is inherently flexible and is calibrated to select novice teachers who will succeed in challenging assignments, so it is calibrated at a high bar. It is also important to note that this effort is understood to be a long-term investment in human capital and a recognition that the extra time and money spent on upfront recruiting via a principled and rigorously implemented system can pay off. Extended research on this kind of process, in multiple contexts, would be useful and could be done along the lines suggested by Wilson.

A Closing Comment

Wilson accurately describes a system that at a national level is incoherent and, in many ways, unprincipled. And yet, from Daly and Keeling, as well as Bersin and Sandy, we see viable models that are far more developed within their local spheres. These models are being used not only to make important decisions about teachers, but also to have a significant impact on practices of teacher preparation and the professional development of teachers early in their careers. So we see some relatively coherent approaches to assessment for professional entry when there is political will and leadership together with the sustained involvement of teaching and measurement professionals. But even these models are only a beginning, and they require the sustained research program about teaching and the assessment of teaching that Wilson so carefully described at the outset.

Reference

Diez, M. E. (2002). The certification connection. *Education Next, 2*(1). Retrieved March 12, 2008, from http://www.hoover.org/publications/ednext/3367226 .html

4 Measuring Teacher Quality in Practice[1]

Deborah Loewenberg Ball[2]

Dean of the School of Education and
William H. Payne Collegiate Professor,
University of Michigan School of Education

Heather C. Hill

Associate Professor, Harvard Graduate School
of Education

One of the most-heard refrains in public debates about U.S. education concerns the state of "teacher quality." Critics argue that U.S. teachers are unprepared to teach in their subject areas. They claim that U.S. teachers have declined in their knowledge and possession of other desirable personal characteristics since the 1960s, when the profession was populated nearly solely by women (Bacolod, 2007; Corcoran, Evans, & Schwab, 2004). They track teacher employment patterns, note a high rate of attrition, and speculate about its causes (Feinman-Nemser, 2003; Ingersoll & Smith, 2003). Many observe that "highly qualified" individuals can earn a greater salary in other professions than they can as teachers (Bacolod, 2007; Dolton & van der Klaauw, 1995; Goldhaber, DeArmond, Liu, & Player, 2007). Other experts examine questions of equity, noting that the least advantaged students often face the least equipped teachers, as measured by both paper qualifications as well as knowledge and skill (e.g., Ferguson, 1991; Hill, 2007; Hill, Rowan, & Ball, 2005; Loeb & Reininger, 2004).

This work on the qualities of the teaching force, done in large part by economists and others working outside the discipline of education per se, has been important. We now understand a great deal more about problems related to teacher quality that are facing the United States, including challenges in recruiting and retaining good candidates and preparing them adequately for their work in classrooms. Our purpose is not to add another perspective to this growing list of concerns about teacher quality, but to offer instead a reframing of the issues. We argue that any examination of teacher quality must, necessarily, also grapple with issues of *teaching* quality. Of course we want high-quality teachers, but we want even more for those teachers to deliver high-quality instruction to their students. If the former ensured the latter, we would have no problems. But we suspect (and the literature confirms) that these are correlated, but not isomorphic, characteristics.

We begin this examination with an excerpt from an actual fifth-grade mathematics classroom.[3] We enter the class as the teacher, Lisa, begins to go over student work. Earlier in the class period, Lisa reviewed adding positive and negative integers using red (negative) and green (positive) chips, by "matching" whole or parts of chips and then noting that they "disappear back out into infinity where all the reds and greens are hanging out." After about ten minutes of independent student work on problems such as $-4\frac{2}{3} + 1\frac{5}{6}$, $-1\frac{2}{5} \times 3\frac{1}{2}$, and $-2\frac{1}{8} \div 1\frac{3}{4}$, she begins eliciting student

solutions. She begins with the problem $-4\frac{2}{3} + 1\frac{5}{6}$:

Lisa:	Negative four and two-thirds. So what does that mean? Xiao-Yun.
Xiao-Yun:	It means that you owe somebody four and two-thirds of something. But you only have one and five-sixths of that thing.
Lisa:	Very good. So I owe somebody four and two-thirds. . . . Let's do pies 'cause I like pie and that always works for me. So I have four and two-thirds of a pie.
	(*Here, Lisa draws four red circles and then attempts to draw two-thirds of a pie. She has some difficulty, taking a minute to erase and correct a partial circle that looks closer to one-third than two-thirds.*)
Lisa:	That's looks like one-third, doesn't it? The way I drew it. We'll get as accurate as we can. . . . What I have, though, to give to the person that I owe four and two-thirds of a pie to, is I have one, and here's my other pie, and if I cut it in six pieces, I have five-sixths of those.

Lisa draws one full green circle, then five-sixths of another. Her representation of the problem looks like this:

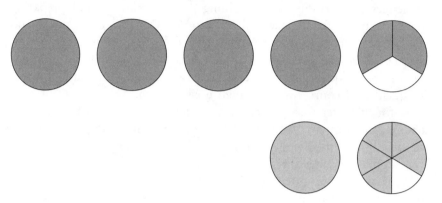

She then continues, pointing to the green pies below:

Lisa: I have one and five-sixths of a pie to give them. So even after I put all of this together, what do I end up with? Those two are gone.

Here, Lisa draws lines through a pair of "matching" red and green pies. She then also crosses out both the two-thirds and five-sixths pies with one stroke of the chalk:

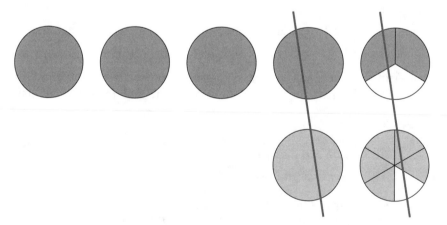

She pauses, notices that she has crossed out two pies that are not equal to each other, and says, "Oops." She recovers by asking a student to report the fraction still owed $\left(2\frac{5}{6}\right)$ and then converts the representation into a correct answer by further crossing out another red pie, leaving two pies, and then draws five-sixths of a red pie.

What can this example tell us about teacher quality? We know from background interviews that Lisa is a highly experienced teacher, having taught for 23 years, 13 of them teaching elementary mathematics and

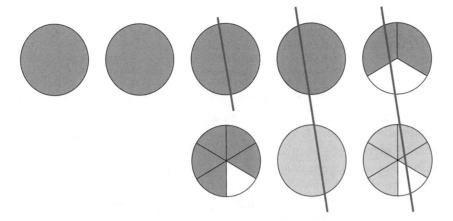

three of them mathematics to fifth graders. She is certified, possesses a master's degree in child development, and is pursuing a doctorate in education. She is also particularly committed to teaching mathematics and believes herself to be a good mathematics teacher. She is an active participant in substantial mathematics professional development opportunities, and in fact, with colleagues, Lisa wrote her own mathematics curriculum, from which she often draws during class. By most conventional standards, Lisa is highly qualified to teach mathematics to her students.

Using other standards, this picture blurs a bit. To start, Lisa scores in the 35th percentile of a large sample of California teachers on a test of mathematical knowledge for teaching (Hill & Ball, 2004). This test focuses on the mathematics teachers know that enables their work with students—not only knowing how to add fractions, for instance, but being able to unpack and explain their key ideas, to produce and link representations of this operation, to explain it in terms comprehensible to students, and to follow students' thinking in this area. If this kind of mathematical knowledge is key to success with students, and many believe it is, then Lisa may not be as qualified as her credentials suggest.

What do we make of Lisa's teaching in this segment? She manages her classroom well, seeks to make the content comprehensible, and focuses on key ideas. However, she lacks precision and makes significant errors in deploying the representation she has chosen. Her language is imprecise and inaccurate (positive and negative numbers do not combine to "go to infinity"). We return to Lisa and an in-depth exploration of this portion of her lesson later in the chapter. First, we consider how teacher quality has been assessed and studied by those who examine the relationship between teacher characteristics and student outcomes. Then we explore how using a mathematical lens to examine classroom teaching offers another way to analyze the quality of instruction. Finally, we discuss Lisa's instruction and how one might use this as the impetus for measuring the quality of *teaching*, as opposed to the quality of the teacher.

Examining Teacher Quality

Here, we sketch in broad outlines how scholars have conceptualized *teacher quality*. As the other chapters in this volume and wider educational debates suggest, there is significant variation in how scholars and policymakers use this term. It can mean knowing enough about a subject to teach it, being culturally responsive, being pedagogically skillful, producing gains in student achievement—in other words, it represents a wide range of different kinds of knowledge and skills. We are far from consensus about the meaning of teacher quality or how to assess it. Yet how one defines this term has important implications, depending on the goals and contexts around its use. If the question is who should be in a classroom teaching students, we might define teacher quality in one way. If we are trying to build theory about the relationship between educational "inputs," including teachers, and student outcomes in the context of large-scale survey research, we might conceptualize it in another way. If we are considering different approaches to teacher education and seek to identify characteristics of good teachers so that we can help prepare preservice teachers for their professional service, we might consider teacher quality in still another way.

So how we define teacher quality depends on our purpose. Yet the proceedings from this conference and evidence from past research show that we too often have not been careful about matching definition and purpose. The case of mathematics education provides an excellent example. Teacher quality in mathematics has been measured with distal indices such as certification and mathematics coursework and degrees, as well as with more direct measures like mathematics assessments themselves. Yet the literature that seeks to identify relationships between these teacher characteristics and student outcomes has not, by and large, carefully considered how the definition of teacher quality enables or impairs accurate conclusions about the relationship between teachers' mathematical quality and student outcomes.

For instance, there are many studies that use teacher certification as a measure of teacher quality and attempt to relate teacher certification patterns to student achievement. Some studies show that high school teachers certified in mathematics produce higher student gains than those who teach mathematics but are certified in other subjects (e.g., Goldhaber & Brewer, 1997; Goldhaber, Brewer, & Anderson, 2000). Yet many other studies, some at the elementary level (e.g., Hill et al., 2005; Rowan, Correnti, & Miller, 2002) and some at other levels (e.g., Goldhaber et al., 2000; Kane, Rockoff, & Staiger, 2006) show no effects of teacher certification on student outcomes. Further, all of these studies are open to criticism on the basis of selection bias or that the teachers who sought certification, or mathematics-specific certification, were somehow different than those who did not. The conclusion we can reach, then, is that teacher certification is not a good indicator of teacher quality in mathematics at the elementary and middle school levels, and an uneven one at the secondary school level. Although this may surprise some, certification status is remote as a measure of teachers' knowledge and skill, much less their effectiveness.

What about course taking or mathematics degree attainment as a measure of teacher quality in mathematics? What do we know here? Studies that use educational attainment as an indicator of teacher quality parse the notion of quality at a finer grain size. Not surprisingly, these studies are somewhat more consistent in showing effects on student achievement gains. However, it is important to note that the effect lies entirely at the secondary school level; we do not see these same effects in studies of elementary teachers. Thus, before recommending an increase in the requirements for teachers' college-level study of mathematics, we must consider the fact that the benefit of doing so applies only to a small fraction of the teachers who provide mathematics instruction in the United States. Another problem rests with selection effects. Just as with studies that examined the effect of certification, it might be that teachers who chose to pursue those degrees or courses were different in "quality" than those who did not. Additionally, we lack evidence about what, in fact, teachers studied and whether they remember (or ever even learned) what was taught in those mathematics courses. Finally, the mathematics taught in college-level courses and that covered in the school curriculum are quite different; even high school teachers who major in mathematics rarely study the content that they actually teach—elementary algebra, geometry, discrete mathematics—focusing instead on abstract algebra, topology, and advanced calculus. For all of these reasons, despite its face validity, college-level mathematics study is an imperfect indicator of teacher quality.

Moving on, when studies measure teachers' knowledge more directly, that is, they attempt to find out what teachers actually know and can do mathematically, the signal is a bit more clear. Although the number of such studies is small (see Harbison & Hanushek, 1992; Hill et al., 2005; Mullens, Murnane, & Willett, 1996; Rowan, Chiang, & Miller, 1997), they do show evidence of teachers' knowledge having a positive impact on student achievement gains.

Given these three ways of defining teacher quality, we ask: What is the strength of the signal about its relationship to students' achievement gains?

We are most sure that actually knowing mathematics is probably a significant factor in teaching it effectively. This may seem obvious, but it was an important issue to examine, for it might have been that the effect of teacher knowledge was swamped by the effects, for instance, of teachers' dispositions toward mathematics, the curriculum they use, the instructional methods they adopt, district policies, or even students themselves—their own predispositions and work habits.

For high school teachers, college-level study predicts their effectiveness only weakly. And college-level study does not predict effectiveness for K–8 teachers. Certification appears to make no difference in most studies, but may make a difference if that certification is in mathematics. Overall, course taking and certification are relatively imprecise discriminators of teacher quality. This is worth noting because these are policymakers' preferred ways of determining whether teachers are qualified. Policies regarding new teacher certification or teacher hiring decisions often rely on these indicators, despite their weak signal strength.

Now pair this with another interesting observation, one made often in these chapters and also in the wider policy community: Teachers do matter. In fact, persistent evidence exists across studies that teachers account for significant amounts of the variability in student achievement gains. Current estimates place the amount of variance explained between 3% and 18%, with one particularly well-designed study (Nye, Konstantopoulos, & Hedges, 2004) showing that figure at 11%. Important to note is that these figures are typically based on state or district assessment data, data not known for their sensitivity to teacher or school effects. Yet despite the fact that most agree that teachers matter, and matter quite a lot, no studies offer much insight into exactly what the teachers who produce greater achievement gains are doing, what characteristics or skills they possess, or what they attend to in their teaching. In fact, at best, these and other studies— some quite nicely done—explain a fraction, what one could even consider a tiny fraction, of that teacher-level effect (e.g., Kimball, White, Milanowski, & Borman, 2004). The need to know more about what the most effective teachers are doing is acute.

Examining Teaching Quality

One way to do this is to study actual practice, and this is what we and our colleagues have been doing for nearly two decades. This program of work began at a time when there were persistent claims that mathematics knowledge matters for teaching, but rather slim evidence on this point. Although researchers had been probing the relationship between teachers' knowledge and students' achievement for several decades, effect sizes were negligible and the methods used to measure teachers' mathematical knowledge relied primarily on proxies for teachers' knowledge. In one study, researchers gave teachers the same assessment their students took; in another, teachers' knowledge was measured by a one-item math test. We would never ask a person to answer one math problem and then make claims about his or her mathematical knowledge based on the performance on that one item. Yet researchers often relied on similarly weak measures of teacher knowledge. But the largest problem we saw in this literature, other than a sheer lack of adequate evidence, was the fact that these mathematics assessments were not grounded in the work that teachers engage in with students. Instead, they assessed the mathematical knowledge that an eighth grader or an adult might know, but not the professionally oriented knowledge of the content that we suspected teachers must possess to provide effective instruction.

Thus, rather than thinking about lists of topics that teachers should know or the courses we wished teachers would have taken, we started by studying the work of teaching to see if we could identify the mathematics that comes up in the course of a teacher's work. What events both are common to instruction and require substantial mathematical insight?

As we identified the work of teaching that seemed likely to involve significant mathematical reasoning and insight, we began to develop a sense of the tasks in which mathematical knowledge and reasoning matter greatly. One large, and immediately obvious, task that teachers engage in is analyzing and understanding student work. For example, suppose a student turns in an assignment on which the answer looks right but the method looks entirely wrong. The fact that a teacher can identify the answer as correct does not get him or her very far, for the teacher still must respond to this student with an assessment of whether the method can or should be used again, and under what circumstances. The teacher's first move might be to analyze what mathematical steps the student took to arrive at that answer. He or she might deploy some knowledge of place value, alternative algorithms, or, if the student is a recent immigrant, even some cultural knowledge about how that procedure is performed in another country. Assuming that some defensible series of steps exists, the next step would be to determine whether the student's work amounts to a method that could be used more generally. Here, too, the teacher might rely on mathematical knowledge and reasoning, asking whether there are mathematical principles (e.g., commutativity, the distributive property) that can help explain and justify the student's method.

An example might help make this clearer. Imagine a teacher who is working privately with a student who has come late to class. The teacher knows that this student has a good grasp of multidigit multiplication and settles the student into class work by reviewing how to calculate multidigit multiplication problems such as the following . . .

$$
\begin{array}{r}
{}^{2}64 \\
\times\ 27 \\
\hline
448 \\
128 \\
\hline
1728 \\
\end{array}
$$

. . . and then assigning the student to work on a similar set of problems.

Knowing multidigit multiplication is certainly a prerequisite for teaching. If a teacher did not know this, he or she could not show this student this procedure, demonstrate multidigit multiplication for the class, or do many of the mundane aspects of teaching such as correcting student work. But this is not all the mathematical knowledge a teacher needs to know. In fact, a few days later, this teacher might have to examine three incorrect answers to the problem 49×25.

In this instance, the teacher needs to analyze the errors to determine the mathematical steps that produced these incorrect answers. Answer B starts from the "bottom" and works upward, multiplying 25×9 and 25×4 (instead of 40). Answer C is produced by multiplying 50×25 and then

(a)	49	(b)	49	(c)	49
	× 25		× 25		× 25
	405		225		1250
	108		100		25
	1485		325		1275

mistakenly compensating in the wrong direction, by adding rather than subtracting 25. In Answer A, the most likely source of the error rests with incorrect management of the carried tens in the conventional algorithm. Multiplying 9×5 yields 45, of which one would carry the 4, which should be added after multiplying 4×5. Instead, here the 4 is mistakenly added to the 4 before the next multiplication, which produces 8×5, or 40—hence 405 on the first line. The same pattern obtains for the second row: 9×2 equals 18, but if the carried 1 is added to the 4 before multiplying 4×2, then the multiplication is 5×2, which equals 10, and produces 108 on the second row.

Beyond simply analyzing these errors mathematically, which clearly requires a substantial amount of mathematical tinkering and reasoning, it is also important to be able to understand how such errors might arise and to explain how a particular process went wrong. Why not do it that way? This last error (Answer A) might result from overgeneralizing the procedure for adding multidigit numbers; in that procedure, you can add the carried tens whenever you want. If you were a fourth-grade teacher, not only would you have to detect this rather predictable error, but you would also have to explain the reasons underlying this step in the procedure. We leave to the reader the task of generating such an explanation for a hypothetical fourth-grade student.

As is apparent from this example, knowledge of how to teach multiplication computation consists of more than being able to perform such calculations oneself. It is also more than knowing fourth-grade math plus a few years beyond that level, as some argue. Instead, it is a rather complex mix of knowledge, skills, reasoning processes, and other habits of mind.

We continued this close study of practice for several years, and as we made progress in identifying and describing these teaching tasks, we began to notice something unusual about them: They seemed somehow special to the work of teaching. For instance, a teacher who can identify a correct or incorrect answer but who cannot reason about student work is as ineffective as a physician who can only tell you that you are sick but cannot diagnose a specific illness. Thus the capacity to see the content from somebody else's perspective and understand what another person is doing is an example of the sort of mathematical reasoning and skill that a teacher needs but a mathematician or physicist does not.

After analyzing records of classroom practice and exploring the dimensions of this special kind of knowledge, we arrived at a name for what we were observing: *mathematical knowledge for teaching* (MKT). This term sounds relatively commonplace, but we mean something rather particular by it. We mean something more than knowledge—it in fact encompasses the skills, habits of mind, reasoning processes, and so on that are required by the work of teaching. So it is more than just what people know. And although our examples are primarily drawn from work within the classroom, by *work of teaching* we mean all the things that teachers do, including meeting with parents to help them understand a student's difficulty, defending the curriculum in front of the school board, or other such tasks that do not take place inside the walls of a classroom. MKT, as we use the term, encompasses a wide range of tasks and responsibilities in which teachers engage. And when we scrutinized these tasks and responsibilities more closely, we saw that teaching is subject matter–intensive in ways that are often overlooked when teacher quality is seen as a matter of what courses one has taken, whether one is certified, or even how well one performs on a test of basic skills.

Once we had developed a descriptive sense for these mathematical tasks of teaching, we moved toward trying to understand how this very specific type of mathematical knowledge was related to practice. Much to the surprise of some of our colleagues, this involved developing multiple-choice measures of teachers' mathematical knowledge for use in a large-scale study that allowed us to examine links between teacher characteristics and student outcomes. As we developed these measures, we focused on several key principles that we hoped would set our items apart from conventional multiple-choice assessments. First, we wrote items to represent this specialized knowledge that teachers might hold: being able to interpret and analyze student work, provide a mathematical explanation that is intelligible to fourth graders, and forge links between mathematical symbols and pictorial representations. Second, we wrote items to represent the mathematical tasks of teaching that recur across different curriculum materials or approaches to instruction; these included analyzing student errors, encountering unconventional solutions, choosing examples, assessing the mathematical integrity and accuracy of a representation used in a textbook, and making up a representation. And we chose to develop measures that could be used on a large scale because the kinds of studies we were contemplating with these measures would require many hundreds of teachers to participate.

Below is an example of one such multiple-choice item:

> Which of the following is best for setting up a discussion about different solution paths for simplifying radical expressions?
>
> (a) $\sqrt{54}$ (b) $\sqrt{156}$ (b) $\sqrt{128}$
>
> (d) These examples all work equally well.

This item is based on a skill that would likely be measured on many tests of mathematical knowledge. Can you simplify a radical expression? A teacher teaching this topic would have to know how to do that, and, in fact, there would be quite a problem if he or she could not. But teaching this topic might also take you into one of the commonplace mathematical tasks of teaching—choosing examples. Suppose you wanted to have a discussion with a group of middle school students about strategies for simplifying radicals and different solution paths for doing so. Would you care which of these three you chose? Or do you think that all of them are equally suitable? Your consideration should focus on the fact that simplifying radicals depends on the factorization of the number under the radical. Once it is expressed in its prime factorization, one inspects the factorization to uncover squares. For example, one way to see this with $\sqrt{54}$ is to note that $54 = 2 \cdot 3^3$, or $2 \cdot 3 \cdot 3 \cdot 3$. The only square is $3 \cdot 3$, or 9, so there is just one way to simplify $\sqrt{54}$, by rewriting it as $\sqrt{6 \cdot 9}$, which permits you to simplify this radical to $3\sqrt{6}$ by extracting he square root of 9 (or 3). Similarly, $\sqrt{156}$ can only be factored to $\sqrt{39 \cdot 4}$, which leads to the simplification $2\sqrt{39}$. A skillful perspective on the mathematics would show that it is only the third example, $\sqrt{128}$, that offers multiple solution strategies because $128 = 2^7$ and so lends itself to more than one way to extract squares.

As this example shows, detecting fine differences in the choice of examples is a mathematically skilled task that is critical to the work of teaching, and one that is not held by many other quite mathematically trained people, including research mathematicians. Teaching requires a particular way of looking at content, one that is not common to those who use mathematics for other purposes. And this only becomes apparent when one gets "below" using high-level indicators, such as mathematics content courses taken or degrees attained, to examine what kinds of mathematical knowledge are used in teaching.

Once we had established a set of items that we thought represented this kind of knowledge, the next step was to validate the items. Who cares how someone performs on a pencil-and-paper assessment if that assessment is not a good indicator of how he or she performs in the classroom with real students? To investigate this question, we conducted validation studies (e.g., Hill, Ball, Blunk, Goffney, & Rowan, 2007; Hill, Dean, & Goffney, 2007). Three main findings stand out from this work. First, when we gave research mathematicians these items, their performance was sometimes less than perfect. Although they did well on the assessment as a whole, there were some notable problems in the area of understanding students' work and methods. This suggests that our idea that the mathematics in these items is "special" to the work of teaching may be at least partially correct.

We also asked whether knowing mathematics in this way has something to do with student learning. To examine the relationship between teachers' scores and student achievement, we asked whether a teacher who performed well on our instrument would also produce greater gains in student achievement compared with a teacher who performed less well. We constructed a questionnaire with 30 items similar to the previous one on radical expressions. We built a statistical model to predict student achievement gains, using teacher content knowledge, teacher and classroom characteristics, and student characteristics (e.g., socioeconomic status, absence rate) as predictor variables. And we found that the teacher content knowledge variable had a significant effect on student achievement gains. It was a small effect, but translated into meaningful terms, it is equivalent to an additional two to three weeks of mathematics instruction for students of teachers who are one standard deviation above average in MKT as opposed to students in an average teacher's classroom. Further, the usual variables in these student outcome models—teacher certification, math methods, and content courses taken—had no significant effect on student achievement gains.

In this study, similar to others that link teacher characteristics and student outcomes, we had really no sense of how the classrooms of higher- and lower-knowledge teachers differed. So we designed yet another study, this one examining the relationship between teachers' pencil-and-paper MKT scores and what actually occurred mathematically in their classrooms.

We drew on the rich tradition of studying teaching through observation. Much of this literature is outlined in a paper we recently wrote on this topic (Hill et al., in press). However, we found that although the insights generated by this literature and our own past work were enormously helpful, none of the coding systems developed to examine video data really fit our purposes. Some schemes were relatively informal and specific to the research questions of each study; others mixed different elements of classroom instruction in ways that were poorly aligned with our ultimate goal, which was to determine whether more knowledgeable teachers handled mathematics differently in their classrooms.

Two years and many arguments later, we completed the development of such a coding system. Along the way, we agreed that the primary construct of interest was the mathematical quality of instruction—or the ways in which mathematics surfaces and is used by teachers and students in a classroom. When we use the term *mathematical quality of instruction* (MQI), we mean a multidimensional framework that captures the richness and accuracy of the mathematics; the degree to which students are engaged in mathematical work; and the ways in which the teacher uses mathematical language, makes and uses representations, and hears and uses student mathematical thinking. We incorporated this framework into an instrument designed to measure these things in the context of videotaped classroom observations.

We can use this instrument to give you a sense of how we might analyze Lisa's instruction. Consider the following three codes:

Selection of numbers, cases, and contexts for mathematical ideas: The teacher uses real-world or pretend contexts as the settings for developing ideas and procedures; selecting numbers for problems and examples; and selecting figures, shapes, and cases (e.g., in geometry).

Selection of correct manipulatives and other visual and concrete models to represent mathematical ideas: The teacher selects pictures, diagrams, and manipulatives or other models to represent a mathematical idea or procedure. Of interest is whether the teacher chooses models appropriate to the mathematics at hand. A model's degree of accuracy should be calibrated to the requirements of the activity at hand.

Makes links among any combination of symbols, concrete pictures, diagrams, and so on: The teacher makes explicit links among multiple models representing mathematical ideas. The links must be mathematically significant—for instance, pointing out connections between representations in ways that allow students to grasp how representations are alike or different, how pieces of one relate to pieces of another, or what one representation affords that another does not. This includes explicit links between pairs of representations (e.g., word problems and symbolic notation, manipulatives and symbolic notation, story problems and manipulatives).

Think back to the segment of instruction from Lisa's class that began this chapter. At the outset, Lisa asks Xiao-Yun to explain what the number $-4\frac{2}{3}$ in the problem $-4\frac{2}{3} + 1\frac{5}{6}$ might mean. Xiao-Yun says that it could mean "that you owe somebody four and two-thirds of something. But you only have one and five-sixths of that thing." Lisa continues this analogy, both verbally elaborating the situation and then drawing red and green pies to represent what is owed and what the person has. What would the first code make of this first section of the clip? Lisa has chosen a problem for her students to work on $-4\frac{2}{3} + 1\frac{5}{6}$, and she and her students have jointly constructed a real-world context for the interpretation of this expression. How appropriate are these selections? When we show this videotape to mathematics educators, one temptation is to argue over whether what Lisa and her student did is the best expression or the best real-world context for this material. But aside from this being nearly impossible to gauge, this is not what we are trying to measure. Instead, we want to understand whether the expression and real-world context are sufficient for supporting high-quality work. First we ask: Is the numeric expression well matched to the level at which students can work on the problem? Giving fifth graders the problem $-4\frac{54}{117} + 1\frac{43}{301}$ would not be particularly fitting, nor could Lisa then easily go on to draw $-4\frac{54}{117}$ "pies." The numbers she chose can be easily understood by students and are reasonably easy to represent visually. Next we ask: Is the real-world analogy chosen by Xiao-Yun and elaborated by Lisa commensurate with the work at hand? We decided that it is mathematically appropriate and could allow students, for whom this problem may otherwise be quite abstract, some insight into its meaning. Again, our code need not establish definitively that an analogy involving having and owing pies is the best way to help students learn, but rather that the representation is accurate and does not distort the mathematics. Thus we coded this segment positively.

The next code asks whether the selection of visual representations or manipulatives could support high-quality mathematical work. Lisa chose to use pies as the currency in which having and owing would be

reconciled, and she drew these on the board, creating the visual representation. Again, the question is not whether this is the best choice—candy
bars, brownies, or other rectangular objects might have made it easier for
Lisa to draw fractional parts—but whether the model of pies is sufficient
for high-quality mathematical work. Here again, we coded positively.

The last code asks about the quality of links made between mathematical
representations—in this case, the story about owing pies and having pies,
and the pictures of pies.[4] Recent thought about students' mathematical
learning suggests that when they are exposed to multiple representations
that are connected, and where the ideas are closely mapped from one representation to another, students' learning increases. But here, Lisa runs into
problems. A strong link between the story situation and the pie figures
would have had Lisa crossing off both a whole negative and a whole positive
pie, matching and crossing off each third of the negative pie to two-sixths of
the positive pie (or converting the two-thirds of the pie to four-sixths, as in
the standard algorithm), then noting that there is one-sixth of the positive
pie left over. This one-sixth of a pie would then cancel one-sixth of a remaining whole negative pie, leaving two and five-sixths negative pies.

Yet this is not what Lisa does; although she does accurately match and
cancel the initial positive and negative pies, she also appears to match and
cancel both fractional parts of the pies, as if they were equal to one
another. She realizes her mistake with an "oops," but rather than retracing
her steps and identifying the extra one-sixth left over, she asks a student for
the correct answer and directly converts the figure to show that correct
answer—but not the steps in the process to get there. Lisa has attempted
to pull off a linkage between two representations, but she is not successful
in doing so; further, what she has done is likely to confuse students, for the
steps performed do not match those from the algorithm she uses later to
perform this computation. We marked "inappropriate" for this code.

Coding is not a quick or easy process. We divide each lesson into roughly
five-minute clips, code each clip by assigning codes for each of 33 instructional variables, combine individual codes into scales, and then aggregate
clips to the lesson level. Because we code multiple lessons per teacher, we can

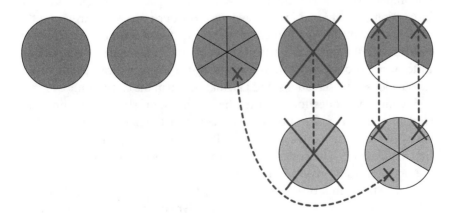

also aggregate from lessons to teachers to arrive at a more accurate picture of the mathematical quality of a given teacher's instruction.

But what can looking closely at instruction tell us that is helpful to this larger conversation about teacher quality? Well, recall that by some standards Lisa is a highly qualified teacher. She was credentialed, obtained a master's degree and was pursuing a doctorate during the study, and was among the more experienced teachers in the U.S. population. She reported that she enjoys teaching mathematics and believes she is a good mathematics teacher. Yet none of these characteristics—ones that policymakers, principals, and others might consider as evidence of teacher quality—ensure that Lisa can teach unproblematic mathematics lessons. In fact, as our coding suggests, Lisa's lessons are a mix of strong and weak moments. In one lesson, she offered the only mathematical justification in the roughly 90 lessons we reviewed for this validation study, but she as often as not got herself into difficulty when her instructional goals overstepped her mathematical knowledge for teaching.

Important here is that following teacher characteristics into the classroom makes it possible to analyze how potential resources affect actual instructional effectiveness. How does a teacher's score on a licensure exam show up in his or her classroom? How does whether or not a teacher is certified make a difference inside the work of teaching? These are questions both of the validity of extant indicators of teacher quality as well as of the role played by teachers' knowledge in classroom practice.

There are a few things to note about our coding instrument. First, it is different from other observational instruments in that it focuses on one element in depth: the *mathematical* quality of instruction. Scholars have long identified important features of the mathematics in teaching, for example, a focus on key mathematical ideas, the quality of mathematical representations and explanations, and the provision of high-quality tasks from which students can learn the subject matter. For the purposes of observing and measuring instruction, however, these descriptive features of the mathematics in classrooms were often integrated within, and thus overshadowed by, larger ideas about how mathematics should be taught (e.g., with attention to students' ideas, with attention to the social processes that occur in classrooms, through direct instruction). As this implies, our instrument is agnostic with respect to the approaches to instruction that are used in the classroom. For our purposes in assessing the mathematical quality of instruction, we are indifferent to whether teachers or students are the ones who articulate particular mathematical explanations. Instead, our codes permit an assessment of the mathematical quality of the explanations, representations, and talk that occurs in the classroom.

Second, our codes focus on teacher, rather than student, actions. If a student gives an explanation that is lacking mathematical rigor, which is likely, this is not what we are coding. Rather, we code the teacher's use of that explanation. The codes focus on the teacher's use of mathematics for the range of tasks involved in teaching.

Third, this kind of measurement instrument provides much richer information about teacher quality than other commonly used indicators.

We define *high-quality teachers* as those who consistently and effectively foster students' learning, but we worry about the many problems with using direct measures of student learning to gauge teacher quality (e.g., Clotfelter, Ladd, & Vigdor, 2004; Hill & Schilling, in press; Kupermintz, 2003; McCaffrey, Lockwood, Koretz, & Hamilton, 2004; Raudenbush, 2004). Thus, this type of instrument comes closer to capturing what we want to, and think we can, measure much more accurately: teachers who provide students with error-free, substantial mathematics and who can manage with mathematical adeptness the range of students' mathematical productions. There may also be other dimensions of instructional quality, such as the cognitive challenge of students' classroom work or the pedagogical aspects of classroom practice, that we would want to include.

This leads us to our fourth point: scale. Our estimates suggest that one must collect and view at least four lessons per teacher before comfortably making a generalization about the mathematical quality of his or her instruction. How realistic is this? Policymakers, district officials, and principals need ways to identify teacher quality among hundreds of thousands of teachers, and the studies that have been discussed elsewhere in this volume enroll hundreds or even thousands of teachers; clearly, collecting observational evidence is not feasible. One solution to this problem would be to use what we have observed on the videotapes to develop measures on which teachers could self-report or indicator variables that work better than measures such as certification or the number of mathematics courses taken. One thing that we do know, from our own validation work, is that the relationship between the mathematical quality of instruction and teachers' MKT is rather high, on the order of a .3–.8 positive correlation depending on what aspects of the mathematics in instruction one is examining. For instance, when Lisa completed the MKT items, we found that she was just below average in a large (but nonrandom) sample of California teachers.

In addition to assessments such as those that measure MKT, there may be other low-cost ways to gather information on instructional quality. One that we have explored in the context of other work is teacher logs, which ask teachers to generate a daily report of the mathematics topics covered as well as some aspects of the pedagogical techniques used. Another might be to take the lead of Hilda Borko and Brian Stecher (see Borko, Stecher, Alonzo, Moncure, & McClam, 2005), who have developed a means for assessing teacher quality based on "scoops" of their classroom practice, in which artifacts of instruction—teachers' and students' work—are gathered and analyzed.

Conclusion

The current enthusiasm for teacher quality requires caution. In the end, what matters is the quality of the instruction that students receive—that is, teaching quality. Certainly it is worth developing and using measures that permit reliable inferences about instruction. But such inferences are not easy to establish with meaningful validity. The temptation is great to use readily available proxies for teachers' practice-based knowledge and skill. As we get clearer about the sort of mathematical knowledge that matters for skillful teaching, or about the sorts of key tasks on which teachers must deploy their specialized knowledge and skill, assessments of teaching quality should become easier. However, given the underdevelopment of the field right now, we need to improve the precision with which we conceptualize and measure teacher quality. We close with a set of key challenges that we recommend for broad discussion and collective effort.

One clearly is the question of which aspects of teaching should be measured. We chose to focus on the mathematical quality of instruction; alternative approaches might focus on the nature and quality of student thinking or work, the nature of student–teacher interactions around content, or even more generic pedagogical skills such as managing transitions or maintaining high student engagement. Yet this discussion is made more complex by the fact that teaching practice itself in this country continues to be highly underconceptualized, with an accompanying lack of language to describe it. This is not true in all countries. Japanese, for example, has many more words than English does to name common acts of teaching. In addition, the lack of a knowledge base about teaching complicates the effort to measure teacher quality. Our efforts to fill the gap between the easiest-to-measure predictors and the fact that teachers do make a difference are limited by the lack of precision with which we can examine instructional practice. It is crucial to get to the technical core and not get stuck in inadequately specified superficial features such as whether teachers conduct whole-group lessons or stage an investigation for students. We need to know about the dynamics of how teachers engage students in adding and subtracting positive and negative fractions, not some global label for a kind of teaching. Would a label for Lisa's teaching help us examine the quality of what she is providing for her students? There are big questions about how much we have to sample practice, depending on the questions we have.

Given where we are in our understanding of the quality of students' opportunities to learn as well as their actual learning, we will have to probe those questions. We will have to delve into instruction and then map backward and forward to specific elements that we can use to predict instructional practice and its quality. Without that, we will be having the same conversation a decade from now.

Notes

1. Research presented in this chapter was supported by National Science Foundation grants REC-0207649, REC-0126237, EHR-0233456, and EHR-0335411, as well as a grant from the Spencer Foundation MG-199800202.

2. We acknowledge the contributions of our research group, which has included Hyman Bass, Merrie Blunk, Charalambos Charalambous, Seán Delaney, Imani Masters Goffney, Jennifer Lewis, Geoffrey Phelps, Stephen Schilling, Laurie Sleep, Mark Thames, and Deborah Zopf.

3. These data come from a study examining links between teachers' mathematical knowledge for teaching and the quality of their instruction. For more information, see Hill et al. (in press).

4. Because symbols were not actively used in the solution to this problem, they were excluded from multiple models. However, links between the visual and symbolic representations were also clearly problematic in this segment.

References

Bacolod, M. (2007). Do alternative opportunities matter? The role of female labor markets in the decline of teacher quality, 1960–1990. *Review of Economics and Statistics, 89,* 737–751.

Borko, H., Stecher, B., Alonzo, A. A., Moncure, S., & McClam, S. (2005). Artifact packages for characterizing classroom practice: A pilot study. *Educational Assessment, 10,* 73–104.

Clotfelter, C., Ladd, H. F., & Vigdor, J. (2004). *Teacher quality and minority achievement gaps.* Durham, NC: Terry Sanford Institute of Public Policy.

Corcoran, S. P., Evans, W. N., & Schwab, R. M. (2004). Women, the labor market, and the declining relative quality of teachers. *Journal of Policy Analysis and Management, 23,* 449–470.

Dolton, P., & van der Klaauw, W. (1995). Leaving teaching in the UK: A duration analysis. *The Economic Journal,* 105, 431–444.

Feinman-Nemser, S. (2003). What new teachers need to learn. *Educational Leadership 60*(8), 25–29.

Ferguson, R. F. (1991). Paying for public education: New evidence on how and why money matters. *Harvard Journal on Legislation, 28,* 458–498.

Goldhaber, D. D., & Brewer, D. J. (1997). Evaluating the effect of teacher degree level on educational performance. In W. J. Fowler (Ed.), *Developments in school finance, 1996* (pp. 197–210). Washington, DC: National Center for Education Statistics.

Goldhaber, D. D., Brewer, D. J., & Anderson, D. J. (2000). A three-way error components analysis of educational productivity. *Education Economics, 7,* 199–208.

Goldhaber, D. D., DeArmond, M., Lui, A., & Player, D. (2007). *Returns to skill and teacher wage premiums: What can we learn by comparing the teacher and private sector labor markets?* (Working Paper 8). Seattle, WA: School Finance Redesign Project.

Harbison, R. W., & Hanushek, E. A. (1992). Educational performance for the poor: Lessons from rural northeast Brazil. Oxford, UK: Oxford University Press.

Hill, H. C. (2007). Mathematical knowledge of middle school teachers: Implications for the No Child Left Behind policy initiative. *Educational Evaluation and Policy Analysis, 29,* 95–114.

Hill, H. C., & Ball, D. L. (2004). Learning mathematics for teaching: Results from California's Mathematics Professional Development Institutes. *Journal for Research in Mathematics Education, 35,* 330–351.

Hill, H. C., Ball, D. L., Blunk, M., Goffney, I. M., & Rowan, B. (2007). Validating the ecological assumption: The relationship of measure scores to classroom teaching and student learning. *Measurement: Interdisciplinary Research and Perspective,* 5, 107–117.

Hill, H. C., Blunk, M., Charalambous, C. Y., Lewis, J., Phelps, G. C., Sleep, L., et al. (in press). Mathematical knowledge for teaching and the mathematical quality of instruction: An exploratory study. *Cognition and Instruction.*

Hill, H. C., Dean, C., & Goffney, I. M. (2007). Assessing elemental and structural validity: Data from teachers, non-teachers, and mathematicians. *Measurement: Interdisciplinary Research and Perspectives, 5,* 81–92.

Hill, H. C., Rowan, B., & Ball, D. L. (2005). Effects of teachers' mathematical knowledge for teaching on student achievement. *American Educational Research Journal, 42,* 371–406.

Hill, H. C., & Schilling, S. G. (in press). Evaluating value-added models: A measurement perspective. *Educational Researcher.*

Ingersoll, R. M., & Smith, T. M. (2003). The wrong solution to the teacher shortage. *Educational Leadership, 60*(8), 30–33.

Kane, T. J., Rockoff, J. E., & Staiger, D. O. (2006). *What does certification tell us about teacher effectiveness? Evidence from New York City* (NBER Working Paper No. 12155). Cambridge, MA: National Bureau of Economic Research.

Kimball, S. M., White, B., Milanowski, A. T., & Borman, G. (2004). Examining the relationship between teacher evaluation and student assessment results in Washoe County. *Peabody Journal of Education, 79*(4), 54–78.

Kupermintz, H. (2003). Teacher effects and teacher effectiveness: A validity investigation of the Tennessee value-added assessment system. *Educational Evaluation and Policy Analysis, 25,* 287–298.

Loeb, S., & Reininger, M. (2004). *Public policy and teacher labor markets: What we know and why it matters.* East Lansing: Michigan State University, Education Policy Center.

McCaffrey, D. F., Lockwood, J. R., Koretz, D., & Hamilton, L. S. (2004). *Evaluating value-added models for teacher accountability.* Santa Monica, CA: RAND.

Mullens, J. E., Murnane, R. J., & Willett, J. B. (1996). The contribution of training and subject matter knowledge to teaching effectiveness: A multilevel analysis of longitudinal evidence from Belize. *Comparative Education Review, 40,* 139–157.

Nye, B., Konstantopoulos, S., & Hedges, L. V. (2004). How large are teacher effects? *Educational Evaluation and Policy Analysis, 26,* 237–257.

Raudenbush, S. W. (2004). What are value-added models estimating and what does it mean for statistical practice? *Journal of Educational and Behavioral Statistics, 29,* 121–129.

Rowan, B., Chiang, F., & Miller, R. J. (1997). Using research on employees' performance to study the effects of teachers on students' achievement. *Sociology of Education, 70,* 256–284.

Rowan, B., Correnti, R., & Miller, R. J. (2002). What large-scale, survey research tells us about teacher effects on student achievement: Insights from the Prospects study of elementary schools. *Teachers College Record, 104,* 1525–1567.

The Policy Uses and Policy Validity of Value-Added and Other Teacher Quality Measures

5

Douglas N. Harris

Assistant Professor of Educational Policy Studies, University of Wisconsin at Madison

The U.S. education system has long tried to maintain and improve the quality of its teaching workforce by requiring and rewarding specific teacher credentials, especially teacher experience and certain types of education. Teachers are prepared in university-based colleges of education that require state government approval. Most of these graduates are then certified to teach, so long as they pass knowledge and/or pedagogy competency tests. Teachers are then hired and compensated based on their years of experience and whether they obtain graduate degrees in education. Not all teachers have high levels of education or experience, but requiring and rewarding these teacher credentials remains the nation's dominant teacher quality strategy.

This traditional credentials strategy and the results it has produced have long been criticized.[1] The systems of public education in general, and human resource management in particular, are seen as less efficient than those used in the private sector. Also, the outcomes of these perceived inefficiencies have been seen as inadequate. The concern is not only the country's low standing in international test score comparisons and perceived slow growth in national test scores (Harris & Herrington, 2006), but that faithfully executing the traditional strategy seems to have no consistent and measurable impact on teachers' effectiveness in raising student test scores. Education production function (EPF) studies by economists have generally found little or no systematic relationship between teacher credentials and student outcomes (Goldhaber & Brewer, 2000; Hanushek, 1986).[2] Levine (2005) reaches essentially the same conclusion in his more recent study and critique of teacher education. The fact that the traditional strategy seems to have little positive impact on student test scores reinforces larger concerns about the country's educational competitiveness.

These research findings, combined with new political pressures, have led to calls for an alternative strategy—teacher quality through accountability.[3] Two major shifts toward this accountability strategy have occurred in recent years: one in the early 1990s, as state governments began to introduce and expand "school report cards," and the second, in 2001, with the passage of the federal No Child Left Behind (NCLB) law that expanded student testing and the use of school report cards as the basis for interventions in schools whose students are not making adequate test score progress. Although focused on holding schools accountable, rather than individual teachers, these pressures were clearly designed to trickle down and influence what teachers do. In many ways, this form of accountability has succeeded in its goals. There is ample evidence that teachers made changes in instructional time and practices to meet accountability objectives (e.g., Booher-Jennings, 2005). In states such as Florida that have long used strong accountability systems, the pressures have apparently permeated schools even more deeply, influencing basic human resource management practices (Rutledge, Harris, Ingle, & Thompson, in press) and policies related to student discipline (Figlio, in press). There is, of course, considerable debate about whether these changes represent genuine improvements, and many of the same studies showing intended change also indicate unintended consequences (Booher-Jennings, 2005), but there is no question that many of the intended effects, such as greater focus on math and reading, have occurred.

The accountability movement has, however, left the traditional credentials strategy largely intact. Although efforts have been made to provide alternative routes to certification, the overwhelming majority of teachers still graduate from university-based teacher education programs, still receive state-sanctioned certification, and still receive compensation based on degrees and experience. Rather than replace the traditional strategy, accountability has simply been layered on top of it.

But perhaps not for long. Many school districts are now experimenting with compensation systems that aim to provide direct incentives for individual teachers, paying them based on the test scores of their own students and therefore implicitly reducing the weight given to university-based teacher education and experience. The federal government is also encouraging these merit or performance pay approaches through a voluntary pilot program, the Teacher Incentive Fund (TIF), and new bills in Congress promise to expand these new pay systems in persistently low-performing schools. (Full disclosure: I am on the federal technical working group that advises TIF districts on their plans.) There are also proposals to use student test scores as a primary basis for making teacher tenure decisions (Gordon, Kane, & Staiger, 2006). Depending on the outcomes of these proposals, the development, implementation, and adoption of similar merit pay policies could greatly expand and even replace the traditional teacher quality strategy altogether.

Yet the debate about both the credential and accountability teacher quality strategies has been confused in a number of ways. The first issue is the way in which empirical evidence has been translated into policy recommendations. Information about statistical validity is far from sufficient to make such recommendations. Therefore, in the second section, I outline the criterion of *policy validity*, or the validity of the use of a teacher quality measure in education policy. The use of a teacher quality measure is valid in this policy sense if the weight given to the measure (in determining who becomes a teacher and how teachers develop their instructional practices) is proportional to the statistical validity and costs associated with the measure. This is an admittedly vague definition, especially in comparison to the related cost-effectiveness concepts typically used by economists. However, I will show later that it does prove useful in interpreting the research evidence and that the more typical and concrete cost-effectiveness frameworks are impractical here because of the complex nature of teacher quality and notable gaps in research.

The debate about teacher quality has also been confused by methodological problems and inconsistent findings in the research studies testing the validity of teacher quality measures. One of the main methodological problems has been the selection bias caused by the nonrandom assignment of both teachers to education and teachers to students (Harris & Sass, 2007b). In the past several years, researchers have begun to develop and use *value-added modeling* to address these problems and more clearly identify the credentials of effective teachers. In the third section, I discuss the basic logic and assumptions of value-added models and provide a summary of recent evidence about the credentials of effective teachers from value-added models as well as some experiments and quasi experiments. I also compare the results of these studies to the older generations of education production function studies, which remain influential in the current debates about teacher quality strategies. All of the research discussed in this chapter focuses on student achievement scores on standardized assessments as the outcome of interest, mainly because there is little evidence about the causal effects of teachers on other important outcomes such as student motivation, creativity, and socialization.

In addition to using value-added models to identify the credentials of effective teachers, a second potential use of value-added models, consistent with the accountability strategy, is to directly measure the effectiveness of individual teachers. By analogy, the credentials approach amounts to measuring how much rain has fallen by the number of clouds in the sky. The accountability strategy would simply put an empty glass on the sidewalk and measure the rain directly—without getting "lost in the clouds." In the fourth section of this chapter, I revisit the assumptions of value-added and show that this rain metaphor is more problematic than it appears at first. The assumptions of value-added modeling are, at best, untested and, at worst, simply wrong, and this has significant implications for using individual teacher value-added measures for accountability. I also summarize recent empirical evidence about the statistical validity of value-added models for accountability.

In the final section, I interpret the recent evidence from value-added studies in terms of policy validity. I conclude that neither the credentials strategy nor the accountability strategy alone is the best approach to improving teacher quality. Just as there is little support for the long-standing tradition of giving higher salaries for having graduate degrees, so too is there little support for the other extreme—compensating and firing teachers substantially on the basis of value-added scores. Instead, what is needed is a coherent and comprehensive strategy that serves all teacher quality functions well and uses resources effectively and efficiently. I provide some specific suggestions at the end of the chapter.

Introduction to Policy Validity

There is no single way to interpret the empirical evidence about teacher quality measures and translate it into clear policy recommendations. Decisions inevitably turn on difficult trade-offs and judgments driven as much by philosophy as by evidence. However, there are some basic elements that are arguably required of any useful decision-making framework related to teacher quality policy. In this section, I discuss three such elements—functions, statistical validity, and costs—and combine these into a framework that I refer to as *policy validity*. I present the different general functions and show how they are intertwined with the meaning of statistical validity.

GENERAL FUNCTION 1: PREDICTING OR "SIGNALING" WHICH TEACHERS ARE MOST LIKELY TO BE EFFECTIVE

A signal is some quality indicating that a person is likely to help the organization meet its objectives and can therefore be used to predict future behavior and effectiveness. For example, suppose that a researcher observes that teachers with academic degrees from particular university programs tend to be more effective than others. A degree from this institution therefore serves as a signal regarding the likely effectiveness of future candidates.[4] Such signals could also be useful at earlier stages in the teacher pipeline. For example, leaders of teacher education programs might observe that teachers who have an above-average grade point average (GPA) in their freshman and sophomore years are more likely to go on to graduate and become successful teachers. Teacher education programs might therefore use GPA as a signal and as a basis for admissions. Of course, to be effective, there must be some relationship between the signal and the contribution to the organization's objectives.

Signals can also be the basis for compensation. As noted earlier, teacher education and experience are used as the basis for teacher compensation in public schools. Using signals in this way, however, can be criticized because compensation occurs after services have been rendered—that is, teachers are paid for work they have already done. Thus, it would only seem logical to compensate teachers primarily on the basis of a signal if what the teachers did—how well they performed—were extremely difficult to measure.[5]

GENERAL FUNCTION 2: IMPROVING TEACHER EFFECTIVENESS THROUGH FORMATIVE ASSESSMENTS OR SUMMATIVE ASSESSMENTS TIED TO INCENTIVES

Signals are useful for identifying potentially effective workers for hiring purposes, but it is also important that organizations develop the skills and effort of their employees after they are hired. There are two ways that a teacher quality measure can aid in this process. First, the measure might suggest ways in which teachers could improve. For example, if professional development appears to improve teacher effectiveness, then a teacher who is performing poorly in a particular area (e.g., teaching fractions) might be encouraged to pursue additional professional development to improve skills in this content area. This would be considered a formative use of the measures.

An alternative use of teacher quality measures is simply to determine who is performing well—a summative assessment—in order to identify the teachers for hiring, promotion, additional compensation, or dismissal. Although summative assessment does not provide advice to teachers about how to improve, it does provide incentives that might induce teachers to seek out paths to improvement or, in the face of repeated low performance, to leave the profession. That teachers often leave the profession well before retirement age is often viewed as a problem, but departures of low-performing teachers are likely to improve outcomes if these teachers can be replaced by more effective ones. It is therefore clear that formative and summative assessments are interrelated. There must be paths to improvement as well as incentives, formal or otherwise, to follow those paths.

MULTIPLE MEASURES

Multiple measures are also necessary to carry out these functions because a teacher quality measure that is useful as a signal may not be useful in improving effectiveness and vice versa. To be useful as a signal, the measure must be a strong predictor of teacher effectiveness (i.e., explain a high degree of the variance in effectiveness). In contrast, to be useful for improving effectiveness, the measure can have more modest statistical explanatory power, so long as it is alterable. Suppose that teachers with particular personality traits tend to make more effective teachers. In this case, the trait might serve as a useful signal, but if personality traits are essentially fixed or at least difficult to systematically alter, they are useless for the purpose of improving an individual teacher's effectiveness. It also turns out, as discussed later, that a measure that is valid for formative assessment might not be valid for summative assessment.

The larger point is that whether an estimate is statistically valid, indeed the very meaning of statistical validity, depends on what type of conclusion one is trying to draw. Further, in trying to improve teacher quality, there are many types of conclusions or functions that are of interest.[6] The multiple functions and meanings of statistical validity help explain why policy validity is a useful term and concept. Policy validity takes into account the specific types of inferences—signaling and improvement—that are important with regard to teacher quality. It also accounts for an additional factor of great interest to policymakers: policy costs. Later in this chapter, I discuss how economists conceptualize and measure costs and provide some back-of-the-envelope calculations about the costs of some aspects of teacher quality policies. In the two sections that follow, I discuss value-added modeling as a source of evidence about the validity of different teacher quality measures.

From Education Production Functions to Value-Added

The impetus for the current reconsideration of the credentials strategy for improving teacher quality, as noted earlier, comes partly from evidence from EPF studies, which suggests that some key teacher credentials (e.g., education, experience, certification) are not closely related to teacher effectiveness. Researchers have been well aware of the questionable validity of these studies, and resulting potential for selection bias, caused by reliance on data from a single point in time. Nevertheless, up through the 1980s, these were some of the best studies available, and researchers and policymakers were right to take them seriously. Now that research methods and data have advanced, however, it is important to revisit the selection bias problems and show how new research methods potentially address them.

There are two main parts to the selection bias problem in this context. First, teachers are nonrandomly assigned to students. For example, some teachers are systematically assigned to teach students who have lower initial achievement. Using data from a single point in time, these teachers will appear less effective. This problem can be partly corrected by controlling for student socioeconomic status (SES) with measures such as student race and income, but recent evidence suggests that variation in initial student achievement is only partly captured by these SES measures (Harris & Sass, 2005).

Second, teachers are nonrandomly associated with their credentials. Most notably, some teachers may be systematically more likely than others to obtain additional education. If the least effective teachers obtain more education to address their deficiencies, then even if teacher education helps, it may appear falsely that teacher education makes teachers worse. Alternatively, better teachers might feel more confident about their potential ability to obtain more education. This would have the opposite effect, making it appear that education made teachers better when, in fact, teachers with more education were better to start with. The net effect of these different forms of selection bias is difficult to determine, but accounting for them is clearly important.

With colleague Tim Sass, I have described a second generation of EPF studies that address nonrandom selection by controlling for a single previous student test score (Harris & Sass, 2007b). If differences across students, such as their access to school resources in the past, affect their propensity for learning in the future, then controlling for a previous test score should account for the differences in past inputs. Put differently, with two scores, we can focus on the change in learning over a very specific time period, one or two years, and more reasonably assume that the change in test scores is due to what happened in the school during that time period.

This *gain score* model partly addresses the nonrandom assignment of teachers to students as long as all students who have the same initial test score have an equal probability of making large gains in the next year. Although this is a more reasonable assumption than the one made in the point-in-time EPF model, it is still problematic. Some students who have the same test score at a point in time may also have different expected rates of learning growth. For example, consider a student who was far behind when starting kindergarten, but who has learned at a fast rate, compared with a student who started kindergarten with a high level of achievement but has been learning at a slow rate. These two students might have the same score at a point in time, but the expected rate of growth in the future is apparently higher for the first student, and teachers assigned to that student will be at an advantage. Also, even if the students have the same expected rate of learning, the gain score model still fails to address the second selection bias problem—nonrandom assignment of teachers to credentials. Therefore, the results from the gain score models are still potentially invalid, in all senses of the term.

Value-added models have the potential to address both selection bias problems. Intuitively, these models start with the average achievement gain of each teacher's students over several years and then adjust these averages based on how much these students would have been expected to learn given their growth trajectory over a long period of time as well as the resources they received in other grades. By including data from multiple years and, in effect, controlling for this adjusted average rate of student learning, researchers can identify the effect of each teacher by calculating for each teacher the average deviation from the students' expected learning trajectories. Teachers whose students systematically beat expectations have above-average value-added. By doing a better job of measuring how much we can expect each student to learn, we can better address the first selection bias problem.

Value-added also addresses the nonrandom assignment of teachers to some types of credentials. Just as with the student assignment problem, the teacher assignment problem can be addressed by using each teacher as his or her own control group. Consider a teacher who takes part in a professional development course. With a value-added model, we could measure the teacher's effect on students before and after the professional development. If teacher effectiveness improves, controlling for other factors such as teacher experience, it is reasonable to conclude that the professional development was the cause—and this is true even if the teacher was nonrandomly assigned to the professional development.[7] It would therefore appear that value-added is a significant advance in identifying the effects of individual teachers and teacher credentials.

Some of the most important early work on value-added was conducted by Hanushek (1979) and Boardman and Murnane (1979). For more recent discussions, which discuss theoretical issues within the context of current data availability, see Harris (in press), Harris and Sass (2005), and Todd and Wolpin (2003).

SOME ASSUMPTIONS OF VALUE-ADDED MODELS

While value-added modeling has some important advantages over traditional EPF and gain score models, this new approach is still based on some important assumptions. I discuss some of the key assumptions here and return later to consider their implications.

Differences in the Expected Achievement Gains Can Be Accounted for by Taking Into Account Their Past (and Future) Growth[8]

I mentioned earlier that an advantage of value-added modeling is that it accounts for the fact that teachers teach different types of students who have different propensities to make achievement gains. More specifically, the student's propensity to make achievement gains has to be fixed. For example, some students have parents who consistently make them do their homework and expect them to go to college, and some children might experience a divorce or other change in circumstances that influences their ability to learn. Although these time-varying changes are not accounted for in value-added models, this does not necessarily bias the estimates of individual teacher value-added. The measured effect of a teacher would only be biased if a teacher were systematically assigned to students who have positive or negative "shocks" in their learning propensities (e.g., divorce of parents).

A 1-Point Increase in Test Scores Represents the Same Amount of Learning Regardless of Students' Initial Level of Achievement or the Test Year

Value-added models are, at a basic level, models of student achievement. Therefore, it is unsurprising that value-added models require strong assumptions about the measurement of student achievement. Specifically, it is assumed that a 1-point change in the score is the same on every point on the test scale—that is, the test is interval-scaled. Even the psychometricians who are responsible for test scaling shy away from making this assumption in the strict sense.

Some adjustments can be made in the value-added analysis to account for the scale problems. For example, some researchers add grade-by-year fixed effects, which adjust each teacher's value-added based on the mean achievement of all students in the respective grade and year. However, this amounts to simply shifting teachers' value-added based on the mean gain in the years and grades in which they have taught. This approach is sufficient so long as the scaling problems influence only the mean gain and not, for example, the distribution around the mean. In that case, an arguably better approach is to "normalize" all the test scores to a mean of zero and standard deviation of one, based on the standard deviation of the respective grades and years. This approach requires the assumption that the differences in the standard deviations (and means) are due to changes in the scale rather than any genuine changes in the learning distribution.[9] The significance of the assumptions about the test scale as well as the adjustments that might be made to account for the assumptions are currently being explored by a number of researchers, though there is little evidence to report at present.

Teachers Are Equally Effective With All Types of Students

A high value-added teacher is one whose students learn at a faster rate than one would expect given their growth rates in other years. These deviations from the expected growth rate are then averaged and adjusted for all of the teacher's students. Because all of the students are averaged together, an implicit assumption is that teachers are equally effective with all groups of students.

To see the problem with this, suppose that the opposite were true and that some teachers were effective with slow-achievement-growth students and other teachers were effective with fast-achievement-growth students. Further, suppose that all teachers were assigned only to students with whom they were most effective. In this case, all teachers would appear equally effective. Now suppose that some teachers were assigned to students with whom they were ineffective, and as a result, their value-added scores decrease. These same teachers who had been judged effective above will now appear ineffective simply because they were assigned to a different group of students. This is problematic because teachers cannot control which students they are assigned to, and it would be difficult to argue that these "misassigned" teachers are really less effective than the others. This example is an extreme case, but it illustrates the general problem with assuming that all teachers are equally effective with all students.

The degree to which this assumption poses a problem depends on the type of statistical validity that is of interest. Although the differences in the ways that teachers are assigned to students are problematic for the sake of summative assessment, these value-added estimates would still be useful for teachers in trying to improve their performance (formative assessment).

Student Test Data Are Missing at Random

Given the complexity implied by the previous discussion, it comes as no surprise that the data requirements for value-added are significant and that data will be missing for a large portion of the students, due to absenteeism, mobility across schools, and data processing errors. Missing data do not bias the results so long as they are missing at random, though missing data significantly diminish the reliability of the estimates. This is a strong assumption and is especially likely to be a problem in high-poverty schools where absenteeism and mobility are high and test-taking rates are lower. It is therefore a significant question whether valid value-added estimates can be made in schools with high mobility.

This discussion has focused on the basic nature of value-added models and their underlying assumptions. In the next section, I discuss some important recent findings regarding value-added. First, I discuss the findings of value-added modeling for program evaluation (VAM-P). Although not referred to specifically above, VAM-P is used to identify the correlations and effects of teacher credentials, such as teacher test scores and teacher professional development. I go on to discuss value-added modeling for accountability (VAM-A), which is used to identify the effectiveness of each individual teacher (ignoring teacher credentials). I also show later why the assumption violations that I have just discussed are much more significant for VAM-A than for VAM-P and therefore why value-added models should be used more cautiously in trying to evaluate individual teachers.

VAM-P Research on the Credentials of Effective Teachers

The previous section shows why the results from value-added models are more likely to yield statistically valid estimates of the credentials of effective teachers—for the simple reason that the two forms of nonrandom selection are addressed with greater care than in EPF and gain score studies. In this section, I summarize recent studies that have used value-added models to examine the credentials of effective teachers. I also discuss some of the difficulties in identifying such credentials, beyond the questionable assumptions mentioned earlier.

Before discussing these findings, it is important to distinguish between two types of teacher credentials: those that vary over time and those that are fixed. Earlier, I discussed teacher personality as an example of a fixed characteristic. Undergraduate education is another example because very few teachers are in the classroom full time before they have their degrees. Other forms of teacher education, such as graduate training and professional development, change over time. The distinction between fixed and time-varying credentials is important partly because it highlights what can be learned about the policy validity of different types of measures. For a characteristic that is fixed in nature, or one that might vary but is only measured at a single point in time in a particular analysis, we can only hope to learn whether the measure is a good signal of teacher effectiveness. We cannot know in this case whether the quality of the signal is due to some unmeasured characteristic of teachers that is correlated with the measured characteristic, or whether improving one's standing on the fixed measure actually causes teacher improvement.[10] In contrast, it is easier to determine the causal effects of alterable and time-varying credentials, such as teacher experience and professional development, because individual teachers can be compared before and after the change takes place.

FINDINGS FROM VAM-P RESEARCH ON
THE CREDENTIALS OF EFFECTIVE TEACHERS

Based on Harris and Sass (2007b), I am aware of 28 studies of the effects of teacher education and experience on teachers' contributions to student achievement, using either the gain score, value-added, or experimental methods. Table 5.1 summarizes the results from these studies, dividing them into two categories based on the methods used. Note that the numbers in the table add to a number considerably larger than 28 because many of the studies have estimates of more than one teacher credential.

Table 5.1 includes the VAM-P studies together with a very small number of related studies that address the issues of nonrandom selection using data where students and teachers are actually or apparently randomly assigned to one another (these address only one form of selection bias). For the reasons stated in the previous section, there are reasons to trust the validity of the value-added studies more so than the gain score studies. Some studies find a positive and statistically significant relationship between the teacher credential and teacher effectiveness, as indicated in the Positive/Significant category. Other studies find either an insignificant relationship or (rarely) a negative and significant one, which are indicated by Insignificant/Negative. Note that only one of the studies (Harris & Sass, 2007b) includes all of the teacher credentials in Table 5.1.

Most Measures of Formal Teacher Education, Especially Graduate Education, Appear Unrelated to Teacher Value-Added

In the gain scores studies, 8 of the 23 estimates of the effects of teacher education (undergraduate, graduate, and professional development) suggest that some aspect of teacher education is positively associated with teacher effectiveness. The same finding holds for 6 of the 15 value-added or related types of estimates that have studied teacher education. Most of the remaining studies find statistically insignificant associations between education and teacher effectiveness. The fact that most forms of formal teacher education are unrelated to teacher value-added does not mean that the same is true of all forms of formal education.

It is also important to emphasize that the measures of teacher education vary considerably across studies. Some look only at whether teachers have degrees from schools of education, whereas others consider training in particular subject areas and/or consider teacher effectiveness in specific school subjects. Gain score studies matching specific undergraduate majors with specific subjects (e.g., the effects of teachers who were math majors on student math achievement) are more likely to find positive effects than those looking at the level of education or whether the degree came from a school of education, but the results are inconsistent even in these cases. Also, note that nearly all of the studies on formal teacher education focus only on the quality of the signal that teacher education provides, not whether it improves teacher effectiveness. (In the case of undergraduate teacher education, this is simply a consequence of the fact that it is not time-varying.)

Wayne and Youngs (2003), in a previous summary of evidence using a broader variety of research methods, conclude that (1) there is a relationship between teachers' mathematics coursework and student mathematics gains in high school, but no such effects are apparent in elementary grades or other subjects, and (2) mathematics certification is related to students'

Table 5.1   Results of Studies of the Effect of Teacher Education and Experience on Student Achievement

Teacher credentials	Gain score studies		Value-added or related studies	
	Positive/ significant	Insignificant/ negative	Positive/ significant	Insignificant/ negative
Undergraduate	5	4	1	2
Graduate	3	10	3	6
Professional development	0	1	2	1
Experience	7	8	8	1
Test score	5	2	1	1

SOURCE: Based on a review by Harris & Sass (2007b).

math scores gains, but there is insufficient evidence with regard to other subjects and grades. However, given the apparent sensitivity of the results to research methods, their inclusion of studies that do not adequately account for nonrandom selection is somewhat problematic.

There Is Some Evidence That Pedagogical Content Knowledge Is Associated With Teacher Effectiveness

This finding is based on analysis of date from Florida (Harris & Sass, 2007b) and is only partially evident in Table 5.1. We used VAM-P to study the time-varying effects of teacher professional development where it is possible to compare each teacher's effectiveness before and after the education takes place. Specifically, we found that "content" professional development was in some cases positively associated with teacher value-added.[11] I interpret this as pedagogical content knowledge because professional development, unlike some courses in undergraduate education, rarely focuses on content alone, so content-oriented professional development is likely to include a mix of pedagogy and content.

Two related findings are noteworthy. First, we found what appears to be a lagged effect of teacher professional development—that is, it can take several years for professional development to produce higher teacher value-added. This is important because it suggests that studies looking for immediate effects will understate the long-term impact. Second, when studying the signal effect of different types of undergraduate teacher education, we found that undergraduate courses mixing content and pedagogy were sometimes positively associated with teacher value-added.[12] Thus, pedagogical content knowledge appears to be the only case in which a particular type of formal education is useful both as a signal and as a path to improvement.

Teacher Experience Is Consistently Positively Associated With Teacher Effectiveness, at Least for the First Several Years

Roughly half of the gain score studies found a positive effect of teacher experience. The effects are overwhelmingly positive in the value-added and related studies, making teacher experience the characteristic that is most clearly related to teacher effectiveness. These results for teacher experience are consistent with evidence on worker experience in other occupations (Harris & Rutledge, 2007). This suggests that teachers, as well as other workers, learn not only through formal coursework, but also by doing—through their own trial and error.

Teacher Test Scores Are Inconsistently Associated With Teacher Value-Added

The gain score studies in Table 5.1 suggest that teacher test scores are consistently positively related with teacher effectiveness. Only two studies have considered teacher test scores with value-added and related methods, but these have yielded more mixed results. Clotfelter, Ladd, and Vigdor (2005) find a positive relationship, whereas Harris and Sass (2007b) find no effect.[13] Both studies focus on college entrance exams (as opposed to certification tests) and on the potential of these scores to serve as valid signals of teacher effectiveness.

Various Forms of Teacher Certification, Including NBPTS, Are Inconsistently Associated With Teacher Value-Added

The research that my colleagues and I have produced in Florida has not focused on state licensure for various reasons, but we have studied a different type of teacher certification: the National Board for Professional Teaching Standards (NBPTS; Harris & Sass, 2007a). In short, we found that NBPTS certification inconsistently identifies more effective teachers. Results from other similar studies find that NBPTS teachers are more effective than others and than those who attempt NBPTS certification but fail to pass (Goldhaber & Anthony, in press), but these, too, are inconsistent.

NBPTS certification also involves a substantial amount of time in the preparation of materials and studying for the required tests. Therefore, it is plausible that this certification, whether or not it is an accurate signal of teacher value-added, still improves teacher effectiveness. In this case, the results are more consistent: None of the value-added studies suggest that teachers improve as a result of going through the process. This is not necessarily a criticism of NBPTS, because directly improving teaching is not the main purpose of the certification, but it is noteworthy because it highlights how a single measure might be useful for one purpose but not another.

While setting aside some important methodological issues that arise even in the most advanced studies,[14] this review summarizes the latest research from value-added and gain score studies. The next section provides a similar review for a very different type of teacher quality measure.

VAM-A Research on Individual Teacher Effectiveness

The traditional strategies for improving teacher quality focus on credentials such as teacher education and experience, as discussed in the previous section. An alternative strategy is to measure teacher effectiveness directly—measuring the rain by putting a glass on the sidewalk, so to speak. In this section, I discuss important findings regarding the VAM-A that inform the feasibility and usefulness of this alternative strategy.

FINDINGS FROM VAM-A RESEARCH ABOUT INDIVIDUAL TEACHERS

Value-Added Varies Considerably Across Teachers

Sanders and Horn (1998) and Rivkin, Hanushek, and Kain (2005), for example, find considerable differences between the most and least effective teachers, based on value-added results. This conclusion is important because it suggests that, even though few teacher credentials are systematically associated with student learning, the teachers themselves clearly do matter—and do vary. This conclusion might not seem very surprising, but remember that earlier studies by Coleman (1966), Hanushek (1986), and others focused only on measurable credentials that ultimately appeared to be unrelated to teacher effectiveness, which led some to conclude that teachers did not generally matter. Although it remains difficult to identify specific credentials that are important, these value-added results suggest that students do better—perhaps substantially so—with some teachers compared to others.

The apparent variation in teacher effectiveness is partly driven by problems with the assumptions of value-added as well as issues such as measurement and estimation error. Nevertheless, the general finding that teacher effectiveness varies is perhaps obvious enough from other types of studies. Studies on student "tracking," for example, suggest that the instruction received by lower-track students is more likely to emphasize memorization compared with the higher-order thinking skills emphasized in higher-track classes (Ogbu, 2003). In this case, the quality of instruction appears to vary across classrooms and teachers, so we would expect value-added to vary as well.

Teacher Value-Added Is Positively Correlated With Other Measures of Teacher Effectiveness

Teacher value-added can be viewed as an objective measure of teacher effectiveness in the sense that the method of calculating it is the same for all teachers and is not filtered through the subjective preferences and beliefs of a supervisor or other evaluator. There is a long history of research studying the relationships between subjective and objective measures of worker productivity as well as the implications of this relationship for employment contracts. As noted by Harris and Sass (2007c) and Jacob and Lefgren (2005), this research suggests that there is a positive, but arguably weak, relationship between subjective and objective measures. There is also a limited amount of literature that specifically addresses this issue. Some studies have examined the relationship between teachers' students' test scores and their principals' subjective assessments (e.g., Milanowski, 2004; Murnane, 1975). All of these studies find a positive and significant relationship despite differences in the degree to which the observations are used for high-stakes personnel decisions.

Some more recent studies have utilized longitudinal data to estimate gain scores models that partly address the selection bias issues described earlier (Medley & Coker, 1987; Peterson, 1987, 2000). Also, Jacob and Lefgren (2005) used value-added models to study 200 teachers in a mid-sized school district and reached two main conclusions: There is a positive correlation between the subjective and objective measures, and this correlation holds even after controlling for teacher experience and education levels, which are currently the primary bases for determining teacher compensation. Harris & Sass (2007c) found similar results from an analysis of a separate midsized school district in Florida. Although the comparison of principal evaluations of teachers with teacher value-added measures cannot be viewed as a validity check per se, it does suggest that value-added measures provide useful information.

Based on these findings—that teacher effectiveness varies and that this measure is correlated with other credible measures—the news on value-added reinforces the potential use of value-added for accountability. This is not the case with the following two findings.

Teacher Value-Added Scores Are Imprecise

There are several sources of error that make estimates of teacher value-added imprecise. This a natural outgrowth of the fact that value-added focuses on changes in student achievement over time, which compounds the measurement error in the achievement scores. Also, by their nature, value-added models involve estimating a large number of parameters (one performance measure per teacher) with relatively few observations per teacher, reducing reliability. Kane and Staiger (2001) provide an excellent discussion of the types of errors involved with VAM-A estimations and their impact on grade-level school performance measures. The problems they describe are worse when data are disaggregated to the individual teachers, as is the case with the VAM-A models of interest here.

Individual Teacher Value-Added Changes Considerably Over Time

Intuitively, we would expect that the actual effectiveness of each individual teacher changes little from year to year. Teachers might gradually improve over time, as suggested by the earlier discussion of evidence on teacher experience,[15] but it is unlikely that they will jump from the bottom to the top of the performance distribution. It is even less likely that teacher rankings on value-added should drop significantly from year to year.

Yet the results imply that teacher value-added estimates are indeed unstable. Koedel and Betts (2005) find that only 35% of teachers ranked in the top fifth of teachers on teacher value-added one year were still ranked in the top fifth in the subsequent year. This suggests that 65% of teachers actually got worse relative to their peers over a short period of time—many dramatically so. It is intuitively implausible that actual teacher effectiveness is this erratic over time. The low reliability and stability of value-added measures therefore reinforce the need to proceed with some caution in using value-added for accountability.

This instability may or may not be a severe problem in VAM-P. If the instability is due entirely to random fluctuations, then this probably introduces no bias in the estimates of teacher credential effects, but only makes it more likely that estimates will be statistically insignificant.

REVISITING THE ASSUMPTIONS

Earlier, I discussed the assumptions of value-added, which apply to both VAM-A and VAM-P. Violations of these assumptions are problematic for both model types, but the assumptions of any value-added model are more problematic for VAM-A. There are two reasons for this. First, achieving valid estimates is always harder in VAM-A than in VAM-P because there are fewer student test score observations to work with for each relevant estimate. Second, many violations of the assumptions may arise only for a small number of teachers or occur randomly so that the problems "wash out" when considering the entire sample of teachers. But when looking at the value-added of individual teachers, this means that the value-added scores for some, perhaps many, teachers will be biased. For example, most teachers may be equally effective with all students or systematically assigned to students with whom they are most effective, but what about the other teachers? What is true on the average will not be true everywhere, which means that many teachers are likely to be inaccurately evaluated when using VAM-A.

The importance of the assumptions, as well as the earlier problematic empirical results, might seem to suggest that VAM-A should not be used. These limitations must be balanced, however, against its main advantages—that it provides a more direct measure of effectiveness and sends a message about the priorities of the school system. Another way to see the difference between VAM-A and VAM-P measures is to observe that, although the "noise" tends to wash out in VAM-P and yields fairly precise estimates of the effects of teacher credentials, these effects are small and explain little of the total variation of value-added; in contrast, VAM-A measures are imprecise, but they imprecisely measure what is of greatest interest.

Also, all of the assumptions of VAM-A apply to other methods of using student test scores to evaluate teachers. For example, suppose we were to evaluate teachers simply on the level of achievement at the end of the school year or even on the simple gains from the previous year. In these cases, all the assumptions discussed earlier (e.g., that teachers are equally effective with all types of students) are still required. These simpler and more common uses of student test scores also require an additional assumption. Instead of adhering to the assumption that student achievement can be accounted for by past and future gains, evaluating teachers based on test score level or gains requires the far less plausible assumption that that there are no differences in the likelihood that students will make achievement gains and, therefore, there is no need to make any adjustments to account for nonschool factors. This is a fundamental flaw because it means that these measures attribute to the school, and to teachers, causes of low achievement that are clearly outside of school control—especially family factors that are well known and powerful influences over student achievement (see, e.g., Coleman, 1966; Harris, 2007). This same assumption is commonly made with school report cards and in defining school success under NCLB, even in states that use growth curve models, though extensive discussion of this topic is outside the scope of the present study.[16]

This leads to two important conclusions. First, the assumptions of VAM-A may be somewhat problematic, but there are clearly fewer problematic assumptions involved with VAM-A than with more common approaches to using test scores. This highlights the fact that VAM-A and its assumptions should not be judged by whether they meet all the desirable statistical properties—they do not and no amount of research will change this—but should be judged relative to the realistic alternatives. When compared with other ways of using student test scores to assess teacher performance, VAM-A stacks up reasonably well.

The other alternative—using VAM-P to identify the credentials of effective teachers—has problems of its own. The fact that VAM-P allows random deviations from the assumptions to wash out when measuring the credentials of effective teachers is an advantage, but these credentials explain little of the variation in teacher value-added and therefore are only modestly helpful in identifying the most effective teachers. These are inherent trade-offs that policymakers must take into account when deciding how to use the various measures.

Policy Validity: Interpreting the Evidence

One possible way to interpret all of this evidence on teacher quality measures is through the economics method of cost-effectiveness analysis—that is, measuring the effects and costs of various options and recommending the set of options that provides the greatest bang for the buck. This framework, however, is impractical for trying to draw policy conclusions from evidence about teacher quality measures. First, there is no agreement on the specific effects and costs of any of the measures. In the case of effects, the previous section shows that this is a result of the variation in results across studies. Although it might be possible to establish reasonable ranges for the effects, there is almost no evidence about the costs of the measures with which to compare them. Second, cost-effectiveness analysis tends to assume that policy options are independent of one another, yet there are multiple functions that the measures play in the process of improving teacher quality, and these are interrelated with one another. In short, teacher quality policy is just too complex to be boiled down to a few simple numbers. Policy validity, therefore, incorporates the cost-effectiveness concept with the specific complex issues that arise in improving teacher quality, taking into account the limits in the research evidence.

After discussing specific policy functions that might be served by teacher quality measures, I present some preliminary evidence about the costs of the measures. Finally, I use this new framework to draw conclusions from the evidence on VAM-A and VAM-P discussed in the previous sections.

SPECIFIC FUNCTIONS OF TEACHER QUALITY MEASURES

To make the functions of teacher quality measures more concrete, it is worth going beyond the general categories of signaling and improvement discussed earlier. Table 5.2 includes four specific functions, broken into two categories depending on the weight given to the measure—that is, the degree to which the measure is relied on to carry out the function and influence the

Table 5.2   General and Specific Functions of Teacher Quality Measures

General function	Specific function with low weight	Specific function with high weight
Signal	Characteristic is recommended as a condition of hiring	Characteristic is required as a condition of hiring
Improvement	Characteristic is required for experienced teachers to maintain certification	Characteristic is the primary basis for compensation or dismissal (firing)

quality of the teacher workforce. Recommending that teachers reach a minimum level of some teacher quality measure obviously involves less weight than firing teachers who are below the minimum. Other cases are less clear. For example, requiring teachers to meet a particular threshold gives significant weight to the teacher quality measure, but not necessarily more than compensating teachers by the measures.

In theory, a teacher quality measure can serve multiple functions. Based on the evidence discussed earlier, pedagogical content knowledge and experience appear to be two cases that serve both the signaling and improvement functions. However, these appear to be rare exceptions. Many measures (e.g., personality, undergraduate education) are essentially fixed and can therefore serve only as signals. Even in these cases, it is not entirely clear that the signaling quality is sufficient to justify excluding potential teachers without observing their actual performance. This means that a combination of measures, each serving its own function in a multifaceted strategy, is the best general approach to improving teacher quality.

COST OF TEACHER QUALITY MEASURES

The focus so far on statistical validity and functions highlights the potential benefits of teacher quality measures. In other work, I have emphasized the fact that the costs of education programs are just as important as their effects (Harris, 2008). In this case, some teacher credentials are much more costly to produce than others.

There are general types of costs that need to be distinguished. Economists define costs as the value of a resource in its next best use—the opportunity cost. For example, for each hour that a teacher spends instructing students, the teacher could have been working in some other job, spending time with family, or engaging in other personally valuable activities. Using the hour to teach children therefore comes at cost in terms of these forgone opportunities. Further, the value of this time can be measured in terms of the compensation paid by educational systems to personnel because compensation is assumed to reflect the opportunity cost of personnel time.[17]

The fact that compensation can be used to measure the economic cost of personnel is intuitive from a practical decision-making perspective. When district administrators are considering a new program that would involve hiring more teachers, they look at the budget and consider whether resources can and should be made available. In the case of teachers, the budgetary, or accounting, impact is often similar to the opportunity costs, but this is not always the case. Some budgetary costs overstate opportunity costs, for example, if a state government decides to provide additional funding for school construction, it may pay for the schools over a 20-year period, but the value of the school, and thus its opportunity cost, is likely to last a half-century or more. Conversely, some opportunity costs may not show up in accounting costs. A notable example is that the teacher time spent in a graduate course does not show up directly in the school district budget, though the teacher could have spent that time developing lesson plans, correcting homework assignments, and so on. When there is a difference between budgetary and opportunity costs, it is recommended that researchers use opportunity costs because this includes all costs to society (Levin & McEwan, 2001).

The most costly teacher quality measure is almost inarguably the master's degree in teacher education, which involves nearly a thousand hours of teacher time spent in class and completing assignments.[18] At $20 per hour, the degree costs at least $20,000 in teacher time alone. This time commitment is five times as long as the time commitment of NBPTS certification and perhaps one hundred times larger than some professional development programs.[19] And these figures ignore the costs of the programs themselves—faculty salaries, university classroom space, and so on. If these were added, the direct costs would only grow.

When the measures are used as the basis of compensation programs, as is typically the case in public (and most private) schools, the costs just listed may be dwarfed by the budgetary costs of additional salaries. If a teacher with a master's degree earns $3,000 more per year than a teacher without the degree, and the teacher stays for 20 years, this could cost the school district $60,000 over the teacher's career—three times more than the costs of teacher time just mentioned. The example of compensation also highlights the fact that the specific functions and costs of the measures, like the functions and meanings of statistical validity, can be intricately related.

FUNCTIONS, COSTS, AND POLICY VALIDITY

Having introduced the basic elements of policy validity—statistical validity, functions, and costs—it is now possible to discuss the relationships among the elements and to draw some general conclusions about valid policy uses of specific measures.

Table 5.3 provides a qualitative assessment of statistical validity. Each of the general functions—signaling and improvement—corresponds to different types of policy inferences or conclusions and therefore involves a separate analysis of statistical validity. (Recall that statistical validity depends on the type of conclusion one is trying to make.) Whereas all of the credentials have evidence regarding the signal, only experience and professional development have evidence regarding improvement. In the case of undergraduate education, the lack of evidence has to do with the nature of undergraduate education and policies that require teachers to have these degrees before entering the classroom on a full-time basis. In the case of graduate education and teacher test scores, it is possible for changes to occur while teachers are in the classroom, but I am aware of no evidence that has considered such effects. The last column provides a qualitative assessment of the costs. Again, the purpose here is to identify teacher quality measures that have high validity and low costs, which in this framework would mean that it is reasonable to give them greater weight in policy uses.

Table 5.3 suggests that teacher experience warrants the greatest weight of all the measures, given its low-moderate statistical validity and low costs.[20] As noted in Table 5.1, experience is consistently found to improve teacher value-added, especially in the early years on the job.

Teacher value-added is not included in Table 5.3 because the nature of statistical validity is somewhat different. Although it is true by definition that a teacher whose value-added has increased has also improved, the larger question is whether teacher value-added measures can be used to facilitate improvement, for example, by providing useful information to teachers and motivating them to get better or informing school leaders about whether to continue employing low-performing teachers and rewarding high-performing ones. Unfortunately, there is little direct evidence on this issue, and given the problems identified in the discussion of VAM-A assumptions and VAM-A findings, value-added currently deserves only a low-moderate rating for statistical validity.

Table 5.3   Statistical Validity and Costs

Teacher characteristic	Statistical validity		Costs
	Signal	Improvement	
Undergraduate education	Low	[No evidence]	High
Graduate education	Low	[No evidence]	High
Professional development	Low-moderate	Low-moderate	Varies
Experience	Low-moderate	Moderate	Low
Teacher test scores	Low	[No evidence]	Very low

The costs of value-added are also relatively low. Certainly, there are upfront costs to creating a data system that can provide the detailed data necessary to make the calculations, but these costs are spread across a large number of teachers. Suppose it costs $100 million to create such a data system in a state that has one hundred thousand teachers. In this case, the cost is only $1,000 per teacher, and some of these costs occur only once.[21] The per-teacher cost of standardized tests such as PRAXIS is also quite low.

In the introduction to this chapter, I described the traditional credentials strategy to improving teacher quality. Table 5.4 compares this current state of affairs with what the evidence from Table 5.3 seems to suggest about policy-valid uses for the two general functions. Notice that, in the signaling category, the current weight given to the various signals is higher than the policy valid weights in all cases except for teacher experience and professional development. The reason for this is simply that the statistical validity of the other measures is weak, and some are costly, so the best overall approach to the signaling function is to avoid filtering out too many teachers, because doing so is likely to result in a lot of effective teachers being excluded. This is somewhat less true of teacher experience, and for this reason the current use of experience as a basis for compensation seems reasonable in terms of policy validity.

Conversely, Table 5.4 suggests that greater emphasis should be given to approaches that improve teacher quality, including measuring teacher performance (through VAM-A and perhaps other approaches) and by providing paths to improvement through professional development. Note that VAM-A is essentially excluded from current uses because it is currently used only in a small number of states and districts and, even in those locations, is given little weight.

Table 5.4   Weight Given to Teacher Quality Measures

Teacher credential	Signals		Improvement	
	Current Policy	Policy Valid	Current Policy	Policy Valid
Undergraduate education	Moderate	Low	—	—
Graduate education	Moderate-high	Low	Moderate-high	Low
Professional development	Low	Low-moderate	Moderate	Moderate
Experience	Moderate-high	Moderate-high	Moderate-high	Moderate-high
Teacher test scores	Moderate	Low	—	—
VAM-A	—	Moderate	—	Moderate

CORRUPTIBILITY AND OTHER POSSIBLE OBJECTIONS

There are a variety of possible objections to the conclusions drawn in the previous discussion. One of the most important is the implicit assumption so far that statistical validity influences the appropriate weight given to any measure in policy, but that the weight does not influence statistical validity. In reality, giving considerable weight to any measure can corrupt and reduce its value as a tool in policy.

Accountability based on student standardized tests is frequently criticized, for example, because it sometimes leads teachers to teach students how to answer particular types of test questions, rather than help them truly understand the content. If the truly lowest-value-added teachers carry out this form of test preparation more than the truly highest-value-added teachers, and if test preparation succeeds in raising student scores, the resulting teacher value-added scores will be corrupted—that is, they will inaccurately measure teachers' genuine contributions to actual student learning.

Teacher credentials are also potentially corruptible. In *How to Succeed in School Without Really Learning*, Labaree (1997) argues persuasively that students' efforts to make high marks makes the entire education system worse. It is reasonable to expect that this same phenomenon applies to teacher education, especially graduate education, where a large percentage of teachers take classes mainly because they are required to do so in order to move into school administration or to obtain a higher salary. Some useful learning certainly takes place in these programs, but these motives are obviously not conducive to genuine learning.

Nevertheless, although all measures are corruptible, it might be reasonable to conclude that measures of teacher performance are more corruptible than those of credentials, based on the simple fact that performance measures directly affect instructional practice. Paying teachers based on their degrees might corrupt teacher education, but have little negative influence on classroom instruction.

There are two other possible objections that warrant brief mention. First, this policy validity framework ignores the relationship between teacher quality measures and other student outcomes and intermediate outcomes such as teacher retention. As indicated earlier, value-added models are based on student achievement scores, which are imperfect in the breadth of student knowledge, skills, and outcomes that they cover. Much has been written on this subject, and even a cursory review is beyond the scope of this analysis. I would only add that I am aware of no evidence about the relationship between student test scores and other student outcomes that would lead to substantially different conclusions than those based on student achievement and value-added methods.

Finally, VAM-A is given the most attention here as a direct measure of teacher performance. Earlier, I mentioned evidence that principals' subjective evaluations are positively (and statistically significantly) related to teachers' success in raising student test scores (Harris & Sass, 2007c; Jacob & Lefgren, 2005). In addition, structured principal evaluations and peer evaluations might also be considered as aspects of teacher quality policies.

Conclusions About Policy Validity

The ideal teacher quality measure is one that has high statistical validity, can be produced at low costs, and serves multiple functions. Although it is obvious that no teacher quality measure lives up to this standard, this does not mean that the imperfect measures discussed earlier should not be used at all. Clearly, there has to be some strategy for improving the nation's teaching workforce, and a viable strategy almost certainly must be based on some combination of the measures considered here. The question is not so much whether the measures should be used, but how.

I argue that neither the traditional credentials strategy nor the alternative strategy provides a sufficient answer to this question and that a policy-valid approach would involve a melding of these general strategies. As shown in Table 5.4, experience and some types of professional development deserve to be given considerable weight, both as signals and as a means of improvement. Further, because even these measures are only proxies for teacher effectiveness, it is also worth giving weight to more direct measures of teacher effectiveness, such as value-added to student achievement.

This analysis also suggests recommendations for what not to do. First, the master's degree is given too much weight in the traditional strategy. Instead of paying teachers based on the master's degree, perhaps it would make more sense to let schools and districts use the degree as one basis for promotion and taking steps up the career ladder (e.g., to the master teacher level). One might say that such a proposal would have the same effect as paying teachers based on the degree because master teachers earn more money, but there are two important ways in which this is not the case: All teachers who get the master's degree would not necessarily be promoted, and master teachers have different responsibilities and part of the logic here is to require the degrees only when it seems plausible that the additional knowledge would contribute to the additional responsibilities. Clearly, a master teacher ought to have more, and more diverse, teaching skills than the average teacher, and the master's degree might help provide those additional skills even if it does not improve individual teacher value-added.[22]

Going to the other extreme, focusing mainly on value-added, would be equally problematic. The unconfirmed assumptions and problematic empirical findings regarding individual teacher value-added (VAM-A) suggest that it, too, should be given only modest weight. The glass on the sidewalk simply does not measure rainfall as well as we might think. One option is to combine value-added with principal and peer evaluations to develop a complete picture of teacher performance when making decisions about hiring, promotion, compensation, and dismissal. Given the limitations of the credentials strategy, experimentation with more direct measures of performance is certainly warranted. At the same time, proposals such as using value-added as the primary basis for teacher tenure decisions (Gordon et al., 2006) arguably gives more weight to value-added measures than seems justified at present.[23]

The discussion of various policy options also highlights their interconnectedness. There would likely be less pressure to compensate teachers based on performance if they could be more easily dismissed on the basis of low performance. Likewise, if a viable accountability system could be established, this would reduce (but not eliminate) the need to identify specific credentials of effective teachers and the priorities given to various credentials in decisions such as hiring. One study found that school principals report that caring is the most important attribute in teachers when hiring teachers (Harris, Rutledge, Ingle, & Thompson, 2006). This may be entirely rational because, if teachers were not caring, there may not be enough other factors to motivate teachers to perform well after tenure. A shift toward accountability might also give principals greater motivation to become instructional leaders because teachers would have greater incentive to improve and, in the case of subjective evaluations, to listen and respond to what the principals suggest. We could therefore expect that a change in external accountability policies would influence a wide variety of internal human resource policies as well.

The point here is less to criticize the traditional teacher quality strategy and more to show how this strategy affects schools and teachers and therefore how alternative strategies might do more to improve schools. Such an effort is no doubt complex and requires a range of considerations regarding the functions of teacher quality measures, the various goals of education, and the larger policy context. The purpose of this study has been to bring order to that complexity and to provide direction for the next generation of teacher strategies that, given the current widespread concern with the present strategy, is already well on its way to being formed. If there is one clear conclusion from this discussion, it is that the general shift toward an accountability strategy appears warranted, but it is also possible to go too far and create new failed policies that, rather than facilitating innovation and success, only serve to reinforce the limitations of the status quo.

Acknowledgments

Many of the studies from which the ideas in this chapter have grown were funded by the U.S. Department of Education Institute for Education

Sciences and the National Board for Professional Teaching Standards. In addition to this support, I gratefully acknowledge comments by Robert Floden, Drew Gitomer, David Monk, and Tim Sass as well as participants in research presentations at the 2007 ETS Invitational Conference in San Francisco and at the University of Colorado at Boulder. The views expressed here are solely mine, and I am responsible for all remaining errors.

Notes

1. Some might refer to the credentials strategy instead as an input-based strategy and the accountability strategy as an output-based strategy. The credentials strategy also might be viewed as process oriented, as reflected in teacher tenure rules and formal, low-stakes evaluations of teachers that are required in most schools and school districts.

2. Others have reached different conclusion even when reviewing the same evidence. Greenwald, Hedges, and Laine (1996) indicate that "school resources are systematically related to student achievement and that these relationships are large enough to be educationally important" (p. 384). Nevertheless, the relationships are inconsistent, a point reinforced by the more recent review in the present study.

3. One might argue that accountability incorporates elements of the accountability strategy (e.g., NCLB includes requirements that schools employ highly qualified teachers). The term *accountability* is no doubt used in different ways by different people, but I define it here as test-based and other forms of outcomes-focused policies, which clearly distinguishes the credential and accountability strategies.

4. When a signal is used by an organization in this way it is considered an act of screening.

5. This chapter does not address whether teachers should be paid more based on the specific subjects and grades they teach. Basic economic theory suggests that teachers should be paid more in fields where teacher supply is lower. For example, it is widely believed that teachers of math and science have greater opportunity costs than other teachers. Supply in specific teaching jobs is also affected by the characteristics of jobs (e.g., school location, student discipline problems, differences in jobs by subjects). In addition to math and science, many schools have difficulty finding qualified special education teachers and this is at least partly due to state and federal regulations that limit the instructional options available to these teachers and impose considerable administrative burdens.

6. There are two general aspects of statistical validity that apply in all cases: bias and precision. However, the meaning of bias depends on what one is trying to estimate. A reviewer of an earlier version of this chapter put this point differently, noting that "statistical validity is a property of an inference not of a test" (R. Floden, personal communication, October 23, 2007).

7. There are still some ways in which the professional developments effects might be biased in this value-added framework. For example, if teachers are assigned to professional development in each period based on achievement growth of students in previous periods, the effects are still biased. Also, there may

be other unmeasured factors that influence the teacher's productivity while the professional development was taking place, but this would not bias the estimated effect unless teachers happened to be assigned to professional development based on unmeasured time-varying teacher credentials. This is possible. Some teachers experience drops in productivity (e.g., when they have personal crises such as divorce from a spouse or the birth of a child), and these same teachers are less likely to take part in professional development for the same reason that reduces their effectiveness—they have less time to devote to it. However, for this to substantially affect the estimated effect of teacher education, a substantial proportion of teachers have to experience such time-varying changes that influence both their classroom effectiveness and their likelihood of receiving professional development. This seems unlikely, though I am aware of no evidence that would shed significant light on the issue.

8. Value-added modeling accounts for student growth both before the teacher taught the student and afterward. For example, if we were studying the effect of a fourth-grade teacher, the student's average rate of growth would be estimated to account for student learning in third and fifth grade as well as fourth.

9. This is not the only assumption required regarding the properties of the student achievement tests. For example, there is also an implicit assumption that the content of the tests is constant over time.

10. In some ways, the distinction between fixed and time-varying credentials reiterates the distinction made earlier between signals and improvement, but there is a subtle difference. Signaling and improvement have to do with the function that the measures serve, whereas the fixed versus time-varying distinction has to do with the type of data that are available to the researcher. Credentials that are fixed in the data can only be used to study the usefulness of the measures as teacher quality signals, whereas time-varying credentials can be used to study both signaling and improvement. Some examples of this distinction are given in the discussion later in this chapter.

11. Other forms of professional development are combined into an "other" category due to the limited distinctions made in the data. All of our results, including this one, tend to show greater statistical significance in middle school math. This is probably partly because, compared with reading, math achievement is determined more by specific math courses (there are few "reading" classes per se) and because, compared with those in elementary schools, middle school teachers are more likely to specialize in specific subjects; they therefore have more student observations from which the estimates can be made. In this particular case, the effect was also significant in some cases for high reading and math.

12. The effects are only statistically significant in elementary and middle school math.

13. This may be because the researchers in this study controlled for a wide variety of other factors such as coursework. If teacher candidates with greater cognitive ability are more likely to take certain types of college courses, then this may make the effect of cognitive ability look smaller than it is.

14 In addition to the twin nonrandom assignment problems, there are two other factors that may make it inherently difficult to identify the true credentials of high-value-added teachers. The first is that the value-added approach necessarily requires very few "degrees of freedom." Consider the simple case of a difference in mean value-added scores between two groups of teachers. Obviously,

the more teachers in the respective groups, the more likely it is that any difference between them would be statistically significant. However, with VAM-P, we are identifying the effects of teacher credentials by comparing each teacher to him- or herself. As discussed later, each teacher's value-added is very imprecisely estimated, and this problem is naturally compounded when analyzing changes in teacher value-added. Precision of course improves after combining the within-teacher differences across teachers in the analysis, but perhaps not enough to identify statistically significant effects even when such effects really exist.

Harris and Sass (2007b) approach this problem by estimating the models with and without teacher fixed effects. In the latter case, the assumptions are more similar to those of the gain score models discussed earlier. As expected, the statistical significance is considerably higher without teacher fixed effects, but this might come at the expense of some estimation bias. In about half of the cases, the point estimates for the effects of teacher experience and professional development were similar (same sign and similar magnitude), implying that the gain score model may not introduce enough bias to change the general conclusions.

A second methodological issue is that the linear regression models, including value-added, may not capture the complexity of how teacher credentials combine to produce student achievement. For example, it may be that no characteristic really matters by itself, but only when it is combined with others. In addition, there may be many contrasting ways to be an effective teacher. For example, some school principals in one of our studies indicated that some intelligent teachers have dull personalities, which makes them less effective in motivating students (Harris, Rutledge, Ingle, and & Thompson, 2006). So suppose that there are two types of teachers: those who are intelligent and unenthused and those who are enthused but less intelligent. Further, suppose that both intelligence and enthusiasm are positively associated with teacher effectiveness, but that very few teachers have both traits. In this case, a standard value-added analysis of these two groups of teachers will conclude—falsely—that neither enthusiasm nor intelligence is important. This is just one example, and the larger point is that the importance of certain traits may be dependent on other traits.

15. In VAM-P studies, teacher experience is generally accounted for directly. This is not the case in VAM-A studies, in which interest lies primarily in determining which teachers are most effective rather than why.

16. Although the specifics vary across states, the general idea is that schools will be judged not on whether their students are making adequate yearly progress, but on whether individual students are on track to being proficient. In some sense, this is a positive move toward value-added modeling, but most of the same problematic assumptions remain. Even with the growth curve analysis, all students still have to be proficient by 2014 in order to avoid sanctions. Thus, the fundamental problem of holding educators responsible for factors outside their control remains firmly intact. It is only the intermediate measures of school performance, between now and 2014, that actually change.

17. The assumption that personnel compensation provides a reasonable measure of opportunity requires some explanation. It is assumed that for-profit firms compensate their workers based closely on each individual's contribution to production. For-profit firms will not pay a worker more than he or she contributes, for doing so would reduce profits. At the same time, for-profits cannot underpay a

worker for risk of losing him or her to another organization. Because for-profits compete for workers with nonprofits and governments, it is reasonable to use the compensation paid to governmental and non-profit workers as a measure of their opportunity cost because these workers have opportunities in for-profit firms.

18. This calculation was made as follows: suppose that master's degree requires 10 semester-long courses, each of which meets three hours per week for 15 weeks and requires an equal amount of time outside the classroom: 10 courses × 15 weeks × 6 hours = 900 hours.

19. Harris and Sass (2007b) report that NBPTS certification requires roughly 200 hours of work. Professional development programs vary widely.

20. The meaning of *costs of experience* requires some clarification. One might argue that the costs are actually high because it takes a teacher a full year in the classroom (at full salary) to gain a year of experience and, on top of that, teachers salaries increase with experience. There are two reasons why this intuition is not quite correct and why it is more reasonable to consider the costs of experience to be low: (1) Experience is naturally occurring so that most learning from experience would occur regardless of whether it is rewarded through salary, and (2) the main activity going on during a school year is that teachers are teaching students and it is difficult to separate how much of the teacher's time is going toward teaching per se versus teacher learning—but surely the benefits received by students from the teaching are substantially greater than zero, thus substantially reducing the potential cost of experience.

21. Harris, Taylor, Albee, Ingle, and McDonald (2008) and Hoxby (2002) discuss the costs of accountability systems, including the cost of data systems. Harris et al. argue that it is difficult to attribute the costs.

22. Using the master's degree for other purposes might address the corruptibility problem by eliminating the least effective master's degree programs and allowing remaining programs to focus on the skills that master teachers need.

23. Gordon, Kane, and Staiger (2006) "propose federal support to help states measure the effectiveness of individual teachers—based on their impact on student achievement, subjective evaluations by principals and peers, and parental evaluations. States would be given considerable discretion to develop their own measures, as long as student achievement impacts (using so-called 'value-added' measures) are a key component. The federal government would pay for bonuses to highly rated teachers willing to teach in high-poverty schools. In return for federal support, schools would not be able to offer tenure to new teachers who receive poor evaluations during their first two years on the job without obtaining district approval and informing parents in the schools. States would open further the door to teaching for those who lack traditional certification but can demonstrate success on the job" (p. 2).

References

Boardman, A. E., & Murnane, R. J. (1979). Using panel data to improve estimates of the determinants of educational achievement. *Sociology of Education, 52,* 113–121.

Booher-Jennings, J. (2005). Below the bubble: "Educational triage" and the Texas Accountability System. *American Educational Research Journal, 42,* 231–268.

Clotfelter, C. T., Ladd, H. F., & Vigdor, J. L. (2005). *Teacher-student matching and the assessment of teacher effectiveness.* Unpublished manuscript, Duke University, Durham, NC.

Coleman, J. (1966). *Equality of educational opportunity* (Report OE-38000). Washington, DC: U.S. Department of Health, Education, and Welfare, Office of Education.

Figlio, D. (in press). Testing, crime, and punishment. *Journal of Public Economics.*

Goldhaber, D., & Anthony, E. (in press). Can teacher quality be effectively assessed? National Board Certification as a signal of effective teaching. *Review of Economics and Statistics.*

Goldhaber, D., & Brewer, D. J. (2000). Does teacher certification matter? High school teacher certification status and student achievement. *Educational Evaluation and Policy Analysis, 22,* 129–145.

Gordon, R., Kane, T. J., & Staiger, D. O. (2006). *Identifying effective teachers using performance on the job* (Discussion Paper 2006–01). Washington, DC: Brookings Institution.

Greenwald, R., Hedges, L., & Laine, R. (1996). The effect of school resources on student achievement. *Review of Educational Research, 66,* 361–396.

Hanushek, E. A. (1979). Conceptual and empirical issues in estimating educational production function issues. *Journal of Human Resources, 14,* 351–388.

Hanushek, E. (1986). The economics of schooling. *Journal of Economic Literature, 24,* 1141–1177.

Harris, D. N. (2007). High flying schools, student disadvantage and the logic of NCLB. *American Journal of Education, 113,* 367–394.

Harris, D. N. (2008). *New benchmarks for interpreting effects sizes: Combining effects with costs.* Unpublished manuscript, University of Wisconsin at Madison.

Harris, D. N. (in press). Education production functions: Concepts. In B. McGaw, P. L. Peterson, & E. Baker (Eds.), *International encyclopedia of education.* Oxford, UK: Elsevier.

Harris, D. N., & Herrington, C. (2006). Accountability, standards, and the growing achievement gap: Lessons from the past half-century. *American Journal of Education, 112,* 209–238.

Harris, D. N., & Rutledge, S. (2007). *Models and predictors of teacher effectiveness: A review of the evidence with lessons from (and for) other occupations.* Unpublished manuscript, University of Wisconsin at Madison.

Harris, D. N., Rutledge, S., Ingle, W., & Thompson, C. (2006, April). *Mix and match: What principals look for when hiring teachers.* Paper presented at the annual meeting of the American Education Research Association, San Francisco.

Harris, D. N., & Sass, T. (2005, March). *Value-added models and the measurement of teacher quality.* Paper presented at the annual conference of the American Education Finance Association, Louisville, KY.

Harris, D., & Sass, T. (2007a). *The effects of NBPTS-certified teachers on student achievement* (Working Paper 4). Washington, DC: Urban Institute.

Harris, D. N., & Sass, T. (2007b). *Teacher training, teacher quality, and student achievement* (Working Paper 3). Washington, DC: Urban Institute.

Harris, D. N., & Sass, T. (2007c, March). *What makes a good teacher and who can tell?* Paper presented at the summer workshop of the National Bureau of Economic Research, Cambridge, MA.

Harris, D. N., Taylor, L., Albee, A., Ingle, W. K., & McDonald, L. (2008, January). *The resource cost of standards, assessments and accountability.* Paper presented at the National Academy of Sciences Workshop Series on State Standards, Washington, DC.

Hoxby, C. (2002). The cost of accountability. In W. M. Evers & H. J. Walberg (Eds.), *School accountability.* Stanford, CA: Hoover Institution Press.

Jacob, B. A., & Lefgren, L. (2005). *Principals as agents: Subjective performance measurement in education* (NBER Working Paper 11463). Cambridge, MA: National Bureau of Economic Research.

Kane, T., & Staiger, D. (2001). *Improving school accountability measures* (NBER Working Paper #8156). Cambridge, MA: National Bureau of Economic Research.

Koedel, C., & Betts, J. R. (2005). *Re-examining the role of teacher quality in the educational production function.* Unpublished manuscript, University of California at San Diego.

Labaree, D. (1997). *How to succeed in school without really learning.* New Haven, CT: Yale University Press.

Levin, H., & McEwan, P. (2001). *Cost-effectiveness analysis* (2nd ed.). London: Sage.

Levine, A. (2005). *Educating school teachers.* Retrieved October, 25, 2007, from http://www.edschools.org/teacher_report.htm

Medley, D. M., & Coker, H. (1987). The accuracy of principals' judgments of teacher performance. *Journal of Educational Research, 80,* 242–247.

Milanowski, A. (2004). The relationship between teacher performance evaluation scores and student assessment: Evidence from Cincinnati. *Peabody Journal of Education, 79*(4), 33–53.

Murnane, R. J. (1975). *The impact of school resources on the learning of inner city children.* Cambridge, MA: Ballinger.

Ogbu, J. U. (2003). *Black American students in an affluent suburb: A study of academic disengagement.* Mahwah, NJ: Lawrence Erlbaum.

Peterson, K. D. (1987). Teacher evaluation with multiple and variable lines of evidence. *American Educational Research Journal, 24,* 311–317.

Peterson, K. D. (2000). *Teacher evaluation: A comprehensive guide to new directions and practices* (2nd ed.). Thousand Oaks, CA: Corwin Press.

Rivkin, S. G., Hanushek, E., & Kain, J. F. (2005). Teachers, schools and academic achievement. *Econometrica, 73,* 417–458.

Rutledge, S., Harris, D. N., Ingle, W., & Thompson, C. (in press). Certify, blink, hire: An examination of the process of teacher hiring. *Leadership and Policy in Schools.*

Sanders, W. L., & Horn, S. P. (1998). Research findings from the Tennessee Value-Added Assessment System (TVASS) database: Implications for educational evaluation and research. *Journal of Personnel Evaluation in Education, 12,* 247–256.

Todd, P. E., & Wolpin, K. I. (2003). On the specification and estimation of the production function for cognitive achievement. *Economic Journal, 113,* F3–F33.

Wayne, A. J., & Youngs, P. (2003). Teacher credentials and student achievement gains. *Review of Educational Research, 73,* 89–122.

Approximations of Teacher Quality and Effectiveness

6

View From the State Education Agency

Mitchell D. Chester

Commissioner of Elementary and Secondary Education, Commonwealth of Massachusetts, and Former Senior Associate Superintendent for Policy and Accountability, Ohio Department of Education

Susan Tave Zelman

Superintendent of Public Instruction, Ohio Department of Education

State approaches to assessing teacher quality and effectiveness represent a range of policy goals and aspirations. Perhaps the least ambitious teacher assessment policy involves the setting of standards that "represent minimal levels of proficiency that are politically acceptable and that do not threaten to reduce the supply of teachers" (Gifford, 1986, p. 253). A somewhat more ambitious policy goal is rooted in a concept of "do no harm," wherein the role of the state is one of risk reduction (Lowi, 1990) by ensuring that those who are licensed to teach meet the minimum qualification necessary to make them eligible to enter the marketplace. A more proactive and aspirational stance assumes that the state's role is to promote effectiveness and not simply certify minimal credentials. This latter conception of the state's role in assessing teacher quality is rooted in a more active licensure role for state government that promotes best professional practices (Chester & Pecheone, 1992).

The distinction between *rules statutes* and *goals statutes* (Lowi, 1990) is a useful starting point for considering the state education agency's role in assessing teacher quality and effectiveness. The rules orientation conveys obligations, such as requiring a subject matter major for teachers, whereas the goals orientation conveys rights, such as providing all students with an effective teacher. This chapter presents the approach of one state, Ohio, to assessing teacher quality and effectiveness. Ohio's approach to assessing teacher quality is grounded in the premise that a definition of teacher quality or teacher effectiveness must include the ability to affect student learning and achievement. We identify a range of approaches that Ohio uses to assess teacher quality and discuss the strengths and weaknesses of these approaches in terms of their proximity to measuring the impact of teachers on student learning. Collectively, these approaches describe a state in pursuit of a teacher policy that balances rules and goals, thus protecting students from unqualified instructors while aspiring to ensure that there is an effective teacher in every classroom. This range of approaches that vary in terms of the nature of evidence of teacher quality and proximity as well as the direct measurement of teacher impact on student learning is the organizing principle for our chapter.

Two caveats about this chapter are appropriate. First, we focus on the efforts that Ohio has undertaken to assess teacher quality and effectiveness. We do not attempt to capture the range of activities that the state education agency sponsors or facilitates that are designed to develop and support teachers. The numerous initiatives that are not outlined in the chapter range from preservice preparation through induction support to inservice efforts.

The second caveat about this chapter concerns the larger context within which the work we are describing sits. We believe that a systems approach to educational policy is critical. We envision five essential systems (one of which is human resources) that are foundational to an effective and efficient educational organization (see Figure 6.1). The organizational core is the system of instructional management, which comprises aligned standards, curriculum, and assessment. The community support system ensures that the collective capital of families and communities are mustered to provide both academic and nonacademic support to students and schools. The fiscal system encompasses both revenue and expenditures and is concerned with the strategic use of funds to support the core instructional mission of schools. Accountability

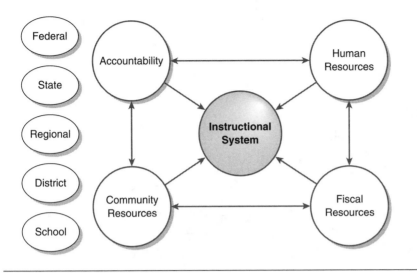

Figure 6.1   A Systems Approach to Education

provides measurement and signals designed to support the pursuit of the most effective practices, and it includes diagnosis and assistance to support and propel school improvement efforts. Coherence and coordination are required within and across the systems. The greater the coordination and coherence across the levels of the educational enterprise—from classroom to school todistrict to state to federal—the stronger the effectiveness and efficiency of each.

A coherent approach to human capital management requires that states adopt complementary policies and practices related to certification, tenure, and compensation. Figure 6.2 identifies elements of a human resource system that are subsumed by certification, tenure, and compensation: preparation, sourcing, induction, training and development, and performance management. Much of the responsibility for these elements lies within the purview of local education agencies and institutions of higher education (in the case of preparation). In many cases, deployment of these elements is promoted and supported by the state education agency. In Ohio, for example, the state accredits teacher preparation programs, manages a database of job openings, funds mentoring programs for teachers and principals, sponsors professional development, and provides educator evaluation guidelines. Each of these areas provides opportunities to incorporate assessment of teacher quality and effectiveness. Again, this chapter focuses on one slice of the enterprise—the state education agency's approach to assessing teacher quality and effectiveness—that is embedded within our approach to human capital management, which, in turn, is but one component of a systems approach to education policy.

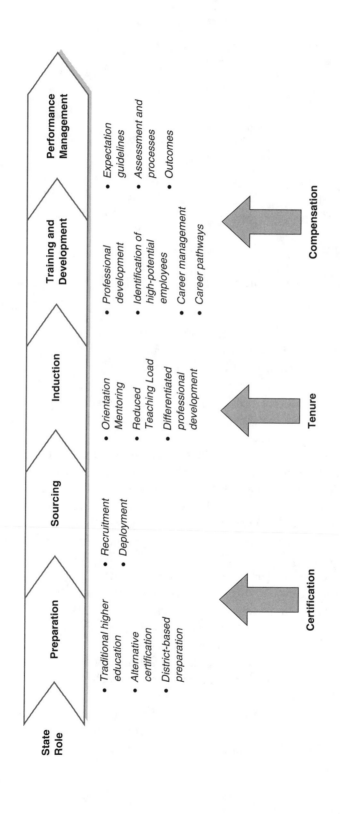

Figure 6.2   Elements of Human Capital Management in K–12 Education

SOURCE: Adapted from Aspen Institute, 2008, p. 3.

Measuring Effectiveness: Levels of Approximation

There is a wide range of data sources (including standardized test scores, classroom observations, and teacher reports) that policymakers draw from to gauge the impact of policies that are designed to influence the quality of classroom events. These sources are employed to draw inferences about the quality of classroom instruction and, in turn, the quality of student learning. Kennedy (1999) examines and compares the potential of different data collection devices to inform policymakers about policy influences on student outcomes. Kennedy identifies four levels of approximation to student learning, which range from the closest measures of student outcomes to the most distant. Level 1 approximations encompass the most direct measures of teaching environments and student learning—classroom observations and standardized tests. Level 2 approximations involve situated descriptions of teaching, whereas Level 3 approximations employ nonsituated testimony about practice. Level 4 approximations—data that are most distant from direct measures of student learning and learning environments—rely on testimony about the effects of policies or programs.

A key application of these four levels of approximation about the quality of classroom instruction and the quality of student learning is the opportunity to quantify the strength of the inferences that can be drawn from different data sources. Because impact on student learning is the core dimension of our definition of teacher quality and effectiveness, it is instructive to examine the relationship between the four levels of approximation and student learning. Newmann, Marks, and Gamoran (1996); Saxe, Gearhart, and Seltzer (1999); and Shavelson, Baxter, and Pine (1992) identify correlations of .59, .77, and .43, respectively, between Level 1 approximations (observations of classroom practice and standardized achievement tests) and measures of complex student learning. Level 2 approximations demonstrate correlations as high as the .70s between teacher reports of practice and observations of their practice (Koziol & Burns, 1986), although Porter (2002) identifies a correlation of .34 between teacher reports of the content of instruction and individual student gains. Level 3 approximations "tend to correlate in the low .30s with first-level approximations, standardized test scores, and classroom observations" (Kennedy, 1999, p. 360). Kennedy is unable to locate research that attempts to correlate Level 4 approximations with closer levels of approximations, let alone with measures of student learning.

Kennedy (1999) identifies two key reasons (apart from their degree of approximation to a direct measure of student learning) for the significance of levels of approximations that are represented by data sources that inform policymakers. First, the different approaches to data collection present different advantages and disadvantages that are related to, among other factors, feasibility (including cost, ease of use, and availability) and susceptibility to errors. In addition to the level of approximation that different data collection methods represent, each approach presents trade-offs among considerations related to feasibility and reliability. The second significance of levels of approximation is that policy researchers lack an agreed-upon model that identifies the path of influence by which more distant approximations to student learning affect more proximal measures. Because policymakers are ultimately interested in how policies influence student learning, and because the relationship between more distant approximations and student learning is not well established, "as researchers move to more distant approximations, they are gathering evidence on outcomes that may be only weakly related to the outcomes policymakers ultimately hope to influence" (Kennedy, 1999, p. 360).

By drawing on Kennedy's (1999) framework, we are able to situate Ohio's state-level efforts to assess teacher quality and effectiveness (see Figure 6.3). We have categorized the different teacher assessment measures into four categories: teacher credentials, teacher knowledge, teacher practice, and change in student learning. Teacher credentials are the most distant measure of teacher effectiveness (they provide the weakest inference about the quality of instruction); measures of teacher knowledge and practice are less distant but still not measures of student learning; and change in student achievement scores provide closer, albeit imperfect, measures of student learning (achievement scores present a stronger basis for drawing inferences about the quality of instruction).

Before providing examples of these four categories of teacher assessment, it is important to identify some of the challenges to measuring teacher quality and effectiveness. First, the more distant the approximation, the less confident we are that we are making an inference about teacher quality and effectiveness; again, our assumption is that the ability to influence student learning and achievement is core to the construct of teacher quality and effectiveness. One of the ironies about this fact is that there is often an inverse relationship between the distance of the approximation and the capacity required to scale the data collection across thousands of teachers (in Ohio, we employ approximately 120,000 K–12 teachers). For example, collecting information on teacher credentials is a less resource-intensive endeavor than is estimating changes in student learning that are linked to individual teacher efforts.

A second challenge to measuring teacher quality is related to the fact that we have limited technologies for evaluating the alignment of the prescribed, assessed, and enacted curriculums. The construct of alignment is central to the standards-based reform movement, yet technologies to assess the decisions that teachers make about the content of instruction are in their infancy. We will illustrate one such emerging technology that we are using in Ohio later in the chapter.

A third challenge to measuring teacher quality relates to that fact that our awareness that teachers need content expertise far outpaces our

DISTANT PROXIMITY TO STUDENT LEARNING PROXIMAL

←——→

Teacher credentials	Teacher knowledge	Teacher practice	Change in student learning
Sources of Evidence/*Types of Measures*			
Transcripts/*Courses taken, exam scores, attestation of preparation institution*	Transcripts/*Courses taken* National Board for Professional Teaching Standards (NBPTS) certification/*Assessment scores* Licensure/*Praxis II scores* Highly qualified teacher certification/*Courses taken, Praxis II scores* Evaluation of professional development (PD)/*Pre- and post-PD assessments of content knowledge*	Licensure/*Praxis III scores* NBPTS certification/*Assessment scores* Teacher Advancement Program Teacher Incentive Fund program/*Evaluations, observations of classroom practice* Program evaluation/*Early Language and Learning Classroom Observation scores, surveys of Enacted Curriculum*	Teacher Quality Partnership Teacher Advancement Program Teacher Incentive Fund program/*Value-added student test scores*

Figure 6.3   Approximations of Teacher Effectiveness in Ohio

understandings of content-pedagogical knowledge. It is our contention that although there is widespread agreement about the importance of content-pedagogical knowledge, our ability to assess content-pedagogical expertise is limited and difficult to reliably apply across many teachers. In the United States, much of what we focus on during most observations of instruction, in fact, may have limited impact on instructional effectiveness. Hiebert and colleagues' (2003) video studies of mathematics instruction help illustrate this point. Observations of mathematics instruction in the United States often focuses on surface features of instruction, such as the use of manipulatives, active learning, and students working in groups. The videos demonstrate that some of the strongest instruction in other nations is characterized by the intellectual rigor of the content and classroom discussion (Stigler & Hiebert, 1999). Many of the strongest teachers in other nations run highly teacher-directed classrooms and would fare poorly in terms of the surface features (e.g., use of manipulative in mathematics classrooms, use of cooperative grouping strategies) on which many of our observations in the United States focus.

Ohio's Approach to Assessing Teacher Quality and Effectiveness

In this section we provide examples of the ways in which Ohio assesses teacher quality and effectiveness. For each category of teacher quality and effectiveness displayed in Figure 6.3, we illustrate data sources from which we draw inferences about teacher quality and effectiveness.

TEACHER CREDENTIALS

Measures of teacher credentials are the most distant approximations of teacher quality and effectiveness that are employed in the system. These measures include transcripts that are incorporated as components of licensure requirements. Transcripts provide evidence of the preparation and training that prospective and current educators have received. Transcripts also provide assurance that teachers have experienced teaching internships (in the case of beginning teachers) and have training in the subject(s) they are to teach—both of which are credentials that are widely accepted as minimal qualifications for teaching. In addition, many states, including Ohio, require attestations of the preparing institutions (in the case of beginning teachers) or of the employing district (in the case of advanced licensure or licensure renewal for current educators). These qualification requirements represent a do-no-harm dimension of teacher licensure, but few would argue that they ensure teacher effectiveness. Instead, most would argue that they are minimal qualifications for accessing employment in the profession.

The "highly qualified teacher" requirement of the No Child Left Behind Act is an example of a measure of teacher credentials, although it includes the demonstration of teacher knowledge. All states are required to report the percentage of courses taught by highly qualified teachers, which includes verification that teachers have taken sufficient coursework in the subject for which they are qualifying. States disaggregate the percentage of highly qualified teachers by high- and low-poverty elementary and secondary schools. In addition, in Ohio we report the percentage of teachers in each district and school who are fully licensed to teach English language arts, mathematics, science, and/or social studies.

Teacher credentials are relatively easy for a state to measure at scale, but they are among the most distant approximations on which to draw inferences about either the intellectual quality of classrooms or the quality of student learning.

TEACHER KNOWLEDGE

The next category of measures relates to teacher knowledge—whether teachers have content expertise in the subjects they teach as well as pedagogical understandings. Although teacher knowledge is not as distant an indicator of quality and effectiveness as are measures of credentials, we consider measures of teacher knowledge to be necessary but not sufficient evidence of teacher quality and effectiveness. In Ohio, examples of how we measure teacher knowledge include the use of Praxis II and licensure requirements related to course taking in the teacher's subject area, Local Professional Development Council attestation of experienced teacher development, assessment of changes in teacher knowledge as a result of state-sponsored professional development, and National Board for Professional Teaching Standards (NBPTS) and highly qualified teacher credentialing.

In Ohio, measures of teacher knowledge and background in the subject(s) that they teach are requirements for licensure and for the highly qualified teacher credential. For each measure, Ohio requires that teachers have majored in the subject in which they teach either at the undergraduate or graduate level and have demonstrated their mastery of the content through the Praxis II, an assessment of content knowledge mastery. Figure 6.4 displays assessment items that illustrate Praxis II assessments in mathematics and science. Renewal of an experienced teacher's license is contingent in part on demonstration of continuing education in areas related to the teaching assignment. This demonstration is overseen and attested to by the local education agency's Local Professional Development Council.

Demonstration of teacher knowledge occurs through other vehicles as well. The Ohio Department of Education has measured gains in teacher knowledge as one component of an evaluation of state-sponsored professional development initiatives. For example, in conjunction with our Mathematics Academy Program for experienced teachers, we developed a pre- and post-measure of teacher knowledge. In each of the academies that we sponsored, teachers demonstrated significant gains in content knowledge. Nonintervention specialists (traditional classroom teachers) registered higher gains than intervention specialists (special education resource teachers). In addition, surveys revealed that participants believed that participation in the academies improved their understanding and application of standards-based instructional models.

Certain aspects of teacher knowledge (such as the kind of content knowledge represented in Figure 6.4) are relatively easy to measure, whether through assessments or documentation of courses taken. Other aspects of teacher knowledge are not as easy to measure. For example, the use of multiple representations of a construct and the ability to quickly understand the implications of a student's error in terms of his or her understanding of the concept are critical components of effective teaching (Ball, Hill, & Bass, 2005). The nexus between teacher knowledge and the quality of instruction and student learning is not straightforward, however. Policymakers accept (and common sense suggests) that a necessary, although not sufficient, requisite of effective instruction is the instructor's grounding in the content that is being taught. It is counterintuitive to expect, for example, that a teacher without a solid science background will

Mathematics	Science
Jerry is 50 inches tall and is growing at the rate of 1/24 inch per month. Adam is 47 inches tall and is growing at the rate of 1/8 inch per month. If they each continue to grow at these rates for the next four years, in how many months will they be the same height?	Which of the following best describes the pathway of a protein from its manufacture to its release from the cell?
(A) 24	(A) Endoplasmic reticulum → Golgi complex → secretory vesicle
(B) 30	(B) Secretory vesicle → endoplasmic reticulum → Golgi complex
(C) 36	(C Secretory vesicle → Golgi complex → endoplasmic reticulum
(D) 42	(D Golgi complex → endoplasmic reticulum → secretory vesicle

Figure 6.4   Sample Praxis II Questions

be an effective science teacher. Strong content knowledge alone, however, does not ensure that a person knows how to represent the subject in ways that will enable students to learn.

TEACHER PRACTICE

The enacted curriculum and the quality of instruction—the environment and content that students experience—are a closer nexus to student learning. In Ohio, examples of measures that we employ to assess teacher practice include the Praxis III, the Early Language and Literacy Classroom Observation (ELLCO) instrument, Surveys of Enacted Curriculum, the Teacher Advancement Program, and the Teacher Incentive Fund program.

The Praxis III—which utilizes direct observation of classroom practice, review of documentation prepared by the teacher, and semistructured interviews—is a requirement for moving beyond initial licensure in Ohio. This assessment yields scores in four domains that collectively provide a profile of teacher practice: *planning,* which encompasses knowledge of students' background, development of clear learning goals, connections to past and future content, selection of appropriate materials and instructional methods, and evaluation strategies; *environment,* which includes classroom climate, fairness, rapport, expectations, positive behavior, and safety; *instruction,* which includes learning goals and procedures, comprehensible content, extended thinking, and adjustment of learning activities based on monitoring of student understanding and feedback; and *reflection,* which involves self-assessment, sense of efficacy, collegial involvement, and communication with parents and families.

The ELLCO instrument employs direct observations of preschool and early-grade classrooms to assess 14 dimensions of classroom practice and environment that have been identified through research to be important elements of effective literacy instruction (Smith, Dickinson, Sangeorge, & Anastasopoulos, 2002). It provides a measure of classroom practice for individuals and can be aggregated to groups of teachers. Figure 6.5 displays the profile of practice across a sample of Ohio Head Start classrooms, rated according to a 5-point scale. The profile suggests that although none of the areas received strong ratings, there is a particular need to improve practice in several areas, including oral language facilitation and assessment approaches. ELLCO assessments are used to provide formative feedback to teachers in Ohio and to inform professional development programs.

Surveys of Enacted Curriculum (Blank, Porter, & Smithson, 2001) codify state standards, state assessments, and teacher content decisions in English language arts, mathematics, and science according to two dimensions: content and cognitive demand. The data can be displayed in several

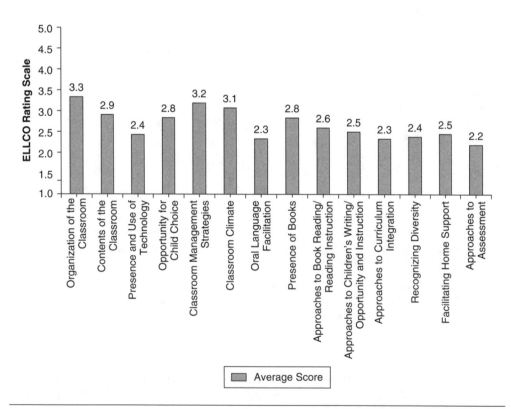

Figure 6.5   Early Language and Literacy Classroom Observation (ELLCO) Results for a Sample of Ohio Head Start Classrooms

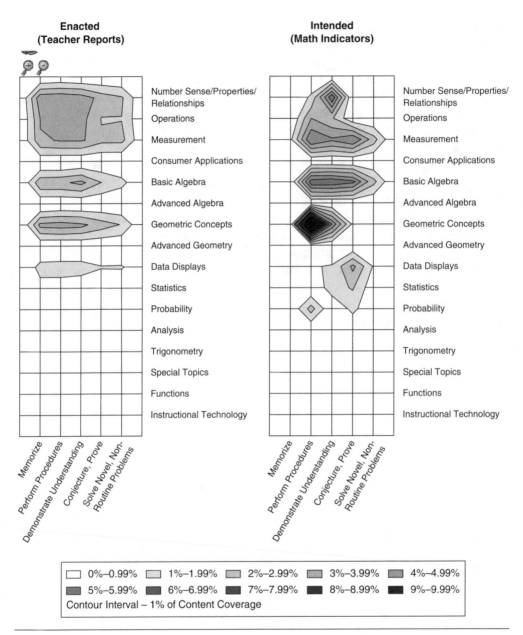

Figure 6.6 Surveys of Enacted Curriculum Results for Grade 7 Mathematics

formats. The Grade 7 curriculum maps shown in Figure 6.6 display teacher decisions about mathematics content and Ohio mathematics standards. The vertical axis identifies content topics, and the horizontal axis displays a cognitive demand scale that utilizes five anchors: memorize, perform procedures, demonstrate understanding, conjecture and prove, and solve novel, nonroutine problems. A third dimension concerns the level of attention given to each content strand at each level of cognitive demand, with darker colors indicating more attention and lighter colors indicating less. The content maps provide a graphic means of identifying alignment or lack of alignment of teachers' content decisions in relation to the prescribed and assessed curricula. Note, for example, the lack of attention of seventh-grade teachers to statistics and probability even though the state standards call for students to perform procedures with probability and to conjecture and prove using statistics.

Other initiatives that involve the assessment of teacher practice include the Teacher Advancement Program and Ohio's Teacher Incentive Fund activities. These overlapping initiatives incorporate teacher evaluations that are tied to measures of teaching skills and practices as well as to measures of student achievement. Compensation is based in part on the demonstration of skills and impact on student achievement.

Each of the efforts designed to assess teacher practice provides evidence that is more directly linked to student learning than are measures of teacher credentials and knowledge.

CHANGE IN STUDENT LEARNING

The closest measures of the effects of curriculum and instruction are measures of student learning, which provide the greatest certainty that teachers are influencing the quality of student learning. In Ohio, we use value-added estimates derived from student assessment scores as outcome measures for several projects (e.g., the Teacher Quality Partnership, which looks for linkages between preservice programs and practices and teacher value-added contributions) and as a component of both the Teacher Advancement Program and the Teacher Incentive Fund grant.

The use of value-added scores is predicated on the concept that, to understand teachers' and schools' contributions to student learning, we need to take into account the prior achievement of students. From year to year, school to school, and classroom to classroom, teachers inherit students who are at different starting points in terms of prior knowledge. Therefore, a method that controls for prior achievement is one that will yield a more accurate assessment of the value that teachers and schools add to student learning than do point-in-time measures of student achievement.

To determine the extent to which Ohio's value-added measure is, in fact, isolating the contribution of teachers and schools, we conducted a number of analyses to determine whether the methodology is systematically biased for or against teachers and schools that serve particular students (e.g., favoring low-achieving, high-poverty schools; favoring high-achieving, low-poverty schools). Figure 6.7 provides an illustration of the relationship between school-level value-added estimates and school-level poverty. The vertical axis displays the level of school value-added gain, where zero is the typical gain. Positive values represent

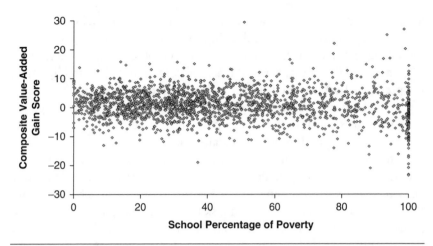

Figure 6.7   Relationship Between School-Level Poverty and Value-Added
                         Achievement Gains

above-average gains, and negative values represent below-average gains. The horizontal axis displays the percentage of students qualifying for free or reduced lunch. Each dot represents an Ohio school. The analysis suggests that the level of school poverty does not predict the gains that we find. We are equally likely to see strong value-added schools across all levels of poverty.

As we noted earlier, central to our definition of teacher quality and effectiveness is the teacher's ability to improve student learning. The closest approximation to assessing this quality is direct measurement of student achievement. With a grade-by-grade assessment system in place and a statewide data system that utilizes individual student longitudinal records tied to teacher assignments, Ohio has the infrastructure in place that is needed to measure student gains.

Discussion

In this chapter we have presented one state's attempt to create a coherent system of assessment of teacher quality and effectiveness—a system that is designed to evolve Ohio's teacher policy from one of a minimalist role for licensure (do no harm) to one of ensuring effective instruction in each classroom. To accomplish this goal, Ohio incorporates a range of measures that represent distant to proximal approximations of teacher ability to influence student learning, from teacher qualifications to teacher knowledge to teacher practice to change in student learning.

Implementing this system is not without its challenges. The effort required to collect data is often in inverse proportion to the level of approximation. Data on teacher credentials and knowledge are relatively easy to collect, yet these have the least established nexus to teachers' ability to improve student learning. Robust assessments of teacher practice require greater effort to implement with fidelity. Our knowledge base for assessing content-pedagogical competence is limited, in part because we have limited understanding of effective content-pedagogical practice.

Core to our understanding of effective practice and systems is alignment—coherence among the learning targets (standards), the content of instruction, and assessment. The construct of alignment is at the heart of the standards-based reform movement. As we write this chapter, the U.S. Department of Education is undertaking its second round of reviews of state assessments. A key element of that review is the alignment of state assessments to state content standards. Several technologies have been developed that allow robust analyses of assessment–content alignment. However, technologies for assessing the alignment of content specifications to the enacted curriculum are not widely adopted at this point.

There are technical limitations to our ability to incorporate at scale measures of teacher practice. The most robust approaches to assessing teacher practice rely on classroom observations that are effort- and resource intensive to implement with consistency. The NBPTS uses video clips and teacher explanations to assess teacher practice. But one concern about this approach relates to the limited sample on which the assessment relies, wherein the judgment reached may have greater validity as a measure of practice for which the teacher is capable rather than as a measure of the teacher's typical practice. As we stated earlier, there are trade-offs between fidelity and feasibility. The development of technologies that permit the assessment of teacher practice at scale, without unduly limiting the construct of effectiveness, will facilitate the incorporation of more proximal measures of teacher quality and effectiveness within federal and state teacher policy.

Although evidence of teachers' impact on student learning is the ideal measure of teacher quality and effectiveness, there are a number of limitations to the use of achievement scores as proxies for student learning. First and foremost, tests do not measure everything that we value. Inevitably, assessments measure only a sample of the content domain that we value and that is specified in the content standards. As a result, within a subject, tests measure a sample of the learning that takes place. In addition, we do not test in every subject. In Ohio, we assess student learning in reading, mathematics, writing, science, and social studies. We do not attempt to assess the arts or foreign languages at the statewide level, for example. Calculating the contribution of individual teachers is further complicated by the fact that, in many schools, teachers work in teams and share responsibility for instruction of the same group of students. The savvy science and social studies teachers may deserve as much credit as the English language arts teachers for the progress of students in reading.

Further limitations of the value-added methodology relate to the precision of the measurement. Even the most sophisticated statistical models result in imprecision of calculation, wherein estimates at the teacher level that are based on observed student gains suggest a range of likely true gain. When confidence intervals are applied to the observed measure, value-added methods do little to discriminate among the contributions of the majority of teachers. It is only with the instructors who produce gains at the extremes that we are confident that the value-added measures truly do identify the most and least effective teachers (McCaffrey, Lockwood, Koretz, & Hamilton, 2003). Finally, a number of concerns have been raised as to appropriate inferences that can be drawn from a given teacher's value-added score. Key to this concern is the degree to which the teacher's contribution is independent of the constellation of students. It is not clear whether teacher effectiveness, as measured by value-added models, is a generalizable calculation that transcends the particular classroom context. Should we expect, for example, that a teacher who demonstrates strong value-added with students from a high socioeconomic background would demonstrate equally strong results with students from a low socioeconomic background?

Much of federal and state policy relies on more distant approximations of teacher quality and effectiveness—primarily focusing on teacher credentials and knowledge, with secondary attention to teacher practice. We lack a robust understanding of the path of influence by which teacher credentials and knowledge impact teacher practice and student learning. In part, this emphasis is one of convenience, since it is more feasible and cost-effective to collect data on teacher credentials and knowledge than it is to assess teacher practice with fidelity. Better understanding of the elements of teacher credentials and knowledge that influence teacher practice and student learning, as well as the nature of their impact, will go a long way toward informing state and federal teaching policy.

There are at least two reasons, in addition to feasibility, that federal and state policy relies largely on distant approximations of teacher quality and effectiveness. Kennedy (1999) identifies as one reason the possibility that some states' reliance on more distant approximations of teacher impact reflects greater interest "in teacher compliance, endurance, or malleability than in student learning" (p. 360). This rationale is consistent with a rules orientation to policy—one that is focused on doing no harm—rather than the more aspirational goals orientation to policy that is associated with ensuring that every child has an effective teacher (Lowi, 1990). This point is not trivial in light of the transformations taking place globally. Barber (2007) identifies as one impact of globalization the shift from a producer-driven to a consumer-driven society. Bobbitt (2002) suggests that the emergence of the "market state" is designed to "maximize the opportunities enjoyed by all members of society" (p. 229). Public expectations and attitudes are marked by declining deference and a rights-based culture (Taylor, cited in Barber,

2007, p. 333). If these are accurate descriptions of the transformations taking place, then educators can expect that parents increasingly will be interested in how teachers and schools are benefiting their own children and will not be satisfied to know simply that their teachers meet baseline qualifications.

The second reason, in addition to feasibility, for basing teacher policy primarily on distant approximations of teacher quality and effectiveness is a matter of political will. There is a political cost to including impact on student achievement in the definition of teacher quality and effectiveness. A vivid illustration of this fact is occurring as we write this chapter, with the reauthorization of the No Child Left Behind Act. Efforts to expand the definition of "highly qualified teacher" to include measures of effectiveness as well as of credentials are meeting strong resistance from the national teacher unions (Hoff, 2007; Klein & Hoff, 2007), resistance that is not automatically present at the local (Gootman, 2007) or state level. Ironically, we have experienced greater willingness on the part of local and state teacher leadership than on the part of national leaders to pilot in Ohio approaches to measuring teacher practice, incorporating evidence of impact on student learning, and providing differentiated compensation. Nonetheless, these pilots are a far cry from the implementation of measures of teacher practice and student learning on a large scale, let alone on a statewide basis.

Conclusion

In this chapter we have presented a schema for organizing the assessment of teachers and teaching that is arranged according to the principle that teachers' ability to influence student learning is central to a definition of quality and effectiveness. We situated the discussion within a larger policy framework wherein the human resource system is but one of five key components, and the assessment of teacher quality and effectiveness is but one element of the human resource system. In Ohio, we employ a teacher assessment framework that balances rules and goals, thus ensuring that students are instructed by teachers who do no harm while aspiring to a standard of effectiveness where all teachers secure improved student learning. To implement this framework, Ohio employs multiple measures of teacher quality and effectiveness, some within the licensing function and others as part of teacher development initiatives. The standards employed include measures of teacher credentials, teacher knowledge, teacher practice, and change in student learning. Measures of credentials and knowledge are more distant proxies for teachers' ability to influence student learning, whereas measures of practice and student achievement are more proximal.

Trade-offs and limitations exist for each type of measure. For example, although measures of teacher credentials have the least direct nexus to student learning, they are among the easiest to collect accurately and to assess. Teacher knowledge is widely assumed to be foundational to effective teaching, yet the nexus between teacher knowledge and student learning is not well understood. Strong knowledge of subject matter content does not automatically translate into effective instruction. Our understanding of the intersection of content and pedagogy is rudimentary. Measures of teacher practice have a close relationship to student achievement, yet these require great effort to conduct with accuracy and at scale. Finally, measures of change in student achievement have their own limitations, including the fact that tests do not measure everything that we value, the imprecision of teacher rankings based on student test score gains, and questions about the generalizability of measures of individual teacher value-added.

It seems to us that a robust teacher assessment policy needs to employ multiple measures of teacher quality and effectiveness. The public relies on the state to diminish risk by limiting the pool of potential teachers to those who are unlikely to do harm—individuals who know the subject matter and have had guided practice to prepare them for their teaching assignment. Increasingly, public policy is consumer driven. Technology and school choice are providing students and parents with increasing options for schooling and education. Consumers are driven by a sense of entitlement to effective services, including schools and teachers who benefit their children in tangible ways. Responsive state policy aims toward schools that work, not simply schools that do no harm. To ignore the importance of measuring teacher quality and effectiveness is to risk making the traditional public schools irrelevant, at least for all but the poor who cannot afford alternative options.

References

Aspen Institute. (2008). *Elements of human capital management in K–12 education: Framework.* Retrieved June 14, 2008, from http://www.aspeninstitute.org/site/c.huLWJeMRKpH/b.3416283/k.DECF/Elements_of_Human_Capital_Management_in_K12_Education.htm

Ball, D. L., Hill, H. C., & Bass, H. (2005, Fall). Knowing mathematics for teaching: Who knows mathematics well enough to teach third grade, and how can we decide? *American Educator, 14–17,* 20–22, 43–46.

Barber, M. (2007). *Instruction to deliver: Tony Blair, public services and the challenge of achieving targets.* London: Politico's.

Blank, R. K., Porter, A., & Smithson, S. (2001). *New tools for analyzing teaching curriculum and standards in mathematics and science.* Washington, DC: Council of Chief State School Officers.

Bobbitt, P. (2002). *The shield of Achilles: War, peace, and the course of history.* New York: Knopf.

Chester, M. D., & Pecheone, R. L. (1992). Assessment-based licensing of school principals. *International Journal of Educational Management, 6*(3), 31–39.

Gifford, B. R. (1986). Excellence and equity in teacher competency testing: A policy perspective. *Journal of Negro Education, 55,* 251–271.

Gootman, E. (2007, October 18). Teachers agree to bonus pay tied to scores. *The New York Times.* Retrieved December 1, 2007, from http://www.nytimes .com/2007/10/18/education/18schools.html?ref=nyregion

Hiebert, J., Gallimore, R., Garnier, H., Bogard Givvin, K., Hollingworth, H., Jacobs, J., et al. (2003). *Highlights from the TIMSS 1999 video study of eighth-grade mathematics teaching.* Washington, DC: National Center for Education Statistics.

Hoff, D. J. (2007, November 14). NEA leads opposition to law's renewal. *Education Week,* pp. 22, 25.

Kennedy, M. M. (1999). Approximations to indicators of student outcomes. *Educational Evaluation and Policy Analysis, 21,* 345–363.

Klein, A., & Hoff, D. J. (2007, September 19). Unions assail teacher ideas in NCLB draft. *Education Week,* pp. 1, 20.

Koziol, S. M., & Burns, P. (1986). Teachers' accuracy in self-reporting about instructional practices using focused self-report inventory. *Journal of Educational Research, 79,* 205–209.

Lowi, T. J. (1990). Risks and rights in the history of American governments. *Daedalus, 119*(4), 17–40.

McCaffrey, D. F., Lockwood, J. R., Koretz, D. M., & Hamilton, L. S. (2003). *Evaluating value-added models for teacher accountability.* Santa Monica, CA: RAND.

Newmann, F. M., Marks, H. M., & Gamoran, A. (1996). Authentic pedagogy and student performance. *American Journal of Education, 194,* 280–312.

No Child Left Behind Act of 2001, Pub. L. No. 107-110, 115 Stat. 1425 (2002).

Porter, A. C. (2002). Measuring the content of instruction: Uses in research and practice. *Educational Researcher, 31*(7), 3–14.

Saxe, G., Gearhart, M., & Seltzer, M. (1999). Relations between classroom practices and student learning in the domain of fractions. *Cognition and Instruction, 17,* 1–24.

Shavelson, R. J., Baxter, G. P., & Pine, J. (1992). Performance assessments: Political rhetoric and measurement reality. *Educational Researcher, 21*(4), 22–27.

Smith, M. W., Dickinson, D. K., Sangeorge, A., & Anastasopoulos, L. (2002). *Early Language and Literacy Classroom Observation (ELLCO) Toolkit.* Baltimore: Brookes.

Stigler, J. W., & Hiebert, J. (1999). *The teaching gap: Best ideas from the world's best teachers for improving education in the classroom.* New York: Free Press.

Measuring Teacher and Teaching Quality

Considerations and Next Steps—Synthesis of Section II

Stephen Lazer

ETS

This session delved into the issues surrounding the measurement of the quality of practicing teachers. On their face, the three chapters would seem to address very different aspects of this general area. Deborah Ball and Heather Hill focus largely on expanding traditional notions of the nature and type of content knowledge needed for effective teaching and examining the relationship between this knowledge and classroom practice. Douglas Harris speaks about the strengths and weaknesses of

This session was composed of papers presented by Deborah Loewenberg Ball and Heather C. Hill, Douglas N. Harris, and Mitchell D. Chester and Susan Tave Zelman. Following these presentations, an interactive panel discussion was held. Panelists were Pamela Grossman, professor of education, Stanford University; Susanna Loeb, associate professor, Stanford University; and Lynn Olson, managing editor, Special Projects, *Education Week*. This chapter represents an attempt to synthesize key ideas from the presentations and papers and the subsequent discussion.

value-added models of teacher effectiveness and quality. And Mitchell Chester and Susan Tave Zelman discuss how a state education agency views and attempts to measure teacher quality. However, although the topics are different, there are substantial commonalities in the themes raised in these chapters. In the pages that follow, I discuss some of the most important of these themes.

It is worth mentioning, if only as an aside, that there are also common themes with chapters in other sections. For example, the topic of this section (Measuring the Effectiveness of Practicing Teachers) would appear to be different than the identification, licensure, and assessment of beginning teachers, but in fact there is substantial overlap.

What Is Teacher Quality?

The three chapters start from a common position perhaps best stated by Ball and Hill: "teachers do matter." Teacher effects explain a notable amount of variance in student performance. Ball and Hill cite studies showing the variance explained as ranging from 3 percent to 18 percent. The studies conducted and reviewed by Harris find wide variation between more and less effective teachers. And as Chester and Zelman point out, Ohio policy is based largely on the axiom that teacher quality matters deeply.

However, although the authors of these three chapters agree that teacher quality is important, they also note that there is little consensus as to how one would define it. They all agree with the seemingly self-evident idea that the goal of teaching, and the ultimate proof of teacher quality, is improved student learning. They all make some attempt to relate teacher quality indicators to measures of student outcomes. They all discuss some of the limitations and problems of their respective approaches. Finally, they all note that the most widely used indicators of teacher quality vary markedly from place to place (and study to study) and have in fact shown little correlation with student outputs.

A bit more detail may be helpful here. First, these authors note that most measures of teacher quality are proxies intended to predict teacher effectiveness. Those most commonly used are the presence or absence of certification (both general and subject specific), educational credentials, experience, professional development activities undertaken, and content area knowledge. These are, of course, attributes of the teachers and not direct measures of their actual teaching. Data shown in the various chapters suggest that most of these indicators have weak relationships to student outcomes. Yet this is not to say that none of the data shows positive relationships to learning. Ball and Hill, when looking at mathematics teachers, found that measures of content knowledge worked better than other indicators to predict student outcomes and that educational credentials (courses taken and degrees earned) did somewhat predict student outcomes at the high school level. Further, their chapter suggests that better measures of what they call "mathematical knowledge for teaching" may predict teaching effectiveness. Harris's chapter similarly suggests that pedagogical content knowledge is associated with teacher effectiveness.

Although there are bright spots, there is general agreement that these sorts of distant measures or proxies are doing an inadequate job of identifying teacher quality. Perhaps more important, as Ball and Hill point out, we should not care solely about *teacher* quality. We should, however, care a great deal about *teaching* quality. Harris as well as Chester and Zelman make similar points when they remind us that the goal is effectiveness in the classroom, not to have a highly credentialed teaching force for the sake of "showing well" in No Child Left Behind reports. In other words, the proxies we use to measure teaching quality are useful only if they predict this or tell us what actions we need to take to improve teaching. We know they do not do a very good job of that; we are therefore left without a common definition of what it means to be a quality teacher and no easy or useful means of finding such teachers or predicting who is likely to be one. As Zelman made plain in her comments at the conference, we have not clearly defined "professional practice," and we have a lot of work to do in this area if we are going to call ourselves a profession.

Why is defining teacher quality so difficult? As these chapters make clear, the problems are real and do not arise from some simple lack of creativity or intelligence on the part of analysts. On the one hand, there is no universal agreement about what characterizes an effective teacher (Lawrence and Gitomer discuss this in their synthesis of Section I in this volume). In addition, professional or guild judgments about teaching effectiveness will always be subject to mistrust if they cannot be shown to improve student learning. But there are serious issues in linking teaching practice to student outcomes.

Despite these problems, each of the chapters does, in the end, try to give some practical advice about getting closer to a shared and measurable understanding of how to identify quality teachers and help others improve the quality of their work.

Content Knowledge and Teacher Quality

Each chapter addresses, in at least some way, the important relationship between teaching quality and teacher knowledge of the content area in which they are delivering instruction. Chester and Zelman describe the steps taken in Ohio to ensure that teachers have appropriate content backgrounds (use of Praxis II, a major in the subject in which they teach, and some demonstration of continuing education in their teaching field as a precondition of license renewal). Harris notes that pedagogical content knowledge is one of the indicators associated with teacher effectiveness in one of his value-added studies. Ball and Hill suggest that, of the three indicators commonly used as proxies of the quality of mathematics teachers (credentialing, college-level course taking, and direct measures of content knowledge), the last is the best predictor of student achievement gains.

Although there is a general sense that content knowledge is important, one of the real contributions of Ball and Hill's research is that they have raised the question of what specific sort of content knowledge is key. They review research studies in which teachers were given content tests (and in which the relationship between teacher scores and student performance was evaluated). They find that these tests might be measuring only limited aspects of the content that is key for teaching effectiveness. As they state, "the largest problem we saw in this literature, other than a sheer lack of adequate evidence, was the fact that these mathematics assessments were not grounded in the work that teachers engage in with students. Instead, they assessed the mathematical knowledge that an eighth grader or an adult might know, but not the professionally oriented knowledge of the content that we suspected teachers must possess to provide effective instruction."

Ball and Hill seek to address this limitation through the definition and assessment of "mathematical knowledge for teaching." It is important to note that this is not general pedagogical knowledge—it is clearly mathematical content knowledge, but a specific form of that knowledge that is needed by teachers to allow them to explain solutions, work with students, identify characteristic flaws in student reasoning, and explain key concepts to other audiences (e.g., parents). It includes, but is not isomorphic with, the ability to solve the mathematics problems presented to students or adults. Nor is it synonymous with the ability to do higher-level mathematics.

Ball and Hill's research in this area is important for several reasons. First, their chapter indicates that knowledge of this sort may be a more reliable way to identify quality teachers than traditional tests of content knowledge or other indicators. This has implications for assessment developers, among others. Perhaps more important, careful educators could be trained in mathematical knowledge for teaching, which should in principle lead to better teaching and learning.

This research, though promising, brings up several questions and suggests certain key next steps. Ball and Hill note that having knowledge is not the same as using that knowledge effectively in instruction. They conducted an observational study to evaluate the "mathematical quality of instruction." As they state, the need for this sort of study raises questions of scalability (more on this later). They also note, more optimistically, that the content knowledge measure itself correlated rather well with their evaluations of instructional quality.

The other key question that arises from this research—an issue that also came up in the subsequent panel discussion—is whether this sort of content knowledge for teaching has been investigated in areas other than mathematics. Two different concerns were raised. The first was about the state of research in areas such as reading, science, history, social studies, foreign languages, and the arts. The second was whether disciplines other than mathematics leant themselves equally well to the identification of such content knowledge. In any case, it is essential that other fields aggressively follow the lead that Ball and Hill have taken.

Value-Added Modeling

All the chapters in this section define effective teaching as leading to improved student performance. Ball and Hill gave students an outcome measure to evaluate the effectiveness of mathematical knowledge for teaching and mathematical quality of instruction. Chester and Zelman highlight that Ohio's system uses changes in student achievement (value-added models) as outcome measures in various parts of its teacher evaluation and research programs.

It seems tautological to state that good teaching will lead to better student learning. However, establishing a statistical relationship between individual teachers and/or certain teaching practices is fraught with challenges and complexities. As Harris makes clear, teachers are not randomly assigned to students and schools, teaching practices are not randomly assigned to teachers (districts adopt curricula, for example), and teachers themselves are not randomly assigned to professional development activities. Therefore, simple use of student outcomes measures as a proxy for teacher quality is clearly inequitable and almost certainly yields misleading results.

For this reason, analysts have tried to use value-added modeling (VAM) to identify good teachers, schools, and programs. The premise of VAM seems simple enough: Researchers can look at average levels of student progress over time, at least as measured on standardized assessments. They can then control those averages for the quality of school-level resources that different children receive. Finally, analysts can identify teachers whose students seem to show higher-than-average growth.

Harris openly discusses some of the challenges associated with VAM; we will come back to those momentarily. However, he also sees real possibilities. They appear to be a distinct improvement over both the simple use of single-point-in-time test scores and the gain-score studies done in the past. In addition, Harris provides some validity evidence: He cites two studies that showed a positive (albeit low) correlation between the VAM scores assigned to teachers and principals' evaluation of the effectiveness of teachers.

Harris also makes an important distinction in the possible uses of VAM. He describes two possible uses of VAM data, one for program evaluation and one for accountability. In the former case, VAM can be used in one of several ways. It may identify groups of teachers who show high levels of value-added. In theory, researchers can search for characteristics or patterns common to those teachers, which can inform policy decisions. In addition, VAM could be used in formal program evaluation settings: Average teacher effectiveness could be evaluated before or after an educational intervention. In general, program evaluation uses of VAM require the models to be useful at a general level.

The other use of VAM is for accountability. Specifically, some wish to use these data to make high-stakes decisions about individual teachers (e.g., decisions regarding promotion, pay, or tenure). As mentioned earlier, Harris shows that teacher effectiveness varies widely. He also discusses value-added studies showing that VAM evaluations of teachers correlate with other measures of teacher effectiveness (e.g., judgments of principals).

However, use of VAM to make individual decisions runs, according to Harris, directly afoul of some of the problems associated with these models. For one thing, measurement of value-added is not particularly precise at the individual teacher level, and telling similar individuals apart may be impossible. Second, VAM estimates are sensitive to the variables included in the models; different models yield different answers. Third, measures of the same teacher taken at different times can change more markedly than seems appropriate for consequential decisions about individual teachers.

Harris seems more comfortable with the use of VAM for program and policy evaluation than for individual accountability. He does not, however, reject either approach, but suggests that some problems have yet to be solved. Other commentators during the conference were far more dubious of the use of these analytic techniques.

It is clear that the debates over VAM will continue for some time. On the one hand, simple use of student test scores should not be the sole basis for evaluating teachers or teaching practices, and VAM seems to offer a more sophisticated approach that attempts to address some of the weaknesses of past practice. On the other hand, there are real and ongoing issues with estimating value-added. These issues may be more than problems associated with the newness of the analytic technique; they may prove intractable.

If this last statement is possibly true, why continue to work on VAM models? There are three reasons. First, the fact that models are imperfect does not necessarily render them useless. It may be important to understand the limitations of VAM, and the nature and size of errors associated with VAM estimates, but still to make use of these data. Second, it may be premature to declare the work either a success or a failure. Third, and perhaps most important, the goal of VAM—to provide objective data about student achievement that can be used to identify effective teachers—will remain of key interest to educators and policymakers.

This last point relates to one other key consideration: VAM models are no better than the tests that they use to chart student progress. If these tests are giving misleading or incomplete pictures, then the VAM results cannot, by definition, be accurate. Furthermore, as Chester and Zelman point out, most states do not even give standardized assessments in areas such as foreign languages or the arts. Teachers in these areas could not be evaluated with the same machinery as those in so-called core areas.

Multiple Measures and Scalability

Ball and Hill as well as Chester and Zelman discuss in different ways the importance of multiple measures. As mentioned earlier, Ball and Hill argue that content knowledge is meaningless unless it is paired with effective implementation in the classroom. Thus the study they describe involved measures of teacher knowledge, tests of student learning, and observations of teacher classroom practice. Chester and Zelman describe a teacher quality system in Ohio that is based on multiple sources of data, including information on teacher credentials, tests of teacher knowledge, observational evaluations of teacher practice, and some attempts to link teachers to student outcomes.

The use of multiple measures is clearly necessary if we are to obtain a complete and nuanced picture of teacher effectiveness. This is true of both research and policy applications. But the need for multiple measures runs directly into an issue raised by Chester and Zelman as well as Ball and Hill: Gaining these measures for large numbers of teachers often at several process points may well prove intractable from a cost point of view. As Chester and Zelman point out, Ohio has 120,000 teachers in 4,000 schools.

This need for scalability places additional pressure on teacher quality researchers. Quality indicators must be designed with the real-life problems of data collection and maintenance in mind. Otherwise, lofty goals may lead to pedestrian practice.

Closing Comment

The chapters in this section examine the measurement of teacher quality from three perspectives. What is perhaps a bit odd is that they all agree that there is no working definition of teacher quality. It is clear that good teaching should lead to student achievement; it is unclear what teacher characteristics are related to such performance or how the relationship with student achievement should be established.

In spite of this lack of clarity, these chapters work to address some of the central issues in this discussion by examining the types of content knowledge and classroom presentation of that knowledge that are necessary for good teaching in mathematics, evaluating statistical models of linking teacher performance and student achievement, and describing a multiple-measures state system for ensuring quality teaching.

Although all three of these chapters make important advances, they also call attention to how much further we have to go. As Ball and Hill state at the end of their chapter, "Given where we are in our understanding of the quality of students' opportunities to learn as well as their actual learning, we will have to . . . delve into instruction and then map backward and forward to specific elements that we can use to predict instructional practice and its quality. Without that, we will be having the same conversation a decade from now."

Section III

Measuring Teaching Quality in Context

7 Mapping the Terrain of Teacher Quality

Arturo Pacheco

Professor and Director of the Center for Research on Educational Reform, University of Texas at El Paso

This chapter maps out in a preliminary way the landscape of teacher quality. It is written in a time of intense discussion of teacher quality, both in the policy community and in the research and measurement community. Although there is a growing consensus among both policymakers and researchers that teacher quality is a critical variable in the improvement of student learning, conversations about teacher quality vary widely and cover much terrain. The range of these conversations is quite broad, depending on both the intent of the participants and the focus of discussion. It makes a difference whether the focus is on teacher characteristics or student characteristics, or, bypassing the attempt to fully describe teacher quality, on the outcomes of teacher–student interaction. There is also a growing recognition that understanding the context in which teachers teach and students learn is important to any definition or measurement of teacher quality.

My goal is to better understand the context of teacher quality, pointing out some obstacles to a more complete understanding. More than three decades ago, in his analysis of the activities of teaching, the philosopher of education Thomas Green (1971) demonstrated that teaching itself is an exceedingly complex set of activities, and any assessment of teacher quality needs to take this complexity into account. In the rush to find measures for the assessment of teacher quality, we may tend to oversimplify this complex phenomenon to make it more amenable to both easier measurement and policy reform. The philosopher Mary Midgley (2001) has pointed out that there is always a great temptation to oversimplify the conceptually complex. One of the goals of this chapter is to make the case that teacher quality is not a fixed set of attributes of a teacher, but rather a construct that arises out of a complex set of social and institutional interactions. Furthermore, it is this complexity that must be taken into account in any assessment framework for teacher quality. Current models of assessment oversimplify and do not attend to these contextual factors.

I begin with two vignettes that illustrate the disparate contexts in which we try to assess teacher quality. I then examine the key concepts associated with teacher quality and identify some of the key variables that have an important role in the assessment of teacher quality. Following this, I identify additional factors that need to be considered in looking at teacher quality in the expanding contexts of the classroom, the school, the community, and the state. I conclude with a discussion of the challenges involved in understanding teacher quality in these multilayered contexts. It is the understanding of this contextual complexity that will assist us in the design of an assessment framework that is both more responsive to the realities of teaching and more useful in improvement of teacher quality. We need an assessment framework that improves the quality of teaching and the learning of students, not one that simply ranks teacher quality as an outcome.

Two Stories to Illustrate the Problem of Contextual Complexity

I had my first classroom teaching experience in 1965, just a few months after my college graduation. It was an experience that had a profound impact on my life, and I have been fascinated by the phenomena of teaching and learning ever since. The context was a classroom of eighth graders in a rural village in southern Thailand. Inspired by the words and legacy of John Kennedy to do something for my country, I had joined the Peace Corps during its early years and, with just a few months' preparation, I was standing before a classroom of 40 well-scrubbed Thai youngsters whose rapid fire Thai I could barely understand. I was their new English teacher.

Although I was young, energetic, and highly motivated to do well, the context presented several challenges. Nearly everything about us was different. I was an inexperienced working-class son of Mexican farmworkers. I had worked my way through a state college to obtain a degree in philosophy, and I had not traveled much beyond the agricultural valley in California where I was born and raised. My students were extremely respectful and soft-spoken in their southern Thai dialect. I do not think they understood much of my English or my rudimentary Thai, and I had lots of trouble even hearing, let alone understanding them. They smiled a lot, at almost anything I said or did. Nearly all of them were Buddhists, had never been more than 20 miles away from their village, but hoped to learn enough English to continue on to secondary school, where English was a required second language.

The texts that were provided by the national education ministry were primers from England, with stories about the British Museum and Hyde Park. On the surface, this context presented a huge disconnect between my experience and background, those of the students, and even the curriculum materials—which were foreign to both the students and me. How would we go about understanding teacher quality, let alone measure it, in this context?

My second example is from the National Board for Professional Teaching Standards (NBPTS) assessments. Flash forward about 30 years to the mid-1990s, when I was the dean of a teacher preparation college and a member of the NBPTS, reviewing videotapes of American teachers in classrooms across the country. I was part of an Assessment Work Group that was examining the criteria for judging the teaching performance of experienced teachers who had applied for certification. These NBPTS assessments were developed by ETS, and they represented some of the best thinking and a pioneering effort in the area of performance assessments for teachers.

I remember viewing one pair of videos that left me feeling particularly befuddled. Both were classroom videos that experienced teachers had submitted as part of their assessments for NBPTS certification. One, from Ann Arbor, Michigan, showed a large, modern, and spacious elementary school classroom. There were several workstations, which were mostly composed of a table and some chairs around it. The teacher was seated at one of these workstations, having a conversation with a group of students. The students were bright and inquisitive and seemed quite comfortable in their discussion, asking questions of the teacher and their fellow students. Most of the students were White and seemingly middle class, as was the teacher. My first impression was very positive—it looked like a good example of inquiry-based teaching and learning at work.

The next video was from an urban classroom in Brooklyn, New York. The classroom was tight and cramped with rows of desks and barely enough room to walk between them. Aside from some low, half-empty bookshelves along the wall and a teacher's desk squeezed into a tight space in the front of the room, there was no other furniture. Most of the students were African American or from other ethnic minority groups and seemingly working class; the teacher, too, was African American. The video showed her teaching from the front of the room, standing in front of her desk and very much in command of the classroom. There was hardly room for her to move or stand anywhere else. It looked like a good example of what we used to call *frontal teaching*—most of the talk and questions came from the teacher, with students alert and responsive to the teacher, answering politely when called on.

If my memory serves me right, I believe that both of these teachers were assessed as high-quality, or accomplished, teachers. Although the NBPTS assessments took several other portfolio entries into account, the conclusions that these were examples of "accomplished teaching" were made independently of any data on student learning.

What Do We Learn From the Two Stories?

I have used these two vignettes for several reasons. First, they serve as dramatic examples of how very different the contexts of teaching can be. Second, they begin to illustrate the difficulty of coming up with common criteria for the assessment of teacher quality. Third, they raise the question of whether the assessment of teacher quality can be made independently of whether we know what and how much students have learned as a result. Finally, the two vignettes illustrate the source of my own long-standing interests in understanding the complexity of teaching and teacher quality as well as my many years as a practitioner attempting to improve teacher preparation.

Let me begin this discussion with a question: Can we assess teacher quality by looking at teacher characteristics alone? This question may seem a bit odd at first. Some people, looking for proxy definitions of teacher quality, have spent much time focusing their attention on identifying teacher characteristics that correlate most closely to a particular definition of teacher quality. This is clearly what the No Child Left Behind Act has done with its definition of a "highly qualified teacher," which is based on three easy-to-measure teacher characteristic (bachelor's degree, adequate test scores, and state licensure), confounding "minimal qualifications" with "highly qualified."

For other people, in an increasing number of contemporary conversations about teacher quality, there is the assumption that defining teacher quality only makes sense in connection with student learning. This is especially true in policy talk, where the focus is almost always on bottom-line outputs. For example, a leading scholar in this area, Eric Hanushek (2002), has provided us with a straightforward definition of teacher quality: "Good teachers are ones who get large gains in student achievement for their classes; bad teachers are just the opposite" (p. 3). This definition of teacher quality serves us both well and not so well. It serves us well in that it is simple and clear, and it reminds us what the central concern is: the improvement of student learning. We need a definition of teacher quality that is connected to some positive outcome in students. Yet it does not serve us well in that it is less a definition of teacher quality than it is a statement of a highly desired outcome of teacher quality, once you have it. It does not help us understand what teacher quality is. Hanushek's definition is a "black box" definition that suggests we should not worry about what is in the black box, but should only be concerned with the outputs. But it is exactly our understanding of what goes on within the black box that is necessary to make improvements in teacher quality. There are good reasons why Hanushek and others have chosen this outcome measure as their definition. I will return to this point later in this chapter.

Even if you accept this end-around attempt at defining teacher quality, as many seem to have done, it does little to help our understanding of what constitutes quality in teaching. Our concerns about measuring teacher quality are not esoteric. Rather, we are concerned about understanding teacher quality so that we can improve it where it needs improving and so that we can better prepare teachers to contribute successfully to the learning that goes on in their classrooms.

Part of the focus in developing the NBPTS assessments was to identify aspects of quality that might be identified in a wide variety of teachers across classrooms in diverse schools around the nation. The videos of classroom teaching submitted by teachers were one part of multi-element performance assessments of teachers in the natural settings of their classrooms. Although it is a commonly heard cliché from experienced instructional leaders that "they know good teaching when they see it," one of the measurement challenges for ETS was whether experienced teachers serving as well-trained assessors could view the videos and identify quality or excellent teachers when they saw them. Could assessment rubrics be developed that would allow fair and accurate scoring of teaching performance in a variety of diverse contexts? Could those people scoring the videos—mostly experienced teachers—do so in a way that was sensitive to context and relatively free of their own biases? Although far from perfect, the NBPTS assessments may be the best performance assessments that have been developed to date.

Examining the Most Basic Teacher–Student Interaction

Let us examine the context of teacher quality by examining the most basic teacher–student interaction (a single teacher and a single student), which may make most sense when described as a dynamic, interactive relational concept. Consider the diagram in Figure 7.1.

Let us begin by describing some of the typical characteristics of the interaction. It is a dynamic two-way relationship with a great deal of interplay in both directions. There are two actors, a teacher and a student. There is an object of understanding, that is, something to be learned. And there is a desired learning outcome or improvement, for example, gains in student learning. The Brazilian philosopher Paulo Freire (1970) called this a

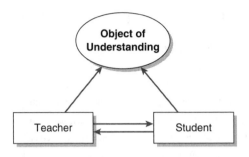

Figure 7.1   The Basic Teacher–Student Interaction

dialogical relationship, with the object of learning mediating a dialogue between teacher and student. It is marked by interaction in two directions, with the possibility of learning through acts of cognition by both student and teacher.

WHAT DO TEACHERS BRING TO TEACHING AND LEARNING?

As we examine this most basic of teacher–student interactions, one of the first questions we could ask is: What do teachers bring to the interaction? Throughout this discussion I use the term *attributes* to cover a variety of different characteristics, including knowledge and skills, attitudes, dispositions, values, beliefs, and other characteristics of human beings, both individual and collective. My general purpose is not so much to make fine distinctions among them as it is to point out how few of them are used as important factors in the determination of teacher quality.

Teachers bring a large set of attributes to the interaction, including specific knowledge, preparation, intelligence, experience, skills, and achievements (on tests or otherwise). Many researchers have focused on these teacher characteristics in attempting to connect particular attributes to student learning outcomes. In addition, teachers bring to the interaction other individual attributes, sometimes called *noncognitive* attributes, such as motivation, expectations, self-identity, values and beliefs, openness, and creativity. Notice that these are quite different from each other and from traditional cognitive attributes. Some are cognitive and some are noncognitive, and there are differences within each of these categories. Yet for our purposes of initially mapping the terrain in this chapter, their exact differences are not so important. What is important is the recognition that each individual teacher brings to the teacher–student interaction a suitcase full of individual characteristics, only some of which are labeled here.

In addition to these individual characteristics, each teacher also brings to the interaction a set of sociocultural attributes. These are the attributes of one's collective identity, including class background, culture, language, race, and gender.

As noted earlier, this limited list of attributes contains very different types. Some are cognitive, some noncognitive. Some, such as race and gender, are ascribed characteristics. Some are much more easily measured than others. We sometimes use some of the more easily measured characteristics as proxies for teacher quality, such as state licensure, a bachelor's degree in a teaching subject area, or test scores in teaching subjects or pedagogy. Taken together, these last three achievements constitute the federal law's definition of a highly qualified teacher. In reality, they say nothing about teaching performance, ability, or effectiveness.

A number of researchers have spent large amounts of their attention trying to measure the impact of one or several of these variables on teaching and learning. Yet looking at them in isolation and independent of the context of the teaching–learning situation is fraught with difficulty. In addition, many of these variables interact with one another. For example, one's motivation can impact one's preparation, and one's class background can impact one's motivation. All of them can be key variables in having an impact on teaching and, consequently, on student learning.

WHAT DO STUDENTS BRING TO TEACHING AND LEARNING?

When we look at the other side of the interaction, and ask what students bring to teaching and learning, it turns out that we find a similar set of attributes, knowledge, skills, and sociocultural characteristics. We now end up with a much more complicated terrain, with many variables that can have a significant impact on both the teaching and the learning outcomes of the interaction. This complex set of interacting variables is displayed in Figure 7.2.

Additional Variables That Impact Teacher Quality

When we take the teaching context into account, the search for significant indicators now takes place in a virtual forest of interacting variables and a great multiplicity of other learning outcomes. A definition of teacher quality, then, needs to take into account these attributes and their interactive effects on both sides of the teacher–student interaction. For example, if there is no response from students, or perhaps a negative response such as boredom or falling asleep, we will probably be hesitant to label the teaching as being of high quality. Or, as in the two NBPTS videos that I described earlier, although the demographics and the classroom conditions were

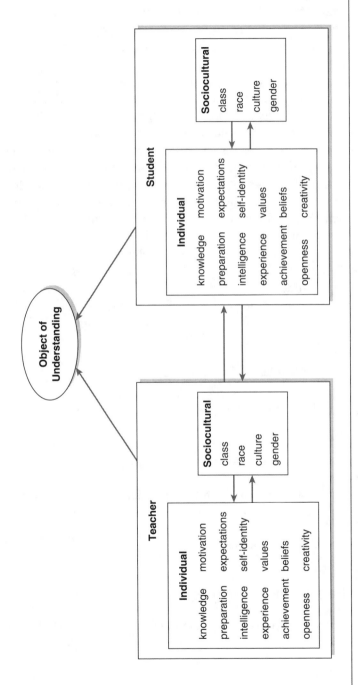

Figure 7.2 The Context of the Teacher–Student Interaction

quite different, one of the things that was apparent in both teaching situations was alert, active, and responsive students. This fact very likely had an impact on the positive response of the assessors scoring the videotaped teaching performances. Thus, the nature of the interaction seems to have a lot to do with whether or not quality teaching is going on. In both cases, the teachers in the videos seemed very sensitive to the responses of their students.

The fact that teaching is an interactive process between teachers and learners, of course, presents one of the great problems in looking for quality only on the teacher side. For example, teacher characteristics by themselves do not determine quality teaching. Some (e.g., possession of a college degree, licensure, a passing score on a test) may be useful and necessary conditions to enter the profession, but are not sufficient to guarantee much else. It is a bit like driving. Almost everyone has a driver's license, but as we all know too well, that does not guarantee quality driving. Quality driving has to do with the interaction with others and being sensitive to a host of other variables. Having a license and a passing score on a test does not lead us to call all drivers "highly qualified."

Partially because of this large set of variables on both sides of the teacher–student interaction, there is a multitude of possible outcomes. Some outcomes, such as achievement gains, are quite desirable. Thus, for example, if the object of learning or understanding is algebra, a successful outcome is evidence of the following:

The student learned a lot of algebra.

Other, less successful outcomes might be these:

The student learned some algebra.

The student did not learn any algebra.

Yet in the same student–teacher interaction, the student might learn several other desirable outcomes:

Teachers care about kids.

Learning is enjoyable.

Learning is important.

There is, of course, the possibility for the student to learn many undesirable outcomes:

Teachers are mean.

Math is not for girls.

I hate math.

I am not very smart.

I hate school.

School is not for people like me.

Our examination of outcomes of the teacher–student interaction, then, has to take into consideration the full spectrum of possible outcomes, both desirable and undesirable. Obviously, we want to create interactions that maximize the desirable outcomes and minimize the undesirable ones.

All of this, of course, takes place not with a single student and a single teacher, but in the natural environment of the classroom (see Figure 7.3), with other students who have similar relationships with the teacher and while many things in addition to teaching and learning are taking place. This context, which Fenstermacher and Richardson (2005) refer to as the *social surround*, is vitally important in any assessment of teacher quality. The multiplicity of interactions, between the teacher and other students, and between one student and another, introduces additional variables that can and do influence teacher quality. Each of the student–teacher interactions can influence the others, as can the interactions between individual students (see Figure 7.4).

Classrooms, of course, exist not in isolation, but in the larger context of schools—a context that introduces new variables that can influence the teacher–student interaction. We know from the landmark works by Seymour Sarason (1996) and John Goodlad (1984) that schools are characterized by cultures that are marked by sets of rules and values, which regulate practice within them and influence the quality of teaching within their walls.

Of course, there is an even broader context—the community—and there may be some unique characteristics of the community that can affect the teacher–student interaction, including its effectiveness in terms of learning outcomes. For example, it is common for classrooms in the urban community of El Paso, Texas, to have significant numbers of children who are both working class and native Spanish speakers. Whether teachers have attributes that include knowledge and understanding of working-class students whose native language is Spanish, not English, could have some influence on the quality of their teaching. Their knowledge and preparation in the teaching of students whose native language is not English will likely influence the overall quality of their teaching. Likewise, these teachers' attitudes, values, and beliefs about the place of other languages in the school and the community could also influence their teaching ability and effectiveness.

Consider a brief example. A few years ago I was teaching a group of teacher interns in their last year of preparation. Half their time was spent teaching in local El Paso elementary schools, and the other half taking classes. A few weeks after the beginning of the school year, they sent notices home to parents to schedule a week of afterschool teacher–parent

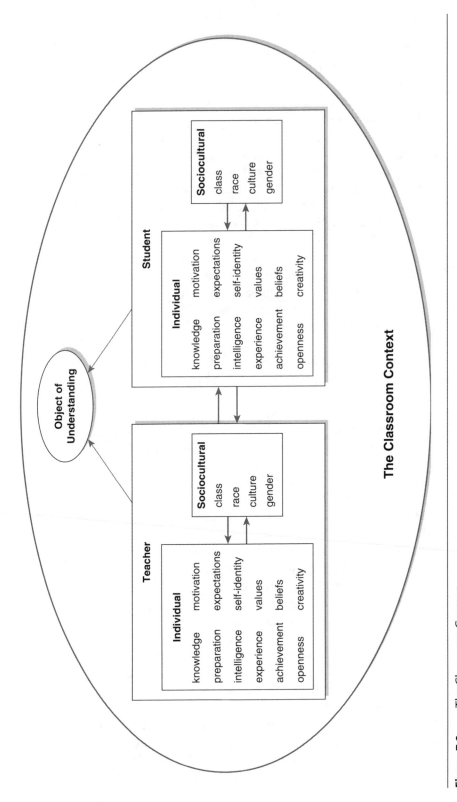

Figure 7.3 The Classroom Context

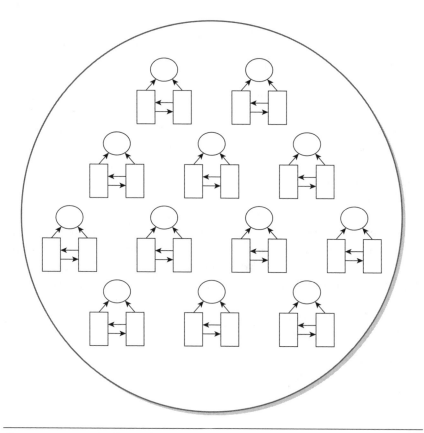

Figure 7.4   Multiple Teacher–Student Interactions

conferences. They were highly motivated interns and thought this would be a great idea to get to know the parents early in the year so that they might better teach the students. When we had a debriefing the week after the parent–teacher conferences, I was surprised that a number of the interns were very disappointed with the outcome. They were disappointed because only a few of the parents had participated. Some parents had even indicated that they would participate, but did not show up at the appointed time. What was even more surprising to me were the attitudes that were beginning to form in the minds of some of the teacher interns. Several of them began to conclude that "these parents" did not seem to care much about schooling or the education of their children.

The interns, of course, got several things wrong. They did not have the knowledge that almost all of the parents were working class and worked in low-level service jobs, where it was impossible to take time off during the regular work day without getting their pay docked or even putting their job in peril, unlike many professional parents who could more easily get time off. Also, many were monolingual Spanish speakers who were hesitant about any meeting in English with a teacher.

Had we left it there, I cannot help but wonder how these new teacher attitudes might have affected their overall teaching quality and effectiveness.

Needless to say, we had to improvise some novel solutions to address the problem. We did several things, including projects involving the interns getting a lot more knowledgeable about the community surrounding the school. This meant gathering information about the community, including the knowledge that many of the primary caretakers of the children were, in fact, grandparents. With the assistance of the local grassroots community organization, it also included early evening visits by the interns to the homes of their students. The home visits often served as eye-openers for the interns; they often found parents who were deeply concerned about the education of their children, but who faced substantial barriers in getting to teacher conferences.

One of the things that this vignette tells us about the assessment of teacher quality is that the teacher's ability to take stock of the sociocultural environment of the school and the community is an important attribute in the overall assessment of teacher quality. Unless they learn to do this, either through teacher preparation or professional development,

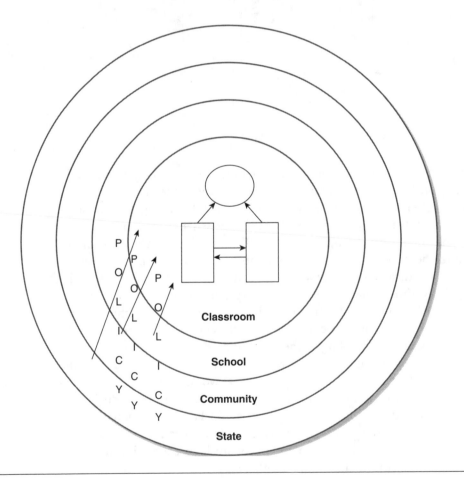

Figure 7.5   Policy Variables

teachers may be more likely to develop attitudes and make decisions that are not in the best interests of student learning. No matter how gifted teachers are academically, they can fail miserably because of these kinds of disconnects with contextual factors.

The Wider Context of the State

There is, of course, the even wider context of the state, where state, and increasingly, federal policies can greatly affect schools, class-rooms, and the quality of teacher–student interactions within them. It is not difficult to come up with examples of such policies. They include the reduction of class size, state and federal definitions of quality and account-ability measures, and high-stakes testing. Various forms of incentive pay, including pay based on student gains, master teacher designations, or NBPTS certification—currently part of the discussions around the reau-thorization of the No Child Left Behind Act—may have important con-sequences on teaching behaviors. Some of these policy levers at the school, community, and state levels are illustrated in Figure 7.5.

The Complexity of Measuring Teacher Quality

Taking all of these contextual layers into account, each with its own sets of variables that can affect teacher quality, is a formidable undertaking. In fact, the complexity of attempting to do so may be overwhelming. The terrain in which we look for teacher quality is immensely complex, so much so that our attempt to isolate individual features, let alone measure them definitively, in the natural multidimensional landscape of the school or classroom is too daunting a task. In such cases, as Midgley (2001) points out, there is a great temptation toward *reductionism,* to oversimplify a very complex task of understanding. This is perhaps why we moved in the early years toward a focus on education inputs in the search for teacher quality. This is a far more stable and knowable terrain; it is easier to isolate a few of these teacher char-acteristics and use them as proxies for teacher quality. With the development of the NBPTS assessments of teacher quality in the past decade, Lee Shulman (2007) has pointed out that any single teacher characteristic was insufficient and there was a movement to identify several important indicators that together could make up a definition of teacher quality. These are what Shulman has called "a union of insufficiencies" (p. 14).

As Hanushek (2002) has pointed out in his discussion of teacher quality, the focus on identifying single teacher attributes that constitute quality has yielded mixed results. Hence, we understand his movement beyond this terrain to the end of the trail to looking at learning outcomes exclusively. He says that "the extensive research over the past 35 years has led to two clear conclusions. First, there are very important differences among teachers. This finding, of course, does not surprise many parents, who are well aware of quality differences of teachers. Second, these differences are not captured by common measures of teachers (qualifications, experience, and the like)" (p. 3). Hanushek goes on to conclude that we have spent far too much time looking at educational inputs and do not know how to identify "a well-defined set of inputs that is either necessary or sufficient for ensuring high quality schooling" (p. 7). This is not a matter of needing more or better educational research, he says; it is just too complex.

Hence, Hanushek's (2002) move to the output end and his "simple definition of teacher quality: Good teachers are ones who get large gains in student achievement for their classes; bad teachers are just the opposite" (p. 3). He is correct in his description of the difficulty of identifying a well-defined set of inputs that make up teacher quality, and he is also correct about the desirability and utility of a simple definition. But it does not follow that the task of defining teacher quality in complex ways is impossible or that his simple definition of teacher quality as student achievement is well conceived. Nor is it the case that student test scores are substitutable for student learning.

To use Midgley's (2001) language, this is a sort of reductionism, a reduction to a single output measure. As we have seen, the output end of the terrain is quite complex, with the possibility of many learning outputs. And although achievement gains may be the most desirable of outcomes, there are many others that may be nearly as desirable, such as sensitivity, respect, and caring for others—skills and understanding for the responsibilities of good citizenship, civility, and decency. We also want to avoid undesirable outcomes that we know are possible as well.

My solution is a different one. Here I agree with Midgley's (2001) conclusions that what we need are not easy answers to complex problems but better maps—conceptual maps—of the contested terrain. In particular, we need to reexamine and remap the terrain of teacher characteristics in a new way—a way that examines them not as static characteristics, but as attributes constantly being shaped by the dynamic contexts of the school and community, and particularly by the attributes brought by the students to student–teacher interaction.

Although there may be some basic attributes that are perhaps necessary in every teacher and are a part of what constitutes teacher quality, there may be some additional ones that are more important in specific contexts, for example, urban classrooms that serve most of the nation's minority and low-income youngsters. We need a better mapping of these contexts, a more finely tuned description of the interplay between urban teachers and the students they serve. Are there other teacher characteristics that impede or facilitate success in these situations, where success is seen as both achievement gains and other outcomes that contribute to the well-being of children? Is the prevailing view of quality and success too narrow? Telling us that teacher quality is defined by student achievement gains is not enough. If we are concerned about assisting existing teachers and helping to select and prepare new ones, we need to know much more. We need an assessment framework that also functions as a feedback system for the improvement of teacher preparation and the further development of existing teachers.

For example, can we identify additional characteristics that are necessary for successful urban teaching and match them with the characteristics that students bring to these classrooms in the context of an urban landscape that influences teachers, students, and the dynamic interplay between them? Here, we may have to do some backward designing. Starting from the study of successful teachers in urban classrooms, can we then design backward to try to better understand the characteristics of those teachers—teachers who are successful in terms of both achievement gains of their students and improvement in the well-being of the students?

Why is this so important? Because minority and working-class children in urban schools are not likely to register achievement gains if they are treated poorly by teachers who, even if prepared well at a general level, do not have sufficient understanding of, experience with, and sensitivity to the needs of the students in their classrooms. These are the students who begin dropping out, at least psychologically, around the ninth grade and often do not finish high school or finish inadequately prepared for either the workplace or college.

This is not a new concern. Descriptions abound of what Martin Haberman (2005) has called the *pedagogy of poverty* and have been steadily put before us since the 1960s, from Jonathan Kozol's (1967) *Death at an Early Age* to his most recent work of the past few years. There has also been much excellent research done in the area of identifying quality teaching in urban classrooms, including the work of two recent presidents of the American Educational Research Association, Gloria Ladson-Billings (1995) and Marilyn Cochran-Smith (1995).

Haberman, at the University of Wisconsin, has devoted decades of work to improving the quality of teachers who end up in urban schools—schools that serve the great majority of working-class and minority students. He sees strong preparation in content and pedagogy as necessary but not sufficient characteristics for being an effective teacher in an urban school (Haberman, 2005). These will not be sufficient if teachers fail to make a connection with the students they serve. In Haberman's view, successful urban teachers believe strongly in the value of diversity and in issues of equity and access to high-quality educational opportunities. For him, success in school is a matter of life and death for children of urban poverty. Haberman has identified 14 attributes that make or break successful teachers in urban schools, including persistence in reaching every student, protecting the learning environment for students, ability to generalize and translate theory and research into practice, deep respect and care for the students they serve, high expectations, organizational ability, and physical and emotional stamina.

If we have had trouble determining what a highly qualified teacher is under the No Child Left Behind legislation, with its lack of distinction between minimally qualified and high-quality teachers, we now have a far more difficult problem. Perhaps this is why Haberman (2005) has put so much effort on the front end, on the initial selection of teachers through alternative means that take into account the attributes listed earlier. For Haberman, many of these attributes come only from experience and maturity, and are often not in the curriculum of preservice teacher preparation programs. He credits much of his understanding to his work in the early 1960s developing the Teacher Corps program at the University of Wisconsin at Milwaukee, which became a model of training for the National Teacher Corps.

Ladson-Billings (1995), citing Haberman's work, draws similar conclusions about the kinds of teachers we need in urban schools and in a democratic society. Good, enthusiastic new teachers who are deeply committed to making a difference often get crushed by the pedagogy of poverty so common in urban schools. This mindless pedagogy is often focused on regimentation and control, giving directions and monitoring behavior. Ladson-Billings adds that teacher quality is only symptomatic of a larger problem, losing sight of the public purposes of teaching and schooling or, as she puts it, "evacuation of the public sphere (p. 158)," which she sees as one of the most dangerous threats to a democracy.

In a similar vein, Mike Rose (2005), in a commentary in *Education Week*, argues that we have developed a restricted vision of what schools ought to be about. Similarly, our discourse about schooling has been limited, and discussions of performance on standardized tests always take center stage. He points out how little we hear about achievement that includes curiosity, reflectiveness, respect, decency, aesthetics, civility, intellect, heart, and mind, let alone public education as the center of a free society.

This concern for the loss of the public purposes of schooling and the teachers that we need in public schools has been a long-standing one in the work of John Goodlad (1984; Goodlad & McMannon, 1997) and Benjamin Barber (1992). They are both deeply concerned about losing sight of an important and vital role that public schools have played in the history of American democracy. Goodlad resurrects the work of John Dewey on the importance of education in a democracy. Barber, in a similar vein, sees public schools as one of the last best hopes for democracy: "This makes formal schooling, however inadequate, our sole public resource: the only place where, as a collective, self-conscious public pursuing common goods, we try to shape our children to live in a democratic world. Can we afford to privatize the only public institutions we possess?" (p. 14).

In summary, let me recap what I have attempted to do here. First, I have mapped in a preliminary way the terrain of teacher quality, that is, where we have to look if we are to find it. Second, I have focused on the teacher–student interaction as a dynamic interactive relationship that is influenced by many variables on either side of the interaction. These variables have to be taken into account in the assessment and measurement of teacher quality. Third, while stressing the importance of achievement gains as an outcome of quality teaching, I have also pointed out a host of other possible outcomes, some of them quite important to successful teaching and learning. In particular, I have suggested teacher characteristics as well as learning outcomes that are very important to the success of urban youngsters in schools. Here I have challenged the prevailing narrow definition of teacher quality as academic achievement gains alone and suggested a measure of teacher quality that includes several other outcomes. Finally, I hope I have highlighted some new measurement challenges to getting at the phenomenon of teacher quality. Rather than moving toward reduction to a few isolated outcomes or proxy characteristics, I have suggested an even more complex terrain for teacher quality that may stress the measurement paradigms currently in play.

References

Barber, B. (1992). *An aristocracy of everyone—The politics of education and the future of America.* New York: Ballantine Books.

Cochran-Smith, M. (1995). Color blindness and basket making are not the answers: Confronting the dilemmas of race, culture, and language diversity in teacher education. *American Educational Research Journal, 32,* 493–522.

Fenstermacher, G., & Richardson, V. (2005). On making determinations of quality in teaching. *Teachers College Record, 107,* 186–213.

Freire, P. (1970). *Pedagogy of the oppressed.* New York: Seabury.

Goodlad, J. (1984). *A place called school.* New York: McGraw-Hill.

Goodlad, J., & McMannon, T. J. (Eds.). (1997). *The public purposes of education and schooling.* San Francisco: Jossey-Bass.

Green, T. F. (1971). *The activities of teaching.* New York: McGraw-Hill.

Haberman, M. (2005). *Selecting and preparing urban teachers.* Retrieved May 26, 2008, from http://www.altcert.org/research/research.asp?page=Research&article=preparing

Hanushek, E. A. (2002). Teacher quality. In L. T. Izumi & W. M. Evers (Eds.), *Teacher quality* (pp. 1–12). Stanford, CA: Hoover Institution Press.

Kozol, J. (1967). *Death at an early age: The destruction of the hearts and minds of Negro children in the Boston Public Schools.* Boston: Houghton Mifflin.

Ladson-Billings, G. (1995). Toward a theory of culturally relevant pedagogy. *American Educational Research Journal, 32,* 465–491.

Ladson-Billings, G. (2005). No teacher left behind: Issues of equity and teacher quality. In C. Dwyer (Ed.), *Measurement and research in the accountability era* (pp. 141–162). Mahwah, NJ: Lawrence Erlbaum.

Midgley, M. (2001). Practical utopianism. In S. J. Goodlad (Ed.), *The last best hope: A democracy reader* (pp. 258–269). San Francisco: Jossey-Bass.

Rose, M. (2005, September 7). In search of a fresh language of schooling. *Education Week,* pp. 42-43.

Sarason, S. B. (1996). *Revisiting "The culture of the school and the problem of change."* New York: Teachers College Press.

Shulman, L. (2007). Highlights from the Carnegie Centennial Conference—Improving quality and equity in education: Inspiring a new century of excellence in teaching and assessment. *ETS Policy Notes, 15*(1), 14.

Measuring Instruction for Teacher Learning

8

Mary Kay Stein and Lindsay Clare Matsumura

Learning Policy Center, University of Pittsburgh

In this chapter, we outline a framework for a new approach to teacher assessment, one that calls for the use of assessment for instructional improvement. This contrasts with the conventional purpose to which teacher assessment is typically applied: teacher accountability and evaluation. Instead, we discuss what assessment for teacher learning might look like and how it could be used in the context of schools and districts. Our argument for this new approach follows the outlines of an argument laid out by Lorrie Shepard (2000) in which she proposed that current methods for assessing students were based on outmoded theories of learning and then proposed how student assessments might change to be consistent with more contemporary views of learning, that is, those based in cognitive, constructivist, and sociocultural theories of learning. We follow a similar pathway but refer to assessment and learning theories as applied to teachers instead of students.

The assessment of instruction for the purpose of teacher improvement has been given short shrift in today's policy climate, a climate that is dominated by debates regarding what it means to be a "qualified" teacher (e.g., Smith, Desimone, & Ueno, 2005), standards for student proficiency (e.g., Kingsbury, Olson, Cronin, Hauser, & Houser, 2003; Linn 2003; Peterson & Hess, 2005), and best approaches to measuring teacher effects on student achievement (e.g., McCaffrey, Lockwood, Koretz, & Hamilton, 2003; Schmidt, Houang, & McKnight, 2005). Although we support the idea of professional accountability (we discuss this issue at the end of the chapter), we argue that the most important reason to measure teachers and their teaching is to improve instruction, not to meet a compliance standard or to weed out the lowest-performing teachers. As such, we shift our attention from the assessment of teachers to the assessment of instructional practice, viewing that practice as a process that can and should be continuously examined and improved. This perspective contrasts with a view of teachers as individuals who can be sorted into those who do versus those who do not "meet the standard."

The improvement of instruction not only is important, but also requires nontrivial changes in teacher preparation and professional support. A range of research indicates that teachers often lack the content knowledge and skills needed to achieve ambitious, standards-based goals for student learning (National Commission on Teaching and America's Future, 1996; Spillane & Zeuli, 1999) and that thoughtful instructional practice has yet to be realized in the majority of U.S. schools. Mathematics instruction remains procedural and disconnected from conceptual understanding (U.S. Department of Education, National Center for Education Statistics [USDE, NCES], 2003); science instruction suffers from an emphasis on breadth at the expense of depth (Berns & Swanson, 2000); reading instruction devotes too little time to comprehension instruction (Snow, 2002); and English language learners typically receive instruction that is passive, teacher directed, and oriented toward low-level skills (Garcia, 2004). Given the state of teaching in U.S. classrooms, it is not surprising that students in this country continue to post substandard performance on assessments in all subjects and at all levels (NCES, 2004; USDE, NCES, 2003).

Meeting and enacting high-level standards for instruction will require a transformation in most teachers' knowledge and practice, not minor adjustments (Ball & Cohen, 1999; Hargreaves, 1994; Thompson & Zeuli, 1999). Teachers must learn subject matter, but, more important, they must learn how to assess and assist students in the learning of that content. In most cases, this means learning to teach in ways that they did not experience as learners in the K–12 system (or, sometimes, even in their teacher education programs).

These new demands for teaching will require attendant changes in schools and districts. We cannot attain ambitious goals for student learning without concurrent changes in the structures and systems that support improved instruction and teacher learning. The present evaluation culture in many districts can be characterized as a series of implicit contracts between players at adjacent levels of the educational system.[1] Students trade good behavior for easy assignments and good grades from their teachers. Teachers trade professional appearance and well-managed classrooms for predictable annual evaluations from their principals. Principals trade a hands-off leadership style for harmonious working relationships with their faculty. And finally, the school as a whole trades lenient grading policies for parental tranquility. Unfortunately, this system of implicit contracts comes at the expense of learning. At each level (students, teachers, principals), individuals opt for familiarity over the anxiety that usually accompanies real learning. Districts and schools that want to engage in the assessment of instruction *for* teacher learning will need to reconstruct the school contract so as to counteract habits acquired under the old system. The challenge is to build enough trust to persuade individuals to let go of predictable behaviors and engage in legitimate discussions of learning performance.

We begin by situating our work historically amid shifting theories of learning and assessment. We then provide examples of what measures for teacher learning might look like and how present-day school and district contexts would need to change in order to make good use of such measures. We conclude with an agenda for policy discussions regarding the measurement of instructional quality in schools and districts.

Historical Perspectives on Teacher Learning, Instruction, and the Measurement of Instruction

Over the past century, there have been dramatic changes in conceptualizations of what it means to be both a learner and a teacher. Unfortunately, models of assessment have not kept pace with the theoretical advances and empirical work related to how we understand the processes of learning (Bransford, Brown, & Cocking, 1999) and the role of teaching as the assistance of learning (Richardson, 2003; Richardson & Roosevelt, 2004; Tharp & Gallimore, 1988). In short, although most theory and research has taken a decided turn toward more complex, constructivist, and social views of the teaching and learning process, our measurement systems continue to be rooted in behaviorist assumptions from the early 20th century (Hull, 1943; Skinner, 1938; Thorndike, 1922). Whereas Shepard (2000) described the mismatches between knowledge about student learning and the assessment of students, we focus on changing conceptions of teacher learning with the purpose of surfacing similar incongruities between new ideas and old approaches to measurement. Following Shepard, we focus on the periods of 1975–1990 and 1990–present.

1975–1990

As shown in Figure 8.1, the period from 1975 to 1990 was dominated by the belief that students learn by accumulating bits of information and that the teacher's role was to teach these bits of information—usually isolated facts, skills, rules, and procedures (Gagne, 1977). Driven by a mechanistic view of teaching and learning (see the top circle of Figure 8.1), teachers were viewed as transmitting information directly to students by

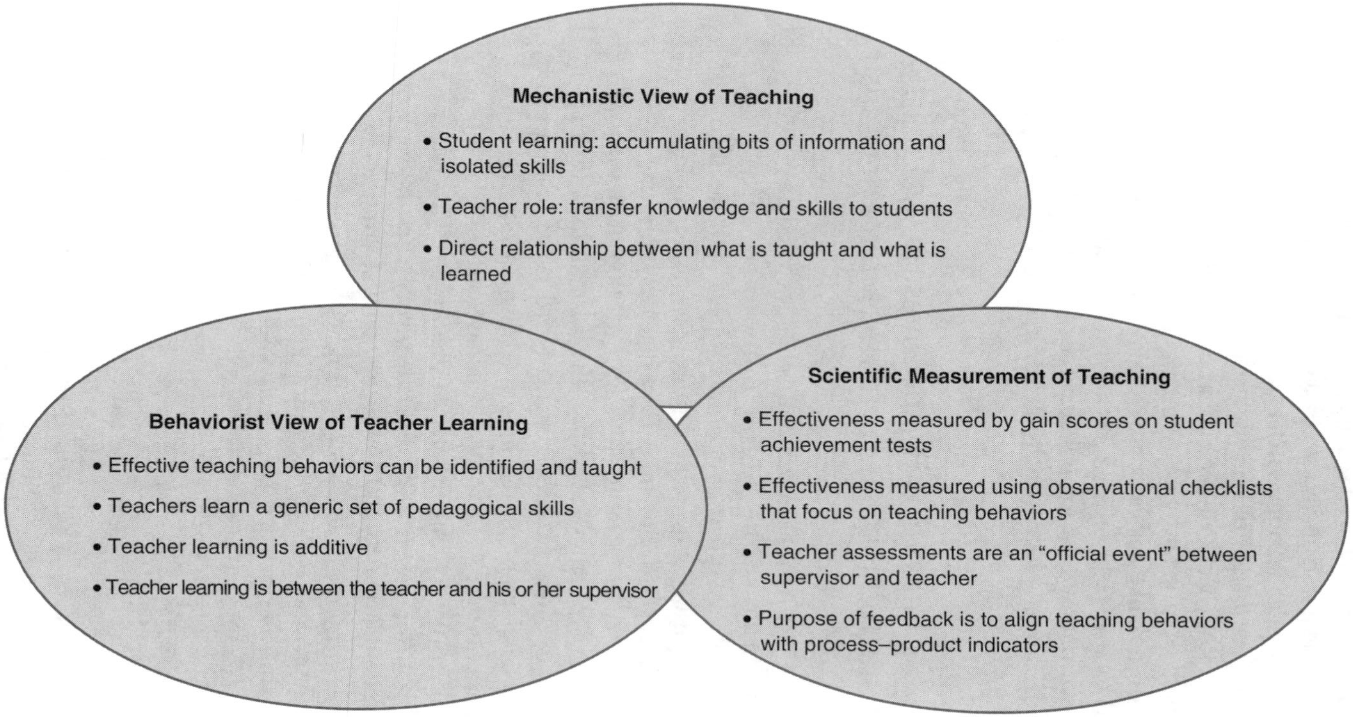

Mechanistic View of Teaching

- Student learning: accumulating bits of information and isolated skills
- Teacher role: transfer knowledge and skills to students
- Direct relationship between what is taught and what is learned

Scientific Measurement of Teaching

- Effectiveness measured by gain scores on student achievement tests
- Effectiveness measured using observational checklists that focus on teaching behaviors
- Teacher assessments are an "official event" between supervisor and teacher
- Purpose of feedback is to align teaching behaviors with process–product indicators

Behaviorist View of Teacher Learning

- Effective teaching behaviors can be identified and taught
- Teachers learn a generic set of pedagogical skills
- Teacher learning is additive
- Teacher learning is between the teacher and his or her supervisor

Figure 8.1   Aligned Relationship Between Views of Teaching, Teacher Learning, and Measurement of Teaching, 1975–1990

explaining concepts clearly, modeling appropriate applications of skills, assigning plenty of practice, and checking student performance on a regular basis (Rosenshine & Stevens, 1986).

Given this uncomplicated view of "teaching," it was not surprising that teachers were expected to learn how to teach in a very basic and straightforward way (see the left circle of Figure 8.1). Features of successful skills training included clear statements of objectives, adequate demonstration, well-designed materials, and opportunities for practice and feedback (Lanier & Little, 1986). Not surprising, teaching was viewed as a skill that could be learned relatively quickly and easily (Peck & Tucker, 1973). Teachers were expected to learn everything they needed to know in college or the first few years on the job. Because teacher learning was viewed as additive (as opposed to transformative), new techniques that were "discovered" later in their careers (e.g., the Madeline Hunter model) were seen as new tools that could be taught in a workshop and easily incorporated into teachers' existing repertoires. Finally, teacher learning was expected to occur between the teacher and his or her cooperating teacher and maybe university supervisor. Seldom, if ever, did teachers share their struggles—or their successes—with peers, and certainly not with their school's principal (Lortie, 1975).

During this time period, the measurement of teaching was viewed as an increasingly "scientific" enterprise with judgments of teacher quality primarily based on two sources of information: students' scores on standardized achievement tests and teachers' profiles on observation checklists (Shavelson, Webb, & Burstein, 1986; see the right circle of Figure 8.1). With goals for student learning that were simple and easy to measure, and the teacher's job defined as the direct transfer of information into students' minds, the view that teacher quality could be measured by student uptake of basic knowledge and skills (as measured in gain scores on standardized achievement tests) made perfect sense. After all, these tests were designed to measure student knowledge of discrete facts and skills in carrying out basic arithmetic procedures and reading processes, the same skills that formed the core of the curriculum. Thus, the curriculum and outcome measures were aligned. Equally important—but not often stated—was the direct and unambiguous relationship that was assumed to exist between what was taught and what was learned. At the time, most research paradigms used in the study of teaching assumed that the actions of teachers were directly related to student achievement. With the advent of the student mediation paradigm (Wittrock, 1986b), researchers began to uncover the many ways in which students interpret instructional information and construct their own understandings (which may or may not be congruent with what was taught). Thus, rather than instruction influencing students' performance on achievement tests, it became widely accepted that instruction influences students' thought processes; these, in turn, influence student performance (Shulman, 1986).

Also during this period, instructional practice was measured using observational checklists that focused on effective teaching behaviors—teaching practices that research had found to correlate with gains in student achievement.[2] With most of these behaviors believed (at least initially) to be universally effective across subject areas and grade levels, questions regarding when, how, and how often to use them were usually not raised. If teacher improvement was deemed to be necessary, it was assumed that such improvement could be achieved through a simple feedback model: If teachers did not explain a procedure clearly, they simply needed to be given feedback in that regard and they would be clearer the next time (Joyce & Showers, 1981). Finally, teacher observations typically occurred infrequently, and when they did occur, they were usually an "official and private event" for the purpose of certifying whether teachers were performing at an acceptable level or were competent to move on to a tenured status (Lortie, 1975).

1990–PRESENT

Turning our attention to the present day, views of teaching and learning have evolved considerably. Building on new theories of teaching and learning that highlighted the constructivist and social/contextual dimensions of learning (Brown, Collins, & Duguid, 1989; Greeno, Collins, & Resnick, 1996; Lave & Wenger, 1991; Rogoff, 1991; Tharp & Gallimore, 1988), teaching was no longer conceptualized as the transmission of facts to students, but rather as facilitating students' learning through engaging them in challenging tasks, asking good questions, orchestrating classroom discussions, and tailoring instruction to individuals' needs (see the top circle in Figure 8.2). Teaching was no longer viewed as directly causing student learning, rather students were viewed as mediating the information and experiences provided in the classrooms (Wittrock, 1986b). The teacher's role was to structure and set up tasks that would encourage students to grapple with important ideas, to listen closely to how students were making sense of those ideas, and to assist their learning in an informed and tailored manner (Tharp & Gallimore, 1988).

Not surprising, teacher educators began to take a second look at the processes of teacher learning at this same time (see the left circle of Figure 8.2). Lists of effective teaching behaviors were replaced with the understanding that teaching was a complex undertaking that was interdependent with what students brought to the table and with the subject matter being taught (Borko & Putnam, 1995). Increasingly, teacher educators saw the need to place prospective teachers into authentic teaching situations in which they engaged with artifacts from practice—sometimes referred to as *practice-based professional development* (Ball & Cohen, 1999). Teacher learning, it was argued, needed to prepare teachers for making online decisions regarding how to lead a class discussion or assist a particular student with a misconception. The role of subject matter knowledge and knowledge for teaching in specific disciplines (Shulman, 1986) became prominent. Finally, based on research showing that the best-performing schools encouraged and provided expert guidance for interactions among teachers (McLaughlin & Talbert, 2006), the contexts in which practicing teachers were expected to learn were revised from workshops to teachers working in school-based communities.

Yet despite these advances in conceptions of learning and instruction, we continue to measure teaching in many of the same ways (see the right circle in Figure 8.2). Judgments of teacher quality still rely on student performance on achievement tests, with a recent turn toward the use of growth models. Although increasingly elegant from a technical point of view, these models continue to be performed on standardized achievement tests that, by and large, focus on the attainment of basic skills and not the higher-level skills called for in standards documents.

Similarly, observation checklists of the so-called effective teacher behaviors from the process–product studies continue to be used in many schools across the country (Danielson & McGreal, 2000). These checklists are problematic because they were designed based on research that used student performance on tests of basic skills as the dependent variable and because they focused on isolated teaching behaviors, not teachers' thinking about, and support of, the interaction of students' current understandings and subject matter goals. Finally, teacher observations remain official events in most schools, performed by principals on teachers primarily for the purpose of evaluation. Despite the fact that these official events often constitute the only time a supervisor observes a teacher, teachers and evaluators pretend that the evaluation is supposed to be in some way helpful. However, teachers are unlikely to be honest about difficulties they are experiencing for fear that the problems will be described as deficiencies. And they may not trust that the evaluator has the subject matter and pedagogical expertise to truly help them.

By continuing to measure teaching in these ways—especially in the context of externally imposed, high-stakes accountability systems—public education will be hindered from realizing the new visions of student learning, teaching, and learning-to-teach that most scholars recognize as important to strive toward. At the student level, the negative effects of high-stakes, low-level tests on opportunities to learn important and worthwhile content have become increasingly clear (Anagnostopoulos, 2003; Koretz & Hamilton, 2006). Although students may be certified as "proficient" on state standardized tests, their impoverished learning becomes evident when they perform poorly on more rigorous assessments (Kingsbury et al., 2003; Linn, 2003; Peterson & Hess, 2005) or when college work is found to be inordinately challenging (California Postsecondary Education Commission, 2007). High-stakes, low-level, checklist-like teacher tests are apt to lead to the same kinds of distortions in teachers' opportunities to learn. Scores on measures of teaching practice may

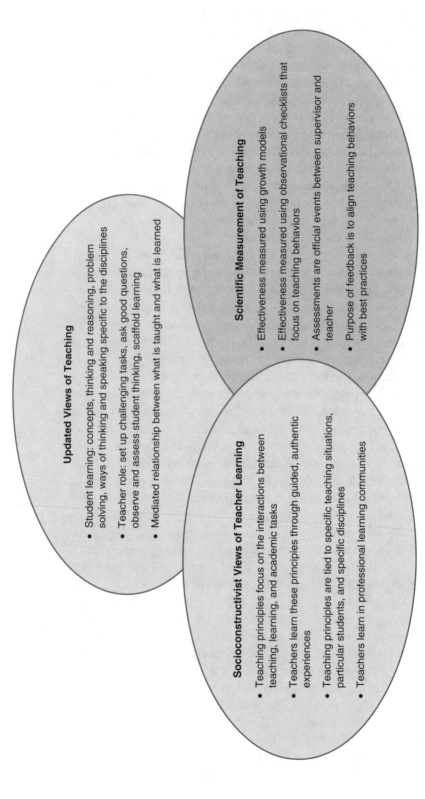

Figure 8.2 Misaligned Relationship Between Views of Teaching, Teacher Learning, and the Measurement of Teaching circa 1990–Present

improve over time, but without a corresponding improvement in the quality of teaching. To foster true improvements in teaching practice, we need more complex measures of teaching practice, measures that reflect our new visions of teaching and learning.

Measures of Instruction for Teacher Learning

So what would these new measures of instruction—measures for teacher learning—look like? Figure 8.3 provides a list of features that we propose would characterize such measures, features that would reintroduce harmony into the fractured system shown in Figure 8.2. First, we propose, as have others, that student growth models be viewed as one, but only one, indicator of instructional quality. Measures of student performance on most of today's state assessments may illuminate a topic that was skipped (or not taught soon enough in the year), but they do not illuminate the *how* of teaching, that is, how teachers present content and help students learn that content. Standardized achievement measures must be supplemented by more complex measures of teaching practice itself, measures that reflect the field's understanding of the teaching practices that support higher levels of student thinking, reasoning, and understanding. Moreover, we argue that the measurement of teaching needs to become less of a private, official event, and more informal, ongoing, and embedded in the day-to-day work of teaching.

Finally, the primary purpose of measuring and discussing instructional practice should be to nudge it toward more thoughtful and challenging forms of practice, not to hold teachers accountable to an externally defined set of effective teaching behaviors. In this view, teachers do not learn from a simple feedback model, but rather benefit from discussions with experts about their practice, how students have responded to it (Were they engaged? What did they learn?), and how it might become more supportive of student learning. Just as students do not learn complex knowledge and skills by having facts poured into their heads followed by simple feedback such as the number correct on a test, teachers do not learn by direct "telling" followed by simple feedback. Contemporary research on the learning of complex knowledge and skills demonstrates that such learning occurs in the interactions between individuals as they work together toward shared goals to create new forms of understanding and meaning (Cole, 1996; Lave & Wenger, 1991; Rogoff, 1991).

Measuring Teacher Practice

How one measures instruction communicates what is valued and thus is a powerful tool in any improvement context. Here we drill more deeply into

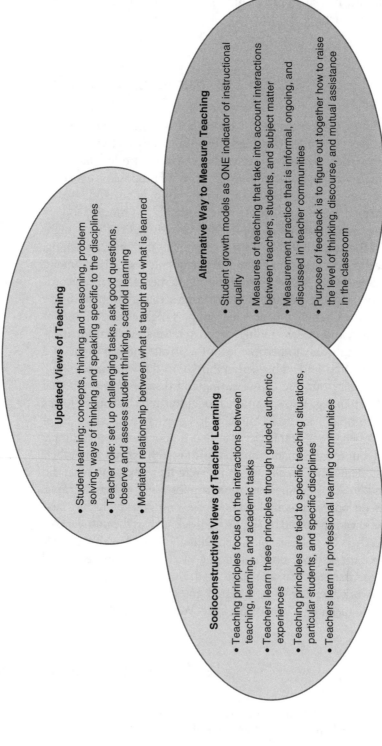

Updated Views of Teaching

• Student learning: concepts, thinking and reasoning, problem solving, ways of thinking and speaking specific to the disciplines
• Teacher role: set up challenging tasks, ask good questions, observe and assess student thinking, scaffold learning
• Mediated relationship between what is taught and what is learned

Socioconstructivist Views of Teacher Learning

• Teaching principles focus on the interactions between teaching, learning, and academic tasks
• Teachers learn these principles through guided, authentic experiences
• Teaching principles are tied to specific teaching situations, particular students, and specific disciplines
• Teachers learn in professional learning communities

Alternative Way to Measure Teaching

• Student growth models as ONE indicator of instructional quality
• Measures of teaching that take into account interactions between teachers, students, and subject matter
• Measurement practice that is informal, ongoing, and discussed in teacher communities
• Purpose of feedback is to figure out together how to raise the level of thinking, discourse, and mutual assistance in the classroom

Figure 8.3   Suggested Realignment of Relationship Between Views of Teaching, Teacher Learning, and the Measurement of Teaching

what it would mean to measure practice in ways that align with what we know about the processes of teaching and learning.

Measures of instruction that are intended to build teachers' capacity should, first and foremost, be rooted in the technical core of instruction—the interaction between teachers, students, and content (e.g., curricula, tasks, texts). Rather than treating teaching behaviors as isolated entities, assessments must focus on the interaction among students, what they are being asked to learn (i.e., the subject matter goal of the lessons), and how instruction does or does not support their learning.

Measures should also be direct and grounded in the real work of teaching (not something that is made up for the purpose of assessment). By direct, we mean that measures for the support of teacher learning should assess the very thing that is of concern. If teacher improvement is needed in terms of how to run a discussion, then how a teacher runs a discussion in her classroom is what should be measured—not a proxy such as a log sheet of the amount of time spent on classroom discussions or students' reports about the number of times such discussions are held.

Additionally, we envision measures of teaching that would embody a coherent, research-based vision of how instructional practice influences student learning. In particular, they should present a vision of exemplary practice that is linked to improved student learning (both theoretically and empirically) and, in so doing, provide a basis for developing an awareness of features of thoughtful practice (see, e.g., Matsumura, 2005). Specifically, we argue that these measures should focus on teaching behaviors that foster students' capacity to think and reason at high levels. Teaching for high levels of understanding, thinking, and reasoning is challenging for teachers (Stein, Grover, & Henningsen, 1996); moreover, these kinds of teaching skills are the ones about which teachers are most likely to disagree (e.g., what it means in practice to apply critical thinking skills, what it means to hold a discussion; Hill, 2006). In this regard, assessments could also help build the professional culture of a school by creating shared understanding of what it means to do intellectually challenging work.

Finally, we argue that to be educative, we need to think about measures of instruction that provide information about the next step that teachers must take to continue to improve and develop.[3] Ideally, measures would be based on articulation of a developmental trajectory of teacher learning. At the present time, such a trajectory has not been worked out empirically, so we can only begin to think about ways in which measures could point the way toward what a teacher would have to do to get to the next level. In the meantime, at the very least, measures that are sensitive to how things can go wrong in practice (e.g., the many ways that the cognitive demands of a mathematical task can be degraded in its implementation) may be helpful. Just as teachers benefit from knowing the variety of ways in which students might arrive at a wrong answer, it would be important for assessors of teachers to be able to spot typical missteps that teachers make.

Measuring Instruction for Teacher Learning

This section provides two examples of measures that are based in every-day practice and have at least some of the characteristics of assessment for teacher learning as described previously. The first example is from a research project that specifically developed and validated a set of measures for assessing the quality of reading comprehension based on the collection of teachers' assignments accompanied by student work—the Instructional Quality Assessment (IQA).[4] The second example comes from observational research conducted as part of the QUASAR project (Silver & Stein, 1996); although the development of measures of instruction was not a goal or specific product of that project, many of the principles that under-girded the observational research have implications for the measurement of teaching practice for teacher learning.

EXAMPLE 1: TEACHER ASSIGNMENTS WITH STUDENT WORK

The tasks teachers assign to students and the criteria teachers' use to grade students' work provide a window on the quality of students' oppor-tunities to think, reason, and support their assertions; teachers' interpre-tation of standards (e.g., what it means to analyze a character, what it means to evaluate a text); and what a teacher values in students' work. As such, we argue that these tasks and criteria capture the interaction among teacher, students, and content—the technical core of instruction.

Research indicates that students achieve at higher levels when they are in classrooms with teachers who provide them with higher-quality (i.e., more intellectually demanding and authentic) assignment tasks (Matsumura, Garnier, Pascal, & Valdés, 2002; Matsumura et al., 2006; Newmann, Bryk, & Nagaoka, 2001). The quality of the criteria teachers use to assess student work also has been associated with improved student learning (Black & Wiliam, 1998). Moreover, and more to the point of this chapter, research indicates that reflection on artifacts of this type can improve instruction (Arbaugh & Brown, 2005; Ball & Cohen, 1999).

Finally, though reliability is not the focus of this chapter, assignments can be reliably scored by multiple raters (Aschbacher, 1999; Clare, 2000; Matsumura et al., 2002, 2006; Newmann, Lopez, & Bryk, 1998). When enough assignments of a specific type are collected, they can yield a gen-eralizable estimate of the quality of the tasks that individual teachers assign to students (Matsumura et al., 2002, 2006).

The IQA rubrics for looking at responses to literature assignments draw on research focused on effective reading comprehension instruction (summarized in Snow, 2002) and the intellectual demands of writing assignments and their relation to student learning (Clare & Aschbacher,

2001; Newmann et al., 2001; Matsumura et al., 2002). Specifically, the rubrics consider the intellectual demands embedded in assignment tasks and the ways in which a task supports (or does not support) students to deeply understand and engage with a text. The features that support high-level engagement with a task include the quality of the text, the intellectual demands of the task, students' opportunity to write extended responses and use appropriate information from a text to support their assertions, and the expectations teachers have and communicate to students for the quality of their work (i.e., the criteria teachers use to grade student work). These dimensions of task quality are described in more detail in the following sections.

Grist Exhibited in a Text

Engagement with high-quality texts is a prerequisite to developing activities and holding discussions that support students to apply higher-level thinking skills in order to deeply understand a text. That is, a text may be so brief, straightforward, and predictable that it offers students nothing about which to make inferences or construct meaning beyond what is written on the page. The IQA ratings thus include a focus on the degree to which the texts read by students contain sufficient *grist* to support analysis and interpretation (Beck, McKeown, Hamilton, & Kucan, 1997). Grist can be exhibited in a number of ways, including a complex, nonpredictable plotline or characters and dilemmas where there is no obvious right or wrong answer (see, e.g., Clare, Patthey-Chavez, & Gallimore, 1996). Grist also could be evidenced in the writer's craft, such as in the language use, vocabulary, and organizational structures employed by an author. Additionally, texts that build students' academic content knowledge and support students to make connections across subject areas (Knapp, Shields, & Turnbull, 1995) could be considered to contain grist for analysis and interpretation.

Intellectual Demands of a Task

Examples of assignments that exhibit a high level of intellectual demand include those that support students to critically evaluate a text, to link ideas within and across texts, to consider the perspective of an author in the writing of a text, to apply a specific lens in the reading of a text (e.g., looking at issues of gender or race), or to reflect on how the meaning of a text is carried through the author's craft. Assignments that require students only to make very surface-level inference or identify specific content verbatim, in contrast, would be considered to exhibit a low level of intellectual demand. The opportunities students have to write extended responses and the guidance students receive to use accurate and appropriate evidence from a text to support their responses also are integral parts of the intellectual demand of a task. These features often distinguish between assignments that support deep engagement with a text and assignments that support basic, surface-level understandings (often through shallow applications of higher-level thinking skills). For example, a task that requires students to analyze a character by completing a short, fill-in-the blank worksheet describing who the characters were, what they did, how they felt, and how they changed would not be considered to exhibit a high level of intellectual demand (at least at the middle and high school levels).

Expectations for the Quality of Student Work

The criteria teachers use to grade students' work is another integral component of the intellectual demand of an assignment task. Research indicates that a teacher's perception of the types of learning opportunities that are possible with a given group of students sets parameters around the level of products and processes for which students are held accountable (Black & Wiliam, 1998). Students are unlikely to spontaneously go beyond what is required by a task or a teacher, but they will adjust their work strategies to correspond to their perceptions of the task's or teacher's requirements (Doyle, 1983). For these reasons, the quality of the expectations teachers communicate to students is an important component of effective practice. The IQA ratings thus focus on the amount and quality of the information (i.e., the clarity and specificity of this information) that teachers provide to students with regard to what good student work should look like, the degree to which a teacher's criteria for good work includes a focus on students developing high-level academic skills, and the way in which teachers communicate this information to students.

The assignments described here are from a pilot study of the IQA in five urban middle schools. These schools are located in a small district in the northeastern United States that serves a very high population of minority English language learners from low-income families. English language arts teachers ($N = 34$) provided four response-to-literature assignments. For each assignment, the teachers completed a two-page cover sheet describing the task and the criteria they used to grade students' work, and submitted four samples of student work (two they considered to be of high quality and two of medium quality).

Results from this study of the IQA indicated that, on the whole, teachers were using high-quality texts (e.g., *Julie of the Wolves*, by Jean Craighead George, 1972; *Maniac Magee*, by Jerry Spinelli, 1990). In fact, 72% of the assignments received the highest rating for this dimension. Students' opportunity to analyze and interpret these texts was much more limited, however. Averaging across all of the schools, the quality of the intellectual demand of the assignment tasks given to students received a score of 1.8 ($SD = .91$; 1 = *poor*, 4 = *excellent*). Although there were a few exceptions, on the whole students were either required to recall isolated facts about a text (e.g., fill-in-the-blank worksheets), write on a topic that did not directly reference information from a text (e.g., after reading the chapter in *Maniac Magee* that describes a baseball game, students were asked to write about a time that they played baseball), or write very short summaries of a text with little or no details from the story.

The rigor of the assessment criteria teachers used to grade students' work also was rated low on average, with a score of 1.9 ($SD = 1.3$; 1 = *poor*, 4 = *excellent*), because these criteria tended to focus on writing mechanics rather than the content of students' ideas related to the text they were reading or their use of appropriate details and evidence to back up their assertions. In many cases, the rubrics used by teachers to grade students' work resembled generic writing rubrics and were not tailored to the response-to-literature task. Moreover, almost no models of high-quality work were given to students to help guide their writing. As exemplified by these findings, knowing only the books (or the curriculum) used in classrooms tells little about the quality of the opportunities that students actually have to learn. Rather, students' opportunities to learn are determined by how the teacher engages students with the book.

We turn now to an example of a response-to-literature assignment typical of those given to many sixth-grade students. The directions given to students and the rubric the teacher used to grade students' work are shown in Figure 8.4.

Assignment: Evaluate *Julie of the Wolves.* You are a writer for the [school's newspaper]. You are to write an article that tells your readers that you either hate this book or like it. Give reasons. Use information from the book to help you convince the readers.

Criteria:

Possible points	
15	Neatness of work
10	Grammar used
10	Spelling
5	Name and date on paper
20	One idea per paragraph
5	Use of periods in the proper places
10	Use of capitals in the proper places
10	Complete sentences
15	Stick to topic

Figure 8.4 Example of a Response-to-Literature Assignment and Grading Criteria

An example of student work judged by the teacher to be of high quality is shown in Figure 8.5.

Looking at the assignment task, the assessment criteria, and the student work, it is possible to imagine that reflecting on these artifacts could be a useful professional development experience. For example, the text received the highest rating because it is a deep and complex story about identity formation, survival, and an evolving relationship between the main character and her father. Some questions that might surface in a collaborative professional development session are: What makes a text high quality? What parts of this story do students have a difficult time comprehending or relating to? What other texts does it relate to?

However, the assignment task received a basic score (2 on a 4-point scale). The assignment contained some of the language found in many state

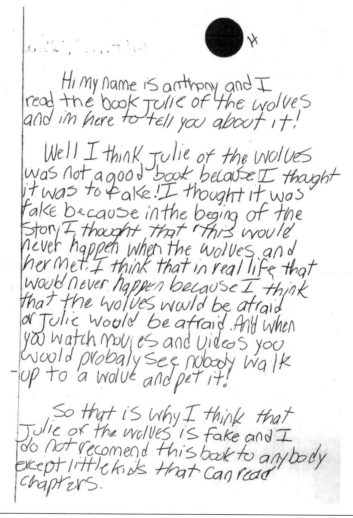

Figure 8.5 Sample of 6th-Grade Student Work Judged by the Teacher to Be of High Quality

and district standards (e.g., *give reasons, use information to convince a reader*), but it did not support students to engage with the rich thematic content of the book or even to reflect on the elements of what makes a book "good" (e.g., engaging characters, a story line that keeps you guessing, interesting or beautiful use of language). Instead, students—even those whose work was judged by the teacher to be of high quality—engaged with only the most surface-level features of the story (and were inaccurate at that). Some questions that might come up in a professional development session are: What would a more rigorous evaluation of a text look like? Why is it not sufficient to simply ask students to give a few reasons for why they liked or hated a particular book? How could the assignment be redrafted so that students have an opportunity to analyze and interpret the text and use appropriate (and accurate) information from the text to support their assertions? What should good student work look like for an evaluation of a text, specifically an evaluation of *Julie of the Wolves*, a text that is part of the district's middle school English language arts curriculum?

The criteria used to assess students' work also received a low score (1). These criteria (used by other teachers in the school as well) focused almost solely on the mechanics of students' writing and provided almost no information to students that could help them be successful at the task (i.e., to write a good book evaluation). Some questions that might surface in a professional development session are: How can we construct rubrics or grading criteria that get at the content of student work, not simply the mechanics? How can we effectively share these criteria with students (e.g., guided joint construction, posted on the wall, discussed in class, models of student work)?

In summary, the kinds of measures that we are advocating for, illustrated in this example as measures of the quality of text, the quality of assignment, and the criteria for judging student work, are measures collected from practice so that they reflect the complexity of practice. Instead of assuming that the quality of a book (or a curriculum) determines the quality of instructional practice, these measures are applied to the practice that surrounds the book. As such, a by-product of these kinds of assessments is that they can produce quantifiable information about the quality of students' opportunities to develop their analytical and academic writing skills. Moreover, assignment tasks can be used as a springboard for discussing and learning about discipline-specific goals for student thinking and teaching, and can be used to create shared understandings about what counts as rigorous, high-quality instruction.

EXAMPLE 2: OBSERVATIONS OF MATHEMATICS LESSONS

Our second example consists of lesson observations as a measure of instruction for teacher learning. Observations are challenging for many reasons, not the least of which is figuring out what instructional behaviors to focus on. In the QUASAR research, Stein and her colleagues argued that the instructional tasks with which teachers and students engage should be the primary focus because tasks form the critical link between what gets taught and what is learned (Doyle, 1988). It is not whether students work in groups or use manipulatives that matters, rather it is the nature of the tasks to which they are exposed, and the maintenance of a high level of cognitive demand, that determine what students learn (Stein & Lane, 1996).

Mathematical instructional tasks can be classified according to the level of cognitive demand that they place on student thinking. High-level tasks foster active inquiry or encourage students to use procedures (broadly defined) in ways that are meaningfully connected to concepts or understanding. Lower-level tasks, on the other hand, encourage students to use procedures in more mechanical ways or consist primarily of memorization or the reproduction of previously memorized facts. More than two decades ago, Doyle (1983, 1988) noted that the nature of tasks changes as they move from the pages of the textbook to enactment in the classroom. Since then, a variety of studies in mathematics have shown that maintaining the cognitive challenge of high-level tasks throughout a lesson is difficult—much more difficult than the initial selection and setting up of high-level tasks (Stein et al., 1996). Results from the TIMSS 1999 Video Study, for example, indicated that less than 1% of the lessons in U.S. classrooms in which the instructional tasks could provide opportunities for students to make meaningful mathematical connections (i.e., tasks with high-level cognitive demands) resulted in students actually making those connections during the lesson (Hiebert et al., 2003). Similarly, only 15 percent of the lessons analyzed by Horizon Research effectively supported students' opportunities for learning mathematics (Weiss & Pasley, 2004).

Tasks not only decline often, they decline in predictable ways. For example, tasks that begin as very open ended, without a predetermined pathway toward a solution, often result in students engaging in unsystematic and nonproductive exploratory activities. Tasks that are more structured with a strong conceptual focus often decline into students using procedures in ways that disconnect them from the conceptual understanding that the task was initially meant to foster. Altogether, Stein, Smith, Henningsen, and Silver (2000) found six different empirical patterns of the cognitive demands of tasks at the set-up and enactment phases, two of which involve the maintenance of high-level demands and four of which involve a decline. This work is helpful for not only providing a vision of what exemplary instructional practice looks like, but also identifying specific ways in which instruction often fails to live up to the potential of the tasks with which teachers and students engage.

Observation of mathematics lessons through the lens of the maintenance and decline of cognitive demand has proven to be a useful and reliable way to code lessons for the purposes of research (NCES, 2004;

Stein et al., 1996). However, this way of viewing instruction has also served as a foundation for the development of measures of teaching practice (Boston & Wolf, 2006; Matsumura et al., 2006) and for the design of professional development with empirically proven improvements in teaching practice (Boston & Smith, in press). What features of this way of viewing and measuring instruction account for its robustness? First, it focuses on the technical core of instruction: the interaction among teacher, students, and content. The final and most crucial phase of the framework draws attention to the manner in which the task is enacted in the classroom, that is, how students engage with the task (not just the quality of the task itself). Second, its documentation of patterns of decline identifies how teachers can get it wrong as well as how they can get it right, enabling observers and teachers to diagnose problems quickly. Finally, it is based on a coherent, research-based model of how high-level instruction unfolds in classrooms, which provides a vision of the elements of instruction that matter most (i.e., how students engage with mathematical ideas). Thus, this way of viewing and measuring instruction can provide a basis from which teachers' can develop an awareness of the characteristics of instruction that support student learning of higher-level thinking, reasoning, and problem solving.

What Would a Learning Culture in Which These Measures Are Embedded Look Like?

Upgrading our measures of instruction is necessary, but it is not sufficient for meeting our goal of measuring instruction to improve teacher learning. The culture of teaching and teacher assessment in most schools and districts can be described as *assigning and assessing*, where assessment usually means making sure that the person below you in the chain of command is performing at minimally acceptable levels (Tharp & Gallimore, 1988). Moreover, in many districts there is a climate of distrust among management (superintendents, principals) and teachers. Teachers feel that the classroom should be private and their practices should not be questioned. The conditions under which teacher evaluations are to be done are spelled out in detail in most union contracts. In this climate, supervisors are tempted to hide behind their evaluations; the more objective, official, and uniform they are perceived to be, the better. In this way, evaluations often become a ritual that everyone has to get through (Danielson & McGreal, 2000). If one drops a new assessment into a traditional school or district culture, it is likely to elicit the same (often nonproductive) reactions as current teacher assessments do.

TOWARD A DISTRICTWIDE
PROFESSIONAL LEARNING SYSTEM

So what can be said about the kind of transformations that are needed in our schools and districts? First, the culture of most schools, as described in the previous section, needs to be renegotiated in more collaborative terms. When supervisors serve solely as critics, teachers are apt to hide the issues that they are struggling with and put on a competent performance. Instead, in recognition of the complexity of teaching and learning, supervisors can become coinvestigators of the improvement process, thereby putting a lot of responsibility on managers to assist teachers in improving their practice.

Nevertheless, leaders would still need to make decisions regarding a teacher's suitability for continuing in the profession. Indeed, one of the greatest strengths of administrators acting as instructional leaders is the accountability they bring to the improvement process by virtue of their position as evaluators. In our judgment, new assessments and professional development are not sufficient to change instruction, especially across an entire system. Teachers must believe that serious engagement in their own learning is part and parcel of what it means to be a professional, and they must expect to be held accountable for continuously improving their practice. Similarly, principals must not only be capable of assisting teachers, but also have the knowledge, skills, and strength of character to hold teachers accountable for integrating what they have learned in professional development into their ongoing practice. District leaders, in turn, must be able to support principals' learning and be knowledgeable enough to be able to hold principals accountable in a fair way. Given their role as both supporters and evaluators, administrators constitute a critical leverage point in the improvement of instruction (Stein & Nelson, 2003).

Taking on the dual roles of assistance provider and evaluator can only happen if leaders spend the majority of their time in classrooms. It is only in this context that assistance and assessment become intertwined—where official evaluations can become an informal, ongoing part of a teacher's professional life and supervisors can become coinvestigators in (and coaccountable for) the improvement process.

An Agenda for Policy Discussions:
How to Measure Teacher Quality

We end with three points for ongoing dialogues between researchers and policymakers around the issue of measuring teacher quality. First, given its prominence in teacher quality discussions today, it is important to articulate why student scores on achievement tests alone cannot shoulder the burden of the improvement agenda. Achievement scores are indicators; as such, they provide little insight into the mechanics of how to improve instruction. Moreover, standardized achievement tests are not designed to test the range of content and skills that students need to learn over the course of an academic year (Hamilton, 2003), but rather focus on narrow slices of learning and content. Basing assessments of teacher quality on these tests means that we are judging teachers on how well they address that narrow content—not the full range of knowledge and skills students need to know and teachers need to teach. Standardized achievement tests also tend to focus on lower-level skills. Again, this encourages teachers to teach only those (lower-level) skills that are tested. In short, basing teacher quality on students' standardized test scores equally rewards those teachers whose instruction resembles "test prep" only and those teachers who are excellent. What is needed are assessments of teacher quality that reward teachers for teaching higher-level skills at least as much as—if not more than—basic skills and that reward teachers for teaching the range and content of the curriculum students need to know.

Second, in this vein, we have to articulate better what we know about how instruction influences students' opportunities to learn and why this is what needs to be mined for creating measures. It is a fallacy that we do not know enough about good instruction to create measures intended to improve teacher learning and instruction. Thirty years of research have been devoted to this issue (e.g., Richardson, 2001; Wittrock, 1986a). Although not all of this research has been good, enough solid evidence of good instructional practice exists to begin constructing measures of quality teaching that could be used in the context of schools and districts.

Finally, if we are serious about the improvement of teaching, we must simultaneously address the culture of professional work and accountability in both schools and districts. Administrators must reconstruct their role to be coaccountable in the instructional improvement process. This means that teachers are held accountable for teaching well and principals also take responsibility for creating the conditions that allow teachers to teach well. In other words, principals should be held accountable for providing high-quality, appropriate professional development for teachers; for creating time in the work day for teachers to meet and plan instruction together and/or with instructional specialists; and for assigning teachers to the grades and the subject areas for which they are specialized to teach (see Ladson-Billings, this volume).

Continuing up the chain, district leaders also should be held accountable for creating the conditions in schools that allow principals and other instructional specialists to serve as instructional leaders and for providing schools with the resources necessary to engage in this process. Likewise, district leaders should be held accountable for providing principals with appropriate, high-quality professional development and support, and time in their day to actually spend in teachers' classrooms, among other things. This means a reduction in the administrative demands made of supervisors. And it may mean holding states and the federal government responsible for providing districts with the necessary funds and resources (not to mention higher-quality tests of student learning and standards).

To close, we echo Shepard (2000) in her concern that dominant theories of the past continue to operate as the "default framework" (p. 4) for how we identify and develop measures of educational processes and outcomes, in this case, measures of instructional practice. Until these outdated ways of measuring instruction are discarded, they will drive current practices toward more mechanistic and less intellectually demanding forms of practice. Moreover, the power of these measurement systems is reinforced by the perspectives of teachers, parents, and policymakers that also derive from these old theories. A break from the past must include a continuing dialogue with these and other constituencies regarding what is important for students to learn and how instruction can influence that learning. New, more complex and thoughtful measures of teaching practice can be a major player in this dialogue and transformation, but only if accompanied by attendant changes in the culture of schools and districts.

Notes

1. This characterization of education cultures as a series of implicit contracts builds on and extends the work of Perrenoud (1991), as cited in Shepard (2000).

2. These so-called effective teaching behaviors were supported by findings from the then-dominant paradigm of research on teaching (known as the *process–product paradigm*) which correlated student achievement gains with particular instructional actions (Brophy & Good, 1986).

3. Shepard (2000) makes this same point about assessments that would foster student learning.

4. This project is a joint collaboration between researchers at the University of Pittsburgh's LRDC and Carnegie Mellon University (e.g., Junker et al., 2005; Matsumura et al., 2006). The specific examples described here are from a pilot study of the IQA in five urban middle schools.

References

Anagnostopoulos, D. (2003). Testing and student engagement with literature in urban classrooms: A multi-layered perspective. *Research in the Teaching of English, 38*(2), 177–212.

Arbaugh, F., & Brown, C. (2005). Analyzing mathematical tasks: A catalyst for change? *Journal of Mathematics Teacher Education, 8,* 499–536.

Aschbacher, P. R. (1999). *Developing indicators of classroom practice to monitor and support school reform* (CSE Technical Report No. 513). Los Angeles: University of California, Graduate School of Education and Information Studies, National Center for Research on Evaluation, Standards, and Student Testing, Center for the Study of Evaluation.

Ball, D. L., & Cohen, D. K. (1999). Developing practice, developing practitioners: Toward a practice-based theory of professional education. In G. Sykes & L. Darling-Hammond (Eds.), *Teaching as the learning profession: Handbook of policy and practice* (pp. 3–32). San Francisco: Jossey-Bass.

Beck, I. L., McKeown, M. G., Hamilton, R. L., & Kucan, L. (1997). *Questioning the author: An approach for enhancing student engagement with text.* Newark, DE: International Reading Association.

Berns, B. B., & Swanson, J. (2000, April). *Middle school science: Working in a confused context.* Paper presented at the annual meeting of the American Educational Research Association, New Orleans, LA. (ERIC Document Reproduction Service No. ED444944)

Black, P., & Wiliam, D. (1998). Inside the black box. Raising standards through classroom assessment. *Phi Delta Kappan, 80,* 139–148.

Borko, H., & Putnam, R. T. (1995). Expanding a teacher's knowledge base: A cognitive psychological perspective on professional development. In T. R. Guskey & M. Huberman (Eds.), *Professional development in education: New paradigms and practices* (pp. 35–65). New York: Teachers College Press.

Boston, M. D., & Smith, M. S. (in press). Transforming secondary mathematics teaching: Increasing the cognitive demands of instructional tasks used in teachers' classrooms. *Journal for Research in Mathematics Education.*

Boston, M., & Wolf, M. K. (2006). *Assessing academic rigor in mathematics instruction: The development of the Instructional Quality Assessment toolkit* (CSE Technical Report No. 672). Los Angeles: National Center for Research on Evaluation, Standards, and Student Testing.

Bransford, J. D., Brown, A. L., & Cocking, R. R. (1999). *How people learn: Brain, mind, experience, and school.* Washington, DC: National Academies Press.

Brophy, J., & Good, T. (1986). Teacher behavior and student achievement. In M. C. Wittrock (Ed.), *Handbook of research on teaching* (pp. 328–375). New York: Macmillan.

Brown, J. S., Collins, A., & Duguid, P. (1989). Situated cognition and the culture of learning. *Educational Researcher, 18*(1), 32–42.

California Postsecondary Education Commission. (2007). *California higher education accountability: Goal—student success, Measure: California community college students' degrees and certificates awarded and successful transfers.* Retrieved December 14, 2007, from http://www.cpec.ca.gov/completere ports/2007reports/07-06.pdf

Clare, L. (2000). *Using teachers' assignments as an indicator of classroom practice* (CSE Technical Report No. 532). Los Angeles: University of California, National Center for Research on Evaluation, Standards, and Student Testing.

Clare, L., & Aschbacher, P. (2001). Exploring the technical quality of using assignments and student work as indicators of classroom practice. *Educational Assessment, 7,* 39–59.

Clare, L., Patthey-Chavez, G. G., & Gallimore, R. (1996). Using moral dilemmas in children's literature as a vehicle for moral education and teaching reading comprehension. *Journal of Moral Education, 25,* 325–341.

Cole, M. (1996). *Cultural psychology: A once and future discipline.* Cambridge, MA: Belknap Press of Harvard University Press.

Danielson, C., & McGreal, T. L. (2000). *Teacher evaluation to enhance professional practice.* Princeton, NJ: Educational Testing Service.

Doyle, W. (1983). Academic work. *Review of Educational Research, 53,* 159–199.

Doyle, W. (1988). Work in mathematics classes: The context of students' thinking during instruction. *Educational Psychologist, 23*(2), 167–180.

Gagne, R. M. (1977). *The conditions of learning* (3rd ed.). New York: Holt, Rinehart, & Winston.

Garcia, G. E. (2004). The reading comprehension development and instruction of English-language learners. In A. P. Sweet & C. E. Snow (Eds.), *Rethinking reading comprehension* (pp. 30–50). New York: Guilford Press.

George, J. C. (1972). *Julie of the wolves.* New York: HarperCollins.

Greeno, J. G., Collins, A. M., & Resnick, L. (1996). Cognition and learning. In D. C. Berliner & R. C. Calfee (Eds.), *Handbook of educational psychology* (pp. 15–46). New York: Macmillan.

Hamilton, L. (2003). Assessment as a policy tool. *Review of Research in Education, 27,* 25–68.

Hargreaves, A. (1994). *Changing teachers, changing times: Teachers' work and culture in the postmodern age.* London: Continuum.

Hiebert, J., Gallimore, R., Garnier, H., Bogard Givvin, K., Hollingsworth, H., Jacobs, J., et al. (2003). *Teaching mathematics in seven countries: Results from the TIMSS 1999 Video Study* (NCES 2003–013). Washington, DC: National Center for Education Statistics.

Hill, H. (2006). How characteristics of language complicate policy implementation. In M. I. Honig (Ed.), *New directions in education policy implementation: Confronting complexity* (pp. 65–82). Albany: State University of New York Press.

Hull, C. L. (1943). *Principles of behavior: An introduction to behavior theory.* New York: Appleton-Century.

Joyce, B., & Showers, B. (1981, April). *Teacher training research: Working hypotheses for program design and directions for future study.* Paper presented at the annual meeting of the American Educational Research Association, Los Angeles.

Junker, B., Weisberg, Y., Matsumura, L. C., Crosson, A., Wolf, M., Levison, A., et al. (2005). *Overview of the instructional quality assessment* (CSE Technical Report No. 671). Los Angeles: University of California, National Center for Research on Evaluation, Standards, and Student Testing, Center for the Study of Evaluation.

Kingsbury, G. G., Olson, A., Cronin, J., Hauser, C., & Houser, R. (2003). *The state of state standards: Research investigating proficiency levels in fourteen states.* Portland, OR: Northwest Evaluation Association.

Knapp, M. S., Shields, P. M., & Turnbull, B. J. (1995). Academic challenge in high poverty classrooms. *Phi Delta Kappan, 76,* 770–776.

Koretz, D., & Hamilton, L. (2006). Testing for accountability in K–12. In R. L. Brennen (Ed.), *Educational Measurement* (4th ed., pp. 531–578). Westport, CT: American Council on Education/Praeger.

Lanier, J., & Little, J. W. (1986). Research on teacher education. In M. C. Wittrock (Ed.), *Handbook of research on teaching* (pp. 527–569). New York: Macmillan.

Lave, J., & Wenger, E. (1991). *Situated learning: Legitimate peripheral participation.* Cambridge, UK: Cambridge University Press.

Linn, R. L. (2003). Performance standards: Utility for different uses of assessments. *Education Policy Analysis Archives, 11*(31). Retrieved March 1, 2008, from http://epaa.asu.edu/ epaa/v11n31/

Lortie, D. (1975). *Schoolteacher.* Chicago: University of Chicago Press.

Matsumura, L. C. (2005). *Creating high-quality classroom assignments.* Lanham, MD: Rowman & Littlefield.

Matsumura, L. C., Garnier, H., Pascal, J., & Valdés, R. (2002). Measuring instructional quality in accountability systems: Classroom assignments and student achievement. *Educational Assessment, 8,* 207–229.

Matsumura, L. C., Slater, S. C, Wolf, M., Crosson, A., Levison, A., Peterson, M., et al. (2006). *Using the Instructional Quality Assessment Toolkit to investigate the quality of reading comprehension assignments and student work* (CSE Technical Report No. 669). Los Angeles: National Center for Research on Evaluation, Standards, and Student Testing.

McCaffrey, D. F., Lockwood, J. R., Koretz, D., & Hamilton, L. S. (2003). *Evaluating value-added models for teacher accountability.* Santa Monica, CA: RAND.

McLaughlin, M., & Talbert, J. (2006). *Building school-based teacher learning communities.* New York: Teachers College Press.

National Center for Education Statistics. (2004). *The condition of education in 2004 in brief* (NCES 2004–076). Washington, DC: U.S. Department of Education, Institute of Education Science.

National Commission on Teaching and America's Future. (1996). *What matters most: Teaching for America's future.* New York: Author.

Newmann, F. M., Bryk, A. S., & Nagaoka, J. K. (2001). *Authentic intellectual work and standardized tests: Conflict or coexistence?* Chicago: Consortium on Chicago School Research.

Newmann, F. M., Lopez, G., & Bryk, A. S. (1998). *The quality of intellectual work in Chicago schools: A baseline report.* Chicago: Consortium on Chicago School Research.

Peck, R., & Tucker, J. (1973). Research on teacher education. In R. Travers (Ed.), *Second handbook of research on teaching* (pp. 940–978). Chicago: Rand McNally.

Perrenoud, P. (1991). Towards a pragmatic approach to formative evaluation. In P. Weston (Ed.), *Assessment of pupils' achievement: Motivation and school success* (pp. 77–101). Amsterdam: Swets & Zeitlinger.

Peterson, P. E., & Hess, F. M. (2005). Johnny can read . . . in some states: Assessing the rigor of state assessment systems. *Education Next, 5*(3), 52–53.

Richardson, V. (Ed.). (2001). *Handbook of research on teaching* (4th ed.). Washington, DC: American Educational Research Association.

Richardson, V. (2003). Constructivist pedagogy. *Teachers College Record, 105,* 1623–1640.

Richardson, V., & Roosevelt, D. (2004). The preparation of teachers and the improvement of teacher education. In M. Smylie & D. Miretzky (Eds.), *Developing the teacher workforce: NSSE Yearbook, 103, Part I* (pp. 105–144). Chicago: University of Chicago Press.

Rogoff, B. (1991). *Apprenticeship in thinking: Cognitive development in social context.* New York: Oxford University Press.

Rosenshine, B., & Stevens, R. (1986). Teaching functions. In M. C. Wittrock (Ed.), *Handbook of research on teaching* (pp. 376–391). New York: Macmillan.

Schmidt, W. H, Houang, R. T., & McKnight, C. C. (2005). Value-added research: Right idea but wrong solution? In R. Lissitz (Ed.), *Value-added models in education: Theory and applications* (pp. 145–164). Maple Grove, MN: JAM Press.

Shavelson, R. J., Webb, N. M., & Burstein, L. (1986). Measurement of teaching. In M. C. Wittrock (Ed.), *Handbook of research on teaching* (pp. 50–91). New York: Macmillan.

Shepard, L. (2000). The role of assessment in a learning culture. *Educational Researcher, 29*(7), 4–14.

Shulman, L. S. (1986). Paradigms and research programs in the study of teaching: A contemporary perspective. In M. C. Wittrock (Ed.), *Handbook of research on teaching* (pp. 3–36). New York: Macmillan.

Silver, E. A., & Stein, M. K. (1996). The QUASAR Project: The "revolution of the possible" in mathematics instructional reform in urban middle schools. *Urban Education, 30,* 476–521.

Skinner, B. F. (1938). *The behavior of organisms: An experimental analysis.* New York: Appleton-Century-Crofts.

Smith, T. S, Desimone, L. M., & Ueno, K. (2005). "Highly qualified" to do what? The relationship between NCLB teacher quality mandates and the use of reform-oriented instruction in middle school mathematics. *Educational Evaluation and Policy Analysis, 27,* 75–109.

Snow, C. (2002). *Reading for understanding: Toward an R&D program in reading comprehension.* Santa Monica, CA: RAND.

Spinelli, J. (1990). *Maniac magee.* London: Little, Brown.

Spillane, J. P, & Zeuli, J. S. (1999). Reform and teaching: Exploring patterns of practice in the context of national and state mathematics reform. *Educational Evaluation and Policy Analysis, 21,* 1–27.

Stein, M. K., Grover, B. W., & Henningsen, M. (1996). Building student capacity for mathematical thinking and reasoning: An analysis of mathematical tasks used in reform classrooms. *American Educational Research Journal, 33,* 455–488.

Stein, M. K., & Lane, S. (1996). Instructional tasks and the development of student capacity to think and reason: An analysis of the relationship between teaching and learning in a reform mathematics project. *Educational Research and Evaluation, 2,* 50–80.

Stein, M. K., & Nelson, B. (2003). Leadership content knowledge. *Educational Evaluation and Policy Analysis, 25,* 423–448.

Stein, M. K., Smith, M. S., Henningsen, M. A., & Silver, E. A. (2000). *Implementing standards-based mathematics instruction: A casebook for professional development.* New York: Teachers College Press.

Tharp, R. G., & Gallimore, R. (1988). *Rousing minds to life: Teaching, learning, and schooling in social context.* Cambridge, UK: Cambridge University Press.

Thompson, C. L., & Zeuli, J. S. (1999). The frame and the tapestry: Standards-based reform and professional development. In L. Darling-Hammond & G. Sykes (Eds.), *Teaching as the learning profession: Handbook of policy and practice* (pp. 341–375). San Francisco: Jossey-Bass.

Thorndike, E. L. (1922). *The psychology of arithmetic.* New York: Macmillan.

U.S. Department of Education, National Center for Education Statistics. (2003). *Teaching mathematics in seven countries: Results from the TIMSS 1999 video study* (NCES 2003-013). Washington, DC: Author.

Weiss, I. R., & Pasley, J. D. (2004). What is high-quality instruction? *Educational Leadership, 61*(5), 24–28.

Wittrock, M. C. (1986a). *Handbook of research on teaching* (3rd ed.). New York: Macmillan.

Wittrock, M. C. (1986b). Students' thought processes. In M. C. Wittrock (Ed.), *Handbook of research on teaching* (pp. 297–314). New York: Macmillan.

9 Opportunity to Teach

Teacher Quality in Context

Gloria Ladson-Billings

University of Wisconsin–Madison

Introduction

Current school reform efforts are linked and informed by school reforms throughout history. According to Rothstein (1998), Americans have always been harsh critics of their public schools. Perhaps because we have always placed a heavy burden on schools for doing the things that we as a society are unwilling to do, schools can never meet our expectations. We expect schools to desegregate a segregated society, feed hungry children, do health screenings, and perform a variety of other functions beyond their expertise. It is no wonder that schools regularly fall short of expected goals.

In 1983 then president Ronald Reagan's Commission on Excellence in Education produced *A Nation at Risk,* a scathing condemnation of the state of America's public schools. This report was quickly followed by a series of reports and indictments of our schools. In President George H. W. Bush's administration (1988–1992) the U.S. Department of Education presented the National Education Goals, a set of six broadly construed statements about the direction of education in the United States. These goals focused on school readiness; school completion; achievement and citizenship; mathematics and science; adult literacy and lifelong learning; and safe, disciplined, and alcohol- and drug-free schools. In President William Jefferson Clinton's administration, the Congress enacted Goals 2000, which added two new goals: teacher professional development and parental participation. This act also established the National Education Standards and Improvement Council "to examine and certify national and state content, student performance, opportunity-to-learn standards, and assessment systems voluntarily submitted by states" (North Central Regional Educational Laboratory [NCREL], n.d.-a, p. 5).

I provide this brief summary of recent national school reform efforts to remind us that our current national reform, No Child Left Behind—which is steeped in a rhetoric of increasing accountability for student performance, focusing on "what works," reducing bureaucracy, and empowering parents—is a logical extension of earlier reform efforts. However, lost in the school reform discussion was the admonition of the Goals 2000 National Education Standards and Improvement Council to ensure that students have an opportunity to learn.

During the transposition of National Education Goals to Goals 2000, there emerged the notion of *opportunity to learn* (Elmore & Fuhrman, 1995; Stevens & Grymes, 1993). A variety of entities have helped define this concept. According to NCREL (n.d.-b), "*opportunity to learn* refers to equitable conditions or circumstances within the school or classroom that promote learning for all students. It includes the provision of curricula, learning materials, facilities, teachers, and instructional experiences that enable students to achieve high standards. This term also relates to the absence of barriers that prevent learning" (p. 1).

The National Council of Teachers of English (NCTE; 1996), in a statement endorsed by the National Council for the Social Studies, the National Council of Teachers of Mathematics, the National Board for Professional Teaching Standards (NBPTS), the National Science Teachers Association, the International Reading Association, the American Association of Colleges of Teacher Education, and ten other professional associations, asserts that

> the opportunity to learn is the inherent right of every child in America. Educators, parents, and other members of a child's many communities share a common interest in the educational success of each child and in the role of education in our democratic society. Full, positive participation in democracy is contingent upon every child's access to quality education. Such access to high-quality education should not be dependent upon the specific community in which a child lives. By focusing and building upon the strengths of learners, opportunity-to-learn standards can help ensure equitable access to high-quality education for all students in America. (p. 2)

I agree that these opportunity-to-learn standards are essential if students are to meet the achievement standards being set for them by federal, state, and local standards and accountability mechanisms. But in addition to these standards, I believe that we must consider what I term *opportunity to teach* standards. Different from teaching opportunities (i.e., the chance to teach), opportunity to teach refers to the ability to use the knowledge, skills, and abilities from one's teacher preparation in an environment conducive to teaching and learning. Teaching opportunities refer to the ability to get a job. For instance, there are few teaching opportunities in White, suburban, high-achieving school districts because few teachers leave those schools. The teachers in those districts stay there, and the school district offices maintain long lists of potential teachers. Indeed, some fully certified teachers would rather accept jobs as substitute teachers in suburban districts than sign contracts for full-time positions in urban school districts.

According to UCLA's Institute for Democracy, Education, & Access (UCLA/IDEA; 2003) opportunity to learn is "a way of measuring and reporting whether students and teachers have access to the different ingredients that make up quality schools" (p. 1). Examples include students' access to qualified teachers, clean and safe facilities, current textbooks and high-quality learning materials, rigorous course content, and school conditions—structures and policies—that provide fair and equal opportunities to learn and achieve.

California is an interesting case study of the notion of opportunity to learn because its schools display incredible discrepancies concerning resources and achievement. These discrepancies are closely linked to issues of race, class, ethnicity, language, and immigrant status. In 2004 *Williams v. State of California* resulted in a settlement that requires that all California public school students have adequate instructional materials in clean, safe, and functional schools. This settlement resulted in five state-level bills attending to minimum standards regarding school facilities, teacher quality, and adequate instructional materials.

Although California has made legal provisions for addressing opportunity to learn via the Williams settlement, the state (as well as most states in the nation) has failed to meet the letter of the law. The evidence in California is startling (UCLA/IDEA, 2003):

- 96,951 students in the class of 2006 failed the math section of the high school exit exam when they took it in tenth grade. This represents 24% of all test takers.

- 96,906 students in the class of 2006 failed the English language arts section of the exit exam when they took it in tenth grade. This represents 23% of all test takers.

- 60% of English language learners in the class of 2006 failed the English language arts section.

- 42% of African American students and 36% of Latino students in the class of 2006 failed the math section.

- 69% of special education students in the class of 2006 failed each section.

- In California schools with severe teacher shortages and dramatic overcrowding, the average failure rate on the math section of the exit exam is 44%. The same schools have an average failure rate of 40% in English language arts.

- The exit exam failure rate in schools affected by the Williams settlement is more than 2.5 times higher than the failure rate in non-Williams schools.

Although these figures illustrate the challenges faced in ensuring that students have an opportunity to learn, in this chapter I attempt to develop the construct of opportunity to teach, which I believe is important to understanding teacher assessment in a more robust way. I explore the notions of restrictive and expansive views of assessing teacher quality and present some alternative views of teacher quality in context.

Opportunity to Teach

One major aspect of opportunity to learn is the context in which teachers do their work. Teachers in inner-city schools and many of their counterparts in poor rural schools teach in places where both the structure and infrastructure interfere with their ability to meet the increasingly high standards expected of all students. This is not to suggest that we do not want students in these contexts to meet high standards. Rather, I am arguing that we place teachers in these contexts in positions that actively work against their meeting these challenges.

Imagine, for instance, that a physician finds herself working in an urban community where all of her patients are on Medicaid or lack any health insurance. As a consequence, the majority of her patients show up for medical care long after they should have. The help she might have provided can do little by the time she sees her patients. Her only solution is to give them stopgap and palliative care. If we were to measure her medical "effectiveness" compared to her medical school classmate who is practicing in an upscale resort community, we might say that she is not a very good doctor. Her survival rate is depressingly lower, and her patients' health remains marginal. But her medical school classmate treats patients for sunburn and tennis elbow. When he has something more serious, he is confident that his patients have adequate medical coverage to allow them to be seen by the area's best specialists. His patient load is stable and reliable, and he gets to see them over their lifespan and even that of some of their children. Everybody believes him to be an "effective" doctor.

If we transpose the image of the two physicians to that of urban schools, we find teachers who want to do a good job with students. But many urban teachers find that the children in their classrooms come to them having been victims of educational neglect. Fourth-grade teachers find themselves in classrooms with children who do not yet know how to read. Eighth-grade teachers find themselves in classrooms with students who cannot do rudimentary mathematics such as fractions or decimals.

Urban teachers may come to work early and stay late, but their efforts may do little to scratch the surface of the problem they are facing.

At the infrastructure level, urban schools and classrooms often lack the number of ancillary personnel (e.g., administrators; specialist teachers in art, music, or physical education; instructional aids; librarians) that their suburban peers enjoy. With these glaring contextual inequities, how can we begin to think that there is enough comparability to measure teacher effectiveness across them and say something meaningful about teacher quality?

By opportunity to teach, I refer to those teachers who have teaching jobs but have to concern themselves with whether or not the context and situation in which they are teaching is conducive to teaching and learning. Provided below are a variety of examples of what constitutes an environment that is conducive to teaching and learning.

TEACHING WHAT YOU KNOW

Ingersoll (2003) has found that the United States produces an abundant supply of teachers (indeed, perhaps an oversupply). However, the number of teachers who either leave the profession or move from one school to another almost equals the number of those who come into the profession each year. Thus, teaching is a field in constant flux, particularly in those schools serving low-income communities, students of color, and students whose first language is other than English. The reasons why teachers leave or change schools are varied, but the majority of teachers claim that they leave because of issues of salary (54%) and poor administrative support (43%).

One of the challenges that teachers face in schools (particularly at the secondary level) is being assigned to teach something they feel unprepared to teach. Administrators often make such teaching assignments in an attempt to staff schools according to district allotments. For instance, in California, teachers may be teaching with a variety of credentials. In the mid-1980s a number of teachers worked with General Secondary Credentials that allowed them to teach in any subject area offered in the school. When schools experienced budget cutbacks and were forced to lay off teachers, fully credentialed but recently hired mathematics and science teachers could be replaced by more veteran teachers of home economics and keyboarding who held General Secondary Credentials. Thus, the schools were forced to place the home economics and keyboarding teachers in mathematics and science classrooms where they were unprepared to teach.

These types of staffing decisions meant that opportunity-to-learn standards were not in place for students (i.e., their teachers were not qualified to teach the subjects to which they were assigned) and teachers were unable to perform the duties required of them. These teachers did not truly have an opportunity to teach. In our current school configuration, middle school teachers who teach core subject areas (e.g., English language arts, social studies, mathematics, science) often are expected to teach two core subjects regardless of their credentials. Their opportunity to teach is compromised in the subject area for which they are less well prepared.

A CLEAN, WELL-LIT PLACE

Teachers expect to teach in classrooms with heat in the winter and reasonable room, and that are free from leaking roofs, pests, and vermin. Unfortunately, far too many of our children in urban and rural schools find themselves in classrooms that fail to meet adequate building code standards (Kozol, 1991). In a graphic description of teaching in Compton, California, new teacher Sarah Sentilles (2005) details the conditions under which she was expected to teach and the students were to learn:

> At Garvey Elementary School, I taught over thirty second graders in a so-called temporary building. Most of these "temporary" buildings have been on campuses in Compton for years. The one I taught in was old. Because the wooden beams across the ceiling were being eaten by termites, a fine layer of wood dust covered the students' desks every morning. Maggots crawled in a cracked and collapsing area of the floor near my desk. One day after school I went to sit in my chair, and it was completely covered in maggots. I was nearly sick. Mice race behind cupboards and bookcases. I trapped six in terrible traps called "glue lounges" given to me by the custodians. The blue metal window coverings on the outsides of the windows were shut permanently, blocking all sunlight. Someone had lost the tool needed to open them, and no one could find another. (p. 72)

Consider another example, this time from a field trial of assessments for National Board certification. A group of teachers attempting to complete the field trial for early literacy (students in Grades K–3) displayed entries for the "creating a literate environment" task. They were asked to show a videotape of what they had done in the physical environment of their classrooms to create an atmosphere that would encourage and support students' literacy competence. One teacher in a wealthy district presented a video showing that she had transformed her classroom into a huge spider's web as she introduced the class to E. B. White's (1952) classic, *Charlotte's Web.* Clearly, she had created a literate environment.

However, the video from one of the other teachers, a woman who taught in one of the state's poorest districts, showed a set of portable bulletin boards that she attempted to use to explore the themes of the books the children read. The space that the teacher was using was not very well lit, and there seemed to be few comfortable places for students to relax and read. Unlike the teacher with the elaborate spider's web, this teacher's room seemed to be a kind of makeshift, hastily organized presentation for the purpose of the assessment activity—not really the creation of a literate environment. When we asked her to explain what we saw in the video she began with what I thought of as the most poignant example of not having an opportunity to teach.

"I don't actually have a classroom," the teacher began. "We don't have enough rooms for all of the classes we have in our school, so I actually float around the building. Every nine weeks or so I am required to pack up my entire classroom and move to some other part of the building and reestablish my classroom. What is on the videotape is what the 'classroom' looked like in the midst of my disassembling for the next nine weeks."

CURRICULUM THAT STANDS IN THE WAY

One of the places that education reform has taken hold is in the curriculum. After the release of *A Nation at Risk* (Commission on Excellence and Education, 1983), the idea of the cafeteria curriculum (where students have extensive course choices) fell into disdain in favor of a more standard and "rigorous" curriculum that required all students (particularly at the secondary level) to take four years of English, four years of mathematics, four years of science, four years of history/social science (including civics and government), and one year of work in computer literacy. Banished to the margins of the school curriculum were courses dealing with the arts and aesthetics, physical and health education, business, and vocational/technical interests.

Curriculum debates are not new to the United States. Eisner and Vallance (1974) assembled a full array of curriculum conceptions that schools, districts, teachers, parents, and others take up as their primary understanding of what the curriculum should be. Briefly, those conceptions include academic rationalism (e.g., an agreed-upon set of the greatest authors and the greatest ideas), the curriculum as cognitive processes (e.g., a set of skills such as literacy, numeracy, or critical thinking that can be applied across content areas), the curriculum as a form of self-actualization (e.g., a more psychologized, personalized curriculum), the curriculum as social control versus social reconstructionist (e.g., the curriculum as a form of either maintaining or reconstructing a society), and the curriculum as technology (e.g., the curriculum as a fully regular, predictable set of activities into which we can plug in particular skills or content).

Despite the utility of Eisner and Vallance's (1974) work, it is important to acknowledge the political nature of the curriculum. As Apple (1993) observes, the curriculum that schools advertise and sanction as a part of their course of study constitutes official knowledge. Indeed, the curriculum has always been a place for societies to embed ideological and national perspectives regarding which knowledge is of most worth. Curricula at the height of war and national threats regularly valorize the nation while demonizing other nations. During World War II, books written by German authors disappeared from library shelves, and during the Cold War, students were regularly taught about the evils of the Soviet

Union. Also, calls for international competitiveness drive the degree to which certain subject areas (e.g., mathematics, science, technology) are included and emphasized.

In today's educational reform environment, with its emphasis on standardized test performance, low-performing schools are being made to adopt scripted and/or highly directive curricula in which the teachers are told exactly what to teach, on what day, and in what manner. Thus, teachers no longer act as teachers but rather as functionaries of the state; their own thinking, creativity, and decision making are not only discredited but are indeed not allowed. Teachers in schools that have adopted scripted curricula do not have the opportunity to teach.

TESTING TOWARD UTOPIA

Perhaps one of the more controversial provisions of school reform is the role of standardized testing. Because we tend to think in dichotomous categories, any objection raised against standardized testing is read as being against improving education. The current federal legislation, No Child Left Behind, requires all schools that receive federal monies to test all students annually in Grades 3 through 8 in the areas of reading and mathematics. Current discussions of reauthorization of the legislation focus on extending the standardized testing mandate to the high school level.

I want to be clear here that testing per se is not the problem. Rather, the concern about standardized testing is how such testing has become the only way of determining what is valued and learned in school. Standardized testing has become the coin of the realm in schools serving low-income students, students of color, and those whose first language is other than English. Such testing is regarded as "high stakes" and has major consequences (e.g., students, teachers, and/or schools are severely sanctioned for not "passing" these tests).

The pernicious nature of standardized testing is that teachers in low-performing schools report that they will teach the curriculum after the tests have been administered. The entire classroom is organized around preparing students for tests, administering tests, and making evaluations about students based on those tests. States such as Texas claim that this system of standards and testing greatly reduced the gap between White students and students of color even before the introduction of No Child Left Behind. However, some researchers are skeptical of these claims:

The [Texas] system of test-driven accountability masks the inequities that have for decades built unequal structures of schooling in [the] state. Test-score inflation, through concentrated test-prep, gives the impression that teaching and learning are improving in minority schools when in fact teaching and learning may have been severely compromised by the attempt to raise scores. The investment in expensive systems of testing, test design, test contracts, and sub-contracts, training of teachers and administrators to implement the tests, test security, realignment of curricula with tests and the production of test prep materials, serve a political function in centralizing control over education and linking public education to private commerce. (Haney, Madaus, & Lyons, 1993, p. 259)

Restrictive Versus Expansive Views of Assessing Teacher Quality

Legal scholar Kimberle Crenshaw (1988), whose work focuses on race and law, makes a distinction between restrictive and expansive views of equality. Briefly, restrictive views of equality are those that suggest that societies are only responsible for creating the legal opportunities to allow people access to particular social benefits. For example, in a restrictive equality view of schooling the society is only responsible for ensuring that all students have access to equal schooling. Thus, laws and judicial decisions look at the legal provisions for education. Are all students permitted to attend school? Do all students have access to the curriculum and cocurricular activities offered at their schools (i.e., can all students enroll in certain classes, try out for teams, and enroll in clubs)?

An example of restrictive equality is what happened in the United States after the landmark *Brown v. Board of Education* (1954) decision and the subsequent consent decree (*Brown v. Board of Education II,* 1955). Upon implementing the *Brown* decision, most schools in the South (at which the decision was primarily aimed because of the existence of separate school systems, not just separate segregated schools within the same system) reluctantly opened their doors (sometimes because of the presence of National Guard troops and federal marshals) but made no special provision or accommodation for the African American students who entered the school. We learned from the narratives of African American students in newly desegregated schools (see, e.g., Beals, 1994) how horribly they were treated by teachers and peers. Though the schools were minimally compliant with the law, this was a very restrictive view of equality.

Although schooling has improved for students of color since those pre-Brown days, the majority of African American and Latino students continue to attend segregated schools. In addition to being in separate schools, per-pupil spending in the schools that are "majority-minority" can range from $3,000 to $11,000 less per year than that of their suburban, mostly White counterparts (Kozol, 2005). How do we justify lower spending on those students whose needs are greatest?

The expansive view of educational equity is concerned with both the equality of access to schooling and the equality of educational outcomes. This expansive notion pushes us to consider whether or not schools actively work to create (more) equal outcomes. It requires schools to look at policies concerning teacher quality and assignment, access to high-quality curriculum, ability grouping and tracking, management and discipline policies, assessment and testing, language, and special education designation and placement.

An imagined example[1] of an expansive view of educational equity is one in which a receiving White school determines beforehand how it will organize and prepare for students of color. Such a school would be careful in monitoring (and asking itself questions about) the number of students of color who participate in high-level course offerings, are assigned to special education, are suspended and expelled, perform at high academic levels, and are included in the entire life of the school. The school would demand an integrated teaching staff and place value on creating an inclusive context. Thus, the sense of belonging, full participation, and high achievement of students of color would be a central focus toward a goal of ensuring that race and/or ethnicity would be less predictive of students' school achievement.

So how do these notions of restrictive and expansive apply to the issue of teacher quality? I argue that at this point we have employed restrictive views of both assessing and determining good teaching. Historically, African American teachers in the South were required to be assessed annually in order to have their contracts renewed. These assessments were often totally arbitrary and capricious. Historian Val Littlefield (1994) documents the ways that White school committee members went into classrooms of African American teachers and made decisions about the worthiness of these women to have their teaching contracts renewed. Sadly, an inordinate number of these decisions were made based on women teachers' acquiescence to sexual harassment and demands.

At the opposite end of this coercive spectrum was the period during which teachers unions challenged the ability of administrators to do any more than rate teachers as satisfactory or unsatisfactory. Teachers in such systems were required to do little more than attend school each day, maintain order, and comply with the secretarial or administrative tasks attendant to the job. These systems required teachers to do enough to earn tenure (usually 2–4 years of satisfactory appraisal) and maintain a minimum competence for the rest of their professional careers.

Sometime after the publication of *A Nation at Risk* (Commission on Excellence and Education, 1983), a number of states began developing merit pay systems in an attempt to reward exemplary teachers. These systems were met with a variety of opposition—some quite valid—about who was meritorious and how to determine what constitutes meritorious practice. This attempt to differentiate and reward outstanding teachers and the consternation about doing so may have been helpful catalysts in the reform and rethinking of teacher assessment. Shulman's (1987) well-known *Harvard Educational Review* article on the knowledge base of teaching was pivotal in helping to reshape the discourse about the way we think about the work of teachers and perhaps assess that work.

Soon after the Shulman article we saw the call for performance-based teacher assessment and the development of the National Board for Professional Teaching Standards (NBPTS). NBPTS worked hard to develop assessments that allowed teachers to demonstrate what they know and are able to do as professionals. Theoretically, NBPTS charts exactly the direction we would want to go in to assess exemplary teachers rather than accepting either arbitrary determination from building principals or narrowly constructed pencil-and-paper tests that allegedly tell us who is and is not a good teacher.

Unfortunately, the practice espoused by the proponents of a performance-based assessment can deviate from theory. So what actually emerged in the development of NBPTS was a set of exercises and activities that teachers participated in throughout the year and used to create their individual teaching portfolios. These assessment exercises included examples of students' work, video representations of teaching, reflection papers, and analysis of issues of teaching that emerge in their domains. On the surface these seemed like exactly the kinds of things we would want teachers to demonstrate—a more "authentic" rendering of teaching. However, the fact that the assessors in this process brought to the assessment their own views of what constitutes good teaching practice meant that certain forms of teaching were privileged over others. Not surprisingly, Black and Latino teachers were adversely impacted by the assessments.

During the art assessment, one African American teacher from a school serving African American students almost exclusively brought in a woman who demonstrated the intricate patterns and designs used in hair braiding to demonstrate how Africans used art to adorn themselves. The NBPTS assessors determined that what the teacher was engaged in was not art but rather vocational education. Thus, the fundamental question of what is art—a question that the art world continues to grapple with—was left to the assessors. Upon further discussion, those of us who were chosen to review the assessments to determine whether or not there was bias and/or adverse impact on African American teachers learned that the assessors felt that the teacher's practice did not reflect *disciplined-based art education* (DBAE). Although widely accepted among arts educators, DBAE is not the only approach to teaching art. We could locate nothing in the Early Adolescence/Young Adulthood Art Certification Standards that requires that teachers take a DBAE approach.

Another example we discovered was that of an African American teacher who failed to earn NBPTS certification in early literacy. As part of her portfolio, she included a video of her second graders reading a book about a man who could not read and encountering the often funny, sometimes disastrous things that occurred because of his misidentification of a variety of items. In addition to reading the story, the teacher had a man as a guest speaker who told the story of his own struggle with literacy and learning to read as an adult. The assessors felt that this teacher was doing a social studies lesson, not a literacy one. Although I cannot be sure that this critique of the teacher's practice is the reason for her failure, it does speak to some of the variance in perspectives that teachers may bring to the performance assessment process.

There was a commonality (other than race) among African American teachers who failed to receive NBPTS certification that is significant. None of them had the support of other colleagues who were themselves going through the certification process. Without a peer group to challenge and endorse what they were doing, these teachers were probably working hard to give the assessors what they thought they wanted.

Interestingly, about 20 years ago, mathematics professor Uri Treisman (Fullilove & Treisman, 1990), seeking to discover why African American students in his college calculus course were struggling, discovered that, unlike the other students in the class, the African American students were not participating in study groups. They had internalized a societal message that they were to "do it on their own." That message worked for them throughout their K–12 schooling and even got them to an elite university. However, once at the University of California the students struggled to keep up. Treisman revamped his course and required all students to be in study groups. At the end of the semester there was no significant difference in the academic performance of the African American students and their White and Asian American classmates. Treisman's pedagogical accommodation resembled Delpit's (1996) strategy of making the tacit rules explicit. Once the students knew the rules about collaborating, they were able to be successful. Similarly, the African American teachers preparing for NBPTS certification need to know the tacit rules that undergird performance assessment.

In a validation study of the NBPTS certification process (Ladson-Billings & Darling-Hammond, 2000), I selected a cadre of 15 teachers from four urban areas and asked them to produce two (out of a possible nine) assessments from the Early Literacy/English Language Arts Assessment. Of the 15, one teacher already had achieved NBPTS certification, five had failed, six were preparing to apply, and the remaining three were not involved in NPBTS certification but were considering it. I also assembled a panel of literacy experts, all of whom were familiar with the NBPTS certification process, to assess the quality of the submissions and respond to the teachers' interview data. More interesting than the assessment results for these urban teachers of color were the contextual factors they faced, including the following:

1. They lack the institutional support to pursue NBPTS certification.

2. They typically teach a greater proportion of students who are underachieving.

3. They typically are rewarded for noninstructional behaviors and activities.

4. They typically teach in isolation from new and exciting teaching practices and knowledge about such practices.

5. They typically attempt to gain certification alone, without collegial support.

6. They may be engaged in family and community activities that are unrecognized and unsupported by conventional professional reward structures.

7. They typically are less familiar with the form and substance of the assessment.

What I learned from the validation study was that the NBPTS certification process at that time was less sensitive to the contextual factors surrounding teaching in urban school communities. We did not conclude that NBPTS certification was invalid in assessing accomplished teaching.

Despite the promise of NBPTS certification, the current demands for public schools to improve student achievement, and do so quickly, have found their way into a discourse that suggests that we can determine the quality of the teachers by the performance of their students on standardized measures (Rivkin, Hanushek, & Kain, 2005). Such a perspective ignores the complex nature of what constitutes student achievement and denies the role of context in either creating or diminishing opportunities for academic success.

Expansive views of teacher quality require a willingness to allow multiple interpretations of what teachers do and to more seriously factor in issues concerning the contexts in which teachers do their work. Teaching is not merely a set of technical tasks that teachers order and perform. Instead, as Shulman (2004) has argued, teaching is such a complex undertaking that no single measure can adequately capture it. Cochran-Smith (2005) cautions that we cannot draw a straight line from teacher education to student achievement. I argue that we cannot draw a straight line from the teacher to student performance on standardized assessments. There is simply too much variance and noise in the system to make that feasible. Even if we conduct randomized trials, we have to acknowledge that students come to the classroom with a variety of context variables that may intervene between what is taught and what is tested. That said, I do not argue that we cannot use standardized testing to tell us something about the nature of the curriculum and what is taught in particular schools.

Throughout this chapter I have made assertions about the role of context in assessing teacher quality. I argue that context may be both contributory and explanatory regarding student performance on standardized measures, not that context is a legitimate excuse for failing to teach all students well. In the final section of this chapter, I propose alternative ways of thinking about teacher quality in context.

Alternative Views of Teacher Quality in Context

In this section, I propose another assessment perspective that incorporates aspects of both the restrictive and expansive models but rearticulates them into what I would term a more holistic or ecological model that looks at student achievement, engagement, and relationships. This type of assessment relies on the cultivation of professional development communities that provide teachers with ongoing opportunities for learning as well as teaching.

I want to make clear that teacher assessment is a complex, nuanced, and nested undertaking. Simply suggesting that teacher quality is directly linked to student achievement on standardized tests is to declare that teachers in the nation's wealthiest schools are the best teachers and those in the poorest communities are the worst teachers when we know that race, class, and achievement are highly correlated. During my graduate preparation I had a statistics professor who was, to put it frankly, terrible. Each day he came into the room, barely looked at the students, and began talking directly to the chalkboard. He never asked any questions. He thought of himself as someone to explain the problems and assign us daily homework. By the third week into the quarter, most of the students stopped attending. They read the text and taught themselves the material. On the day of the final, the room was filled as it was on the first day of class. Most of the students did quite well in the class. However, it would be a mistake to say that the professor was a good teacher. If we attach teacher quality only to student achievement, teachers like him will be regarded as good merely because they happen to be teaching in an elite university setting.

If we want to take serious the assessment of teacher quality, we have to look at assessments that include teachers' opportunity to teach. My statistics professor had an opportunity to teach. He had students who were willing to do the work, he had extensive resources, and he knew his subject matter even though he was not very good at explaining what he knew to the students. I relate his story to illustrate the need to think of teaching as a very complex undertaking. At the K–12 level teachers are asked to make hundreds of decisions each day, and each decision has the potential to change students' learning experiences.

The other thing we must do if we are serious about alternative forms of teacher assessment is move away from a notion of good teaching that is linked to one particular style of teaching—even if it is a style we like. Here I am arguing that sometimes more traditional styles of teaching are both appropriate and effective. Some teachers are gifted lecturers, and we should recognize their lecturing skill. Other teachers are great at conducting discussions in which, to the casual observer, it seems that they are not really doing much. However, such teaching requires a tremendous amount of planning and structure that is not readily apparent to the observer, who nevertheless may recognize that most of the class seems to be taking part in a spirited discussion. On the other hand, we could see a classroom full of activity and instructional materials. That teacher could have students using manipulative materials, using a variety of visual aids, and sitting in cooperative groups. That same busy classroom can be a place where little learning is taking place. Teaching style does not always equal quality teaching.

Although some measures of teacher quality do consider teaching context, context generally accounts for a small part of teacher quality. I argue that the context in which teachers (or any professionals) do their work is a central aspect of how effective their practice can be. As I discussed earlier in this chapter, doctors who work in poorly staffed, overcrowded hospitals that serve uninsured and underinsured patients are more likely to be faced with higher mortality rates than doctors who work in state-of-the-art medical facilities serving high-income, well-insured patients. Likewise, attorneys who serve poor clients tend to have lower rates of successful court decisions than those who have wealthy clients. We cannot conclude from this that the rich are more moral. The resources available to their lawyers allow them to present more elaborate defenses. The context in which lawyers and doctors do their work has a direct bearing on their effectiveness, and the same is true of teachers. How we account for context is yet to be determined, but we must account for it.

There are subtleties to every context that static measures are sure to miss. Not only are the objective measures of school and community contexts relevant here, but the less visible aspects of these contexts are also helpful in determining factors that impact teacher quality. For example, a new teacher placed in a school with a large proportion of new and inexperienced teachers is at a marked disadvantage compared to a new teacher placed in a school with teachers who have many years of experience. The differing environments may encourage one while discouraging the other. Factor in things such as administrative support, academic press, professional development opportunities, sociopolitical climate, and cultural mismatch, and it is possible to create a complex matrix of teaching contexts that have a profound impact on teacher effectiveness.

And what if we determine that someone is a good teacher? Does that mean that he or she is a good teacher in all contexts? This is perhaps one of the more challenging aspects of determining teacher quality. The NBPTS understood this in its decision to allow teachers to sit for specific subject areas in teaching (e.g., early adolescence mathematics, early childhood and middle childhood literacy, adolescence and young adulthood science). However, the NBPTS does not differentiate between and among the contexts in which teachers teach. So we must ask: Does being an excellent teacher in a suburban school serving high-income students mean that you will also be an excellent teacher in an urban school serving students who are low income, recent immigrants, and/or English language learners? Such context questions are the crux of the issue when it comes to determining alternative assessments for teacher quality.

If we are going to be serious about factoring context into assessments of teacher quality, then we will have to think more creatively about how to do so. From my own work (Ladson-Billings, 1994), it is clear to me that this type of assessment is labor intensive. Assessors must be willing to spend enough time *in* the classroom and school context to make meaning from what they see transpire in a classroom. They have to see practice over time to determine its effectiveness. They have to provide teachers with opportunities to describe their practice. And they need to have more robust measures of student achievement.

What I have described requires a major commitment of time and resources. It means that teachers must have the opportunity to work with knowledgeable others in order to look at their practice and improve it. It means that single, static measures of achievement (such as annual standardized achievement tests) cannot be used as the sole measure of teacher quality. It means that teachers must have the opportunity to teach.

Note

1. I choose to offer an "imagined" example because I am unaware of a school desegregation example that used an expansive model.

References

Apple, M. W. (1993). *Official knowledge.* New York: Routledge.

Beals, M. P. (1994). *Warriors don't cry: A searing memoir of the battle to integrate Little Rock's Central High.* New York: Pocket Books.

Brown v. Board of Education, 347 U.S. 483 (1954).

Brown v. Board of Education II, 349 U.S. 294 (1955).

Cochran-Smith, M. (2005). The new teacher education: For better or worse? *Educational Researcher, 34*(7), 3–17.

Commission on Excellence and Education. (1983). *A nation at risk.* Washington, DC: Author.

Crenshaw, K. (1988). Race, reform and retrenchment: Transformation and legitimization in antidiscrimination law. *Harvard Law Review, 101,* 1331–1387.

Delpit, L. (1996). *Other people's children: Cultural conflict in the classroom.* New York: Free Press.

Eisner, E., & Vallance, E. (1974). *Conflicting conceptions of the curriculum.* Berkeley, CA: McCutchan.

Elmore, R. F., & Fuhrman, S. H. (1995). Opportunity to learn standards and the state role in education. *Teachers College Record, 96,* 433–458.

Fullilove, R. E., & Treisman, P. U. (1990). Mathematics learning among African American undergraduates at the University of California Berkeley: An evaluation of the Mathematics Workshop Program. *Journal of Negro Education, 59,* 463–478.

Haney, W. M., Madaus, G. F., & Lyons, R. (1993). *The fractured marketplace for standardized testing.* Boston: Kluwer-Academic.

Ingersoll, R. (2003). *Is there really a teacher shortage? Report to the Center for Policy and Research in Education and the Center for the Study of Teaching and Policy.* Philadelphia: University of Pennsylvania, Graduate School of Education.

Kozol, J. (1991). *Savage inequalities: Children in America's schools.* New York: HarperCollins.

Kozol, J. (2005). *The shame of the nation: The restoration of apartheid schooling in America.* New York: Crown Books.

Ladson-Billings, G. (1994). *The dreamkeepers: Successful teachers of African American children.* San Francisco: Jossey-Bass.

Ladson-Billings, G., & Darling-Hammond, L. (2000). *The validity of National Board for Professional Teaching Standards (NBPTS)/Interstate New Teacher Assessment and Support Consortium (INTASC) assessments for effective urban teachers: Findings and implications for assessments.* Washington, DC: National Partnership for Excellence and Accountability in Teaching. (ERIC Document Reproduction Service No. 448152)

Littlefield, V. (1994). A yearly contract with everybody and his brother: Durham County, Black female public school teachers, 1885–1927. *Journal of Negro History, 79,* 37–53.

National Council of Teachers of English. (1996). *Opportunity-to-learn standards, statement of principles.* Retrieved August 14, 2007, from http://www.ncte.org/about/over/positions/category/rights/107677.htm

North Central Regional Educational Laboratory. (n.d.-a.). *Summary of Goals 2000: Educate America Act.* Retrieved August 14, 2007, from http://www.ncrel.org/sdrs/areas/issues/envrnmnt/stw/sw0goals.htm

North Central Regional Educational Laboratory. (n.d.-b.). *Opportunity to learn.* Retrieved July 26, 2007, from http://www.ncrel.org/sdrs/areas/issues/methods/assment/as8lk18.htm

Rivkin, S., Hanushek, E., & Kain, J. (2005). Teachers, schools and academic achievement. *Econometrica, 73,* 417–458.

Rothstein, R. (1998). *The way we were? The myths and realities of American school achievement.* New York: Century Foundation Press.

Sentilles, S. (2005). *Taught by America: A story of struggle and hope in Compton.* Boston: Beacon Press.

Shulman, L. S. (1987). Knowledge and teaching: Foundations of the new reform. *Harvard Educational Review, 57,* 1–22.

Shulman, L. S. (2004). *The wisdom of practice: Essays on teaching, learning, and learning to teach.* San Francisco: Jossey-Bass.

Stevens, F. I., & Grymes, J. (1993). Opportunity to learn: Issues of equity for poor and minority students. Washington, DC: U.S. Department of Education, National Center for Education Statistics. (ERIC Document Reproduction Service No. 356306)

UCLA's Institute for Democracy, Education, & Access. (2003). *Opportunity to learn (OTL): Does California's school system measure up?* Retrieved August 17, 2007, from http://justschools.gseis.ucla.edu/solution/pdfs/OTL.pdf

White, E. B. (1952). *Charlotte's web.* New York: Harper & Row.

Williams v. State of California (County of San Francisco), No. 312236 (Sup. Ct. December 10, 2004).

Crisp Measurement and Messy Context

A Clash of Assumptions and Metaphors—Synthesis of Section III[1]

Drew H. Gitomer

ETS

Sophisticated measurement tools, data systems, and research studies are being developed to assign particular value to teachers and to factors that may be associated with teacher effectiveness. Elaborate and expensive randomized trials are being conducted to examine the impact of certain aspects of teaching (e.g., Decker, Mayer, & Glazerman, 2004), and sophisticated analyses of the relationship of teachers to student achievement are being carried out on a regular basis (see www.caldercenter.org for a broad set

---

Following the papers presented by Arturo Pacheco, Mary Kay Stein and Lindsay Clare Matsumura, and Gloria Ladson-Billings, an interactive panel discussion was held. Panelists were Joan Baratz-Snowden, president, Education Study Center; Kenji Hakuta, professor, Stanford University; Lloyd Bond, professor emeritus, University of North Carolina, Greensboro, and senior scholar, Carnegie Foundation for the Advancement of Teaching; and Carol Dwyer, distinguished presidential appointee, Educational Testing Service. This chapter represents an attempt to synthesize selected ideas that were brought forth through the papers and subsequent discussion.

of such studies). Even amid this ambitious activity, pursuit of rigorous research data that can help us understand personal, program, and institutional factors that might be associated with effective teaching remains a nascent effort (e.g., Cochran-Smith & Zeichner, 2005).

When I review this research, I am struck by how unimpressive the findings are that policies and practices about teachers can fundamentally shift educational outcomes. In many studies, relationships are not found between a particular teacher characteristic and student outcomes. In other studies, the findings may be statistically significant, but quite small in terms of practical import for that same characteristic. Nonexistent is the finding related to a teacher's characteristics such that, if we could somehow increase its presence in the teaching force, we would be able to transform the quality of education and/or fundamentally alter the achievement gap history in this country.

Why Are the Effects So Small?

The difficulty in locating robust and consistent findings can mean one of three things. First, one could conclude that nothing about teachers matters much—not academic preparation, coursework, licensure test scores, pedagogy, experience, or National Board certification. This is not to say that effects have not been identified for these characteristics; they are simply so small when considered in light of the educational challenges we face. For example, a rough estimate of the Black–White achievement gap across different tests and different age groups is about 1 standard deviation. Teacher effects are seldom one-tenth of that, and typically range around .05 standard deviation, or one-twentieth of the achievement gap difference (see, e.g., Clotfelter, Ladd & Vigdor, 2007; Goldhaber, 2007). Even with an impressive body of research, the ability to account for student achievement by examining teacher characteristics is small.

Certainly the argument can be made that many other factors outside of the school and the classroom are more influential in determining student outcomes. Rothstein (2004) has made a powerful case that factors associated with race and class swamp any influence that schools have on educational outcomes. Hanushek and Rivkin (2006) have demonstrated that the demographic characteristics of students have far more to do with student achievement growth than do certain teacher factors, such as years of experience.

Nonetheless, the idea that teacher qualities do not have a dramatic impact not only is deeply troubling, but also defies all of our personal experiences with our own teachers, in academic as well as nonacademic contexts. Many adults can identify particular teachers who made profound differences in their lives. Parents who can afford it (and some who cannot) spend great resources to get their children the right tutor, coach, or piano teacher. Research has also identified particular teachers who do produce large learning gains in student achievement (e.g., Sanders, Saxton, & Horn, 1997), though associating such changes with particular characteristics of teachers and teacher policies remains elusive

So from a variety of perspectives, anecdotal and empirical, there is compelling evidence that teachers matter. A second possible explanation for the lack of strong observed patterns of relationships is that there are particular characteristics of teachers that make them effective, but these characteristics are not readily captured with any available metrics. Like trying to describe good art or music, the characteristics of effective teaching may be elusive and ineffable. In fact, as with what makes for good art or music, there may be so many avenues to being an effective teacher that it holds little promise to define teachers in terms of characteristics that receive typical attention. Accepting such a premise is inherently frustrating to almost all stakeholders in teacher education because it argues that there are limited consistent actions we can take to improve teaching outside of differentially encouraging those who demonstrate positive outcomes, for apparently unknown and unknowable reasons. Such a counterintuitive view should be accepted only when all other plausible explanations have been eliminated.

Therefore, a third possible explanation is that the methods being used in this research are not sensitive to any relationships that may actually exist. The less-than-compelling results could be due to limits in the measures of student achievement and/or the methods applied to those measures.

THE LIMITS OF ACHIEVEMENT MEASURES

Student achievement measures may be inadequate proxies to capture the impact of teachers. Such tests have been criticized for the following reasons:

- measuring a limited and impoverished set of desired learning outcomes (see, e.g., Bennett & Gitomer, in press)
- relying on items that are most impervious to instruction when vertically scaling tests across grades—a procedure necessary for value-added analyses (see, e.g., Schmidt, Houang, & McKnight, 2005)
- addressing a narrow curricular scope (usually reading and math) so that large parts of the curriculum (art, music, history, science) are not examined
- excluding secondary subjects, which do not have annual subject matter tests; thus, the vast majority of studies about teachers are based only on reading and mathematics scores of students at the elementary level

Comparing measures inappropriately by attempting to generalize findings across different studies is problematic as well because measures used in each state are different. Particular questions are evaluated by examining findings across studies as if the units of measurement are the same thing. They are not and are not easily compared (see, e.g., Feuer, Holland, Green, Bertenthal, & Hemphill, 1999).

Despite these limitations, the achievement test continues to be the currency by which many studies evaluate teacher effectiveness. The use of this currency underlies two of the key metaphors that have been used to guide much of the policy research: the medical or pharmaceutical model of gold-standard and randomized trials (e.g., Whitehurst, 2003) and the economic metaphor that considers achievement benefits in the same way as economic benefits characterized by gains or losses in currency units. Both metaphors have significant limitations in light of the use of standardized test scores.

Using either metaphor, the outcome measure is assumed to have relatively equivalent meaning across studies. An economic benefit of one hundred dollars means the same thing in Florida as it does in Idaho. Also, this same one hundred dollars has some external reality, for it can be compared with what goods can be purchased and how many hours of labor would be needed to earn such money.

A decrease in the rate of medical events through the use of a particular drug also means the same thing across studies and also has an external reality. Fewer people dying has an economic cost and benefit that can be assigned to the use of a particular drug. Findings are replicable across study locations. Of course, an additional attribute of medical studies is that they are typically highly focused on individuals with particular characteristics (e.g., men between 30 and 40 with high blood pressure), and reports of the effectiveness of the treatment are highly contextualized to the characteristics of the experimental groups only.

Contrast this with achievement tests when used across studies in different states. There is no legitimate way of comparing results. One-tenth of a standard deviation in student achievement scores does not mean the same thing in Idaho as in Florida. Also, there is no external reality. What does one-twentieth of a standard deviation in achievement test impact mean in terms of educational or other gains for a student or a population of students? In concrete terms, these kinds of effects might be translated to answering correctly, on average, one more item correct on a typical standardized multiple-choice test. What are the practical implications of such an effect?

Unlike pharmaceutical research, in education we do not ask whether a particular teacher is effective with a particular group of students sharing certain characteristics. Rather, we look for effects across all individuals most of the time. To the extent that there is some attempt to focus the effects of treatments on particular classes of individuals, the typical lens used is race/ethnicity, gender, and/or socioeconomic status. We group students not because they have particular individual educational characteristics, but because they are members of groups with different achievement profiles.

The fact is that large-scale, state-specific standardized achievement tests are often the only available metric to use to study the impact of teaching. But using measures because they are convenient rather than because they are clearly appropriate to the task has its costs, one of which may be a profound insensitivity to teacher impact.

THE LIMITS OF OUR METHODOLOGIES FOR DETERMINING EFFECTIVENESS

An important second possible reason for the lack of compelling findings concerns the assumptions underlying the analytic methods and models typically used to study teacher quality issues. It may be that there is a fundamental incompatibility between these assumptions and the phenomenon that is being analyzed: effective teaching. Specifically, the issue of diverse teaching contexts challenges the core methodological assumption, the stable-unit-treatment-value assumption (SUTVA; Rubin, 1990), used in identifying teacher effectiveness. In trying to make causal inferences about the impact of some treatment on an outcome (e.g., teacher preparation on student achievement), SUTVA assumes that any individual (unit) will have one and only one outcome to a particular treatment and there is no interaction between units. Though these assumptions lie at the heart of what we have called gold-standard research, they seem particularly difficult to accept when we consider the reality of teaching contexts (for a fuller discussion of related issues, see Hong & Raudenbush, 2006; Raudenbush, 2008). Once again, the metaphor of medical research used to champion this kind of research on teaching may be inappropriate. Indeed, Richard Berk (2005), in considering the SUTVA dilemma, cleverly described randomized experiments in these kinds of studies as a bronze standard.

In the medical metaphor, a study might give 20 mg of drug X and a placebo to different groups of subjects with a particular disease. The first assumption is that the 20 mg of the drug is the same treatment for each and every subject. Indeed, the pharmaceutical industry takes great pains in quality control to make sure that the treatment is absolutely consistent all of the time. The second assumption is that whether or not Patient A gets better has no bearing on the outcome of Patient B.

Now, consider a typical research design to explore teacher effectiveness. Imagine a study that compared the effectiveness of teachers prepared in

traditional teacher education programs with those who have been prepared through alternate route programs. Here the treatment is program
type, and the units are students. Rubin (1986) argues that the two most
common ways that SUTVA can be violated appear to occur when there are
versions of each treatment varying in effectiveness or there is interference
between units. For SUTVA to hold, we need to assume that the treatment,
or educational preparation intervention, is stable across all teachers who
participate in each of the program types. We also need to assume that
there are no interactions (interference) between students that influence
their respective achievement outcomes.

On the face of it, we know these assumptions do not hold in the study
of teacher effectiveness. Arturo Pacheco, in mapping the terrain of teacher
quality, provides great insight into the complex set of interactions that
occur within a classroom community, not only between teacher and student but between and among all combinations of community members
(i.e., units of treatment). He also draws on the work of the National Board
for Professional Teaching Standards (NBPTS), which has been a subject of
intense study of educational impact. In his vignette comparing two teachers in urban and suburban schools, he brings home the point that two
teachers offering the same "treatment" (NBPTS certification) are actually
operating in such different contexts that it is wrong to conceive of the
treatment as stable.

Gloria Ladson-Billings introduces the concept of *opportunity to teach,*
making it clear that trying to place the complexity and nuance of teaching
within simple categorical boxes is a fool's errand, particularly amid the
diverse contexts in which teaching occurs. Also drawing on her experience
examining NBPTS performances in context, she forces the question of
whether any analytic model that assumes a lack of critical and consequential interactions is appropriate.

Interestingly, Pacheco, Stein and Matsumura, and Ladson-Billings all
begin with a critical assumption of their own. They take the position that
the fundamental purpose of assessing teaching ought to be to improve it,
which directly echoes the premise of Ball and Hill's chapter in this volume
as well. It is not enough to simply rank teachers by some outcome measure; assessment must provide insight into acts and contexts of teaching to
provide a basis for some type of informed action.

Stein and Matsumura begin to address how such a model of assessment
might work. They describe measures of teaching that can be used to support communities of practice in professional feedback collaborations (i.e.,
teacher learning communities) that take into account the complex interactions of teachers, students, and subject matter. Rather than focusing on
any single outcome, they suggest the consideration of multiple measures
in judging teacher quality.

If SUTVA assumptions do not hold, then the validity of inferences based on an analysis of student achievement scores may not be supportable. Carol Dwyer reminded us of the tight linkage required between the targets of inference and the measures employed: "What are we gathering evidence of and what inferences are we trying to make from that evidence?" She argues that understanding evidence in the complicated contexts of classrooms is not straightforward and "you are never going to get to that target set of skills unless teachers are very, very deeply involved with specifying what's important about teaching and with helping you interpret your data."

Lloyd Bond also raised validity concerns that he confronted as part of the NBPTS effort: "How can you come with an assessment and a score that can be validly applied to a teacher in small-town Iowa and [one] in a city like Detroit? How do you do that? It's an enormously difficult task, and it begs a profound question: Is there a deep structure to the teaching profession? Are there principles that ignore surface features? Hell, I don't know, but I actually think there are."

Joan Baratz-Snowden framed the same issue in a slightly different manner by comparing methods for evaluating other professions, again drawing on a medical metaphor. She spoke of examining physician quality through the appropriate application of established protocols even though they may manifest differently in different medical contexts with different resources available. By identifying core principles, she hopes that "we can know how protocols are manifest in different settings, instead of needing protocols for every setting."

Yet the principles that Bond posited have been difficult to empirically support in research efforts, possibly due to the role of context and the insufficiency of analytic models to address its impact. Kenji Hakuta captured the tension: "In behavioral sciences especially, context is used as kind of error variance; it's one thing that you can't explain once you've considered other factors and everything is left over—well, it's context. Then the sociologist comes along and says, no, you really have the figure and ground reversed. You really need to think about context as driving the things that happen."

So part of what may be happening is that our analytic models are attempting to detect a consistent signal in an exceedingly noisy environment. And the fact that weak signals are often detected does not necessarily mean that the signal is weak, only that the other noise is so overwhelming. An alarm clock just does not sound loud in the subway.

This contextual complexity does not imply that one cannot study teaching in a principled way, but that it needs to be done with extreme care and modesty. Baratz-Snowden heeded Einstein's wisdom that "not everything that counts can be counted and not everything that can be counted counts," but urged the field to move forward "on the things we can get a handle on now, as discussed by Deborah Ball, and use outcomes to go to those kinds of things that Arturo Pacheco was talking about with civic values and beyond simple and limited tests."

RESOLVING THE METHODOLOGICAL ISSUES

The context–SUTVA dilemma may also be at the root of many methodological limitations that are being raised in evaluating a variety of value-added methodologies (e.g., Braun, 2005; McCaffrey, Lockwood, Koretz, & Hamilton, 2003) and may contribute to the weakness of teacher effectiveness findings more broadly. Although all sorts of statistical procedures are designed as attempts to control for some of these context effects, they appear to be inadequate in light of the complex nature of contextual interactions inherent in teaching and highlighted by all of the papers and commentaries. Hong and Raudenbush (2008) have attempted to address at least some of these shortcomings in educational research more generally, but these methods have not been generally applied to the study of teaching.

How the field confronts the context–SUTVA dilemma has important consequences for policy decisions that arise out of teacher effectiveness research. On the one hand, methods have been developed that require a given set of assumptions. These assumptions are necessary to garner the statistical power needed when making inferential comparisons. Without SUTVA, analytic methods that require a sufficient number of replicates of some educational treatment are not viable. Yet there is every reason to believe that the key SUTVA assumptions are not valid for policy-related studies of teaching. By developing ever more sophisticated procedures to smooth out the "noise" of context from teacher effectiveness, we may in fact be eliminating the factors that are most critical to teacher effectiveness.

A Closing Comment

Of course, all metaphors are imperfect, and most statistical assumptions are violated to some extent for much of educational research. For example, some analytic methods require assumptions that the population is normally distributed with respect to a particular variable. Research generally does not require that assumptions are met perfectly, nor is it necessary that the pharmaceutical and educational studies can be equated on all dimensions that serve the metaphor. Nevertheless, there comes a point at which the key assumptions and metaphorical premises are violated to such an extent that the methods are no longer appropriate. Given the compelling discussions of context we heard throughout this conference, I believe that we will find the currently popular and dominant analytic models for examining teaching to be viewed as increasingly unsatisfactory.

It appears possible to improve on the application of current analytic methods in order to reduce SUTVA discrepancies. However this will be an expensive proposition because such studies require far more attention to the consistency of the treatment within a condition. Examining effects on groups that are more consistent with respect to a particular set of educational characteristics (e.g., difficulty with reading comprehension) will also allow for more focused studies and more focused measures of impact. However, such studies imply that simply using available achievement tests will have limited utility.

But even these studies, no matter how many resources are available, will, in the end, be of limited use because they are not designed to illuminate the nature of teaching and how teaching can be improved. Although there may continue to be a place for such studies in serving some piece of the accountability puzzle, they will be of limited use in informing educational policy.

If we are to use metaphors to guide a new generation of educational research, then we need to take those metaphors seriously and see where they do and do not apply. If we are to use analytic methods that violate key assumptions of the phenomenon being studied, then we should not be surprised if we do not find overwhelming evidence of the effect of particular educational interventions. In the pursuit of developing a rigorous and scientific approach to the study of teaching, we will need to continue to grapple with the complexity of the phenomena of teaching and all of its messy context. For as Kenji Hakuta noted, we do very different work if we treat the context not as noise, but as an inseparable part of teaching activity.

Note

1. I would like to thank Joan Baratz-Snowden for helpful comments on this chapter.

References

Bennett, R. E., & Gitomer, D. H. (in press). Transforming K–12 assessment. In C. Wyatt-Smith & J. Cumming (Eds.), *Assessment issues of the 21st century*. New York: Springer.

Berk, R. (2005). *Randomized experiments as the bronze standard* (Paper 20050800201). Los Angeles: University of California, Los Angeles, Department of Statistics. Retrieved March 24, 2008, from http://reposito ries.cdlib.org/cgi/viewcontent.cgi?article=1019&context=uclastat

Braun, H. I. (2005). *Using student progress to evaluate teachers: A primer on value-added models* (Policy Information Center Report No. 730194). Princeton, NJ: Educational Testing Service.

Clotfelter, C. T., Ladd H. F., & Vigdor, J. L. (2007). *Teacher credentials and student achievement in high school: A cross-subject analysis with student fixed effects* (Working Paper No. 11). Retrieved March 24, 2008, from http://www.calder center.org/PDF/1001104_Teacher_ Credentials_HighSchool.pdf

Cochran-Smith, M., &. Zeichner, K. M. (Eds.). (2005). *Studying teacher education: The report of the AERA panel on research and teacher education.* Mahwah, NJ: Lawrence Erlbaum.

Decker, P. T., Mayer, D. P., & Glazerman, S. (2004). *The effects of Teach For America on students: Findings from a national evaluation.* Princeton, NJ: Mathematica Policy Research. Retrieved March 24, 2008, from http://www.mathematica-mpr.com/publications/pdfs/teach.pdf

Feuer, M., Holland, P. W., Green, B. F., Bertenthal, M. W., & Hemphill, F. C. (Eds.). (1999). *Uncommon measures: Equivalence and linkage among educational tests.* Washington, DC: National Academy Press.

Goldhaber, D. (2007). *Everybody's doing it, but what does teacher testing tell us about teacher effectiveness* (Working Paper No. 9). Retrieved March 24, 2007, from http://www.caldercenter.org/PDF/1001072_everyones_doing.PDF

Hanushek, E. A., & Rivkin, S. G. (2006). *School quality and the black-white achievement gap* (NBER Working Paper No. 12651). Cambridge, MA: National Bureau of Economic Research.

Hong, G., & Raudenbush, S. W. (2006). Evaluating kindergarten retention policy: A case study of casual inference for multi-level observational data. *Journal of the American Statistical Association, 101,* 901–910.

Hong, G., & Raudenbush, S. W. (2008). Causal inference for time-varying instructional treatments. *Journal of Educational and Behavioral Statistics.* Available from http://jeb.sagepub.com/cgi/content/abstract/1076998607307355v1

McCaffrey, D. F., Lockwood, J. R., Koretz, D. M., & Hamilton, L. S. (2003). *Evaluating value-added models for teacher accountability.* Santa Monica, CA: RAND.

Raudenbush, S. W. (2008). Advancing educational policy by advancing research on instruction. *American Educational Research Journal, 45,* 206–230.

Rothstein, R. (2004). *Class and schools: Using social, economic, and educational reform to close the achievement gap.* Washington, DC: Economic Policy Institute.

Rubin, D. B. (1986). Statistics and causal inference: Comment: Which ifs have causal answers? *Journal of the American Statistical Association, 81,* 961–962.

Rubin, D. B. (1990). Formal modes of statistical inference for causal effects. *Journal of Statistical Planning and Inference, 25,* 279–292.

Sanders, W. L., Saxton, A. M., & Horn, S. P. (1997). The Tennessee value-added assessment system, a quantitative, outcomes-based approach to educational measurement. In J. Millman (Ed.), *Grading teachers, grading schools: Is student achievement a valid evaluation measure?* (pp. 137–162). Thousand Oaks, CA: Corwin Press.

Schmidt, W. H., Houang, R. T., & McKnight, C. C. (2005). Value-added research: Right idea but wrong solution? In R. Lissitz (Ed.), *Value-added models in education: Theory and applications* (pp. 272–297). Maple Grove, MN: JAM Press.

Whitehurst, G. J. (2003, April). *The institute of education sciences: New wine, new bottles.* Paper presented at the Annual Meeting of the American Educational Research Association, Chicago. Retrieved March 24, 2008, from http://www.eric.ed.gov/ERICDocs/data/ericdocs2sql/content_stor age_01/0000019b/80/1b/42/99.pdf

Assessment *of* Teaching or Assessment *for* Teaching?

Reflections on the Invitational Conference

Lee S. Shulman

The Carnegie Foundation for the Advancement of Teaching

How can anyone attempt to offer an adequate synthesis of this rich, varied, and often contradictory conference? Assessment has never been a hotter topic, and the quality of teaching has rarely attracted so much attention. Thus the intersection of assessment and teacher quality is necessarily both a contested and a challenging corner of the educational world. I therefore offer a set of reflections on the conference, thoughts stimulated by a number of the papers that were delivered, and memories of the history of this field in which I have been engaged for more than a quarter century, triggered by discussions at the conference.

Twenty years ago, I gave a plenary presentation to the 1988 ETS Invitational Conference on testing devoted to the topic New Directions for Teacher Assessment. Does that sound vaguely familiar? We were then deeply engaged with the development and testing of the forms of teacher assessment that would become the National Board for Professional Teaching Standards. My paper was titled "The Paradox of Teacher Assessment" (L. S. Shulman, 1989). Although the particular contradictions may have changed somewhat, the condition of paradox continues two decades later.

At that time, the paradox was that the quality of teaching was powerfully domain and context specific, while the assessment of its quality continued to emphasize what was generic and context free. Those of us engaged in research in the field, and in the development of new forms of assessment, emphasized the complexity of domains and settings, and of rich and complex task environments that we designed into new types of exercises. Those responsible for deploying tests of teachers that could be administered to thousands of candidates across all fifty states in a low-cost, efficient manner were skeptical of the much more elaborate, labor-intensive approaches that we innovators were advocating. I still recall Carol Dwyer characterizing the immense difference between developing an experimental assessment to field test with several dozen simulated candidates with the reality of preparing and administering the National Teachers Examination (NTE). She reminded me that Ginger Rogers had to match every dance move Fred Astaire so effortlessly produced, but backwards and in high heels!

The central feature of this 2007 conference was also the inescapability of its inherent contradictions. On the one hand, beginning with Suzanne Wilson's powerful opening paper, we were presented with new data and arguments that once again emphasized the fundamental complexity, contextuality, and domain specificity of teaching, and hence the impossibility of understanding its quality or its impact at the individual or aggregate levels without appreciating and taking account of that richness. Deborah Ball and Heather Hill illustrated those principles with vivid examples from the teaching of elementary mathematics. Arturo Pacheco described the power of context in determining teacher quality, a perspective strongly supported by Gloria Ladson-Billings. On the other hand, we heard a number of presentations that offered newer approaches to the assessment of teaching quality that fall broadly under the rubric of value-added and have attracted a great deal of attention, especially within the policy community. These approaches "work" by exercising remarkable acts of simplification, acts of either audacity or faith that call on educators and policymakers to suspend disbelief in quite significant ways in order to achieve powerful forms of quality assessment. Doug Harris was particularly helpful in candidly discussing both the virtues and the liabilities of value-added models and the purposes for which they might be more and less legitimately employed.

On the one hand, we were told that teaching quality could only be understood, much less assessed, through confronting its inherent complexities. On the other hand, we are in an era when the assessment of teacher quality is being led by a set of approaches that work primarily through simplification. How do we manage those contradictory messages?

They Can't All Be Right

I was reminded of an old story of the rabbi who was sitting in his study when two men came before him, each holding one leg of a worse-for-wear chicken. The first man said, "This is my chicken," and offered his argument. And the rabbi said, "You know, you're right, that's certainly your chicken." And the second fellow said, "Not so fast," and he gave his argument. And the rabbi said, "You know, you're right, that's clearly your chicken." Meanwhile the rabbi's very wise wife was watching the proceedings and whispered quietly to him, "Rabbi, you know, they can't both be right." He looked up and said, "You know, you're right also."

On this occasion, it's hard for all of the speakers to be right. Can the chicken of teacher quality indeed be both complex and simple, both utterly context specific and broadly generic? I agree with Gloria Ladson-Billings when she reminds us that we have been at this question for quite a while, and there is no basis for insisting that we don't know anything. We do know that every time you add a layer of complexity, the analyses and evaluations can change dramatically. Even if many of the new statistical models elect to ignore these variations, those of us engaged in policy and practice cannot afford to do the same. Nor can we avoid the consequences of such ignorance (a word that has the same etymological root as *ignore*) by rapidly repeating the mantra *ceteris paribus*—all other things being equal.

What Economists Have Wrought: A Cacophony of Counterfactuals?

I don't want to pick on economists. Some of my best friends are economists. But economists thoroughly dominate the field of policy studies of teacher quality these days, and their analyses are too often accepted without raising needed critical questions. That's why I so appreciated Doug Harris's candor and openness as he reviewed all of the premises that are built into the value-added models and where he felt the models worked most and least effectively.

He carefully distinguished between two quite different uses of the increasingly popular value-added models—to evaluate educational programs such as teacher education and professional development and to evaluate individual teachers and their quality. These are distinctly different uses, he emphasizes, and should not be confused with one another. But as he reviewed the assumptions underlying each of those uses, it became increasingly clear that these models require that those who employ them accept a troubling variety of premises. These premises pertain to the assignment of teachers to classes, the patterns of effects that teachers can have on pupil learning, and the extent to which circumstances in which neither students nor teachers have been randomly assigned to settings or to one another can be appropriately analyzed *as if* those conditions did not matter. As these premises were articulated, I became increasingly aware of how significant they are. Indeed, in many cases the premises are distinctly counterfactual, that is, those who understand the complexities of teaching and learning know that the premises are patently false. All else is not equal.

In these value-added models we confront a cacophony of counterfactuals. The faltering logic comes in a number of forms. First, as discussed earlier, the indicators that are used both to define the teacher's characteristics and to measure the teacher's impact on student learning are subject to serious questions. They are, at best, proxies at both the independent and dependent variable ends. Indeed, as if the standardized tests were not sufficiently questionable as reflections of achievement, the analyses of change, replete with corrections for initial differences and measurement unreliability, as well as the needed premises about equal impact of teachers across all students are seriously deficient. The uses of these models run up against the messages of the other papers presented at the conference. They work only by ignoring the complexities so vividly portrayed by our other colleagues. It is as if we were building a new Golden Gate Bridge, with each end anchored in unsettled ground and with a suspension system of questionable stability connecting San Francisco and Marin County.

A few days after I originally offered these remarks to the conference attendees, I received an e-mail from Heather Hill and Steve Schilling, who were completing a careful critical review of value-added models. In their paper (Hill & Schilling, 2007), they argued that these models function like high-stakes teacher tests and therefore should be evaluated from the perspective of the standards for educational and psychological testing. They observe that "the reliability of the teacher estimates is low (between .3 and .5) and the validity evidence is nearly non-existent." Their conclusion, after conducting a much more careful analysis than I have and an extensively detailed set of critiques, is unambiguous: "Based on the evidence, one might say that VAM [value-added] models estimate teacher effects, not teacher effectiveness or quality. Alternatively, one may say that these models estimate teacher effectiveness or quality, but quite poorly" (Hill & Schilling, 2007).

We have to take the rabbi's wife seriously here. I have come to the conclusion that we should stop investing so heavily at this point in more large policy studies of value-added models. We should continue only those studies that combine large-scale longitudinal data analysis with careful qualitative analyses of the conditions of teacher preparation and professional development and of student learning, such as those employed in the work that Pam Grossman and Susanna Loeb pursue. But the "black box" studies just are not moving us very far. With limited funding for education research, I don't think that multiplying the number of value-added studies will be helpful. Without the qualitative element, they tend to provide not-so-precise estimates of teacher failure, but not add to the promotion of quality for all students in all settings. Assessment is a powerful tool for raising the quality of teaching and learning. It should be used diagnostically and interactively, not as a form of autopsy. To put it another way, we have to stop thinking of what we're doing as, if you will, the retrospective assessment *of* teaching quality, and replace it with the notion of assessment *for* teaching quality. It's a very small grammatical change, but represents a huge difference in how we invest our time and energy.

Neither Economists nor Other Professions Use These on Themselves

How seriously do economists themselves take the importance of value-added approaches for evaluating the quality of teaching or teachers in their own field? Do you know a single economist who in his or her academic economics department uses a value-added model for determining which teachers of economics ought to be promoted and given salary raises? Have you seen a value-added analysis of economics teaching that has become the basis for curriculum revision at the undergraduate or graduate level? I haven't. I hold to a principle I learned many years ago: to distrust people who give you all kinds of very firm advice about how to run your life but are not prepared to apply the same advice to themselves.

I have been studying the education of professionals for forty years, especially education in the teaching and medical professions. It is quite striking that no profession other than teaching has attempted to conduct the kinds of studies that relate either the characteristics of training programs or individual characteristics of practitioners to client outcomes. In that context, they have certainly not attempted to study the value-added that can be attributed to type or amount of training, individual certification test scores, or the like. There are a number of reasons for this lack of interest or initiative. First, teaching is among the few learned professions that, although it requires general baccalaureate academic preparation, nevertheless permits college graduates to practice without professional training through the use of alternate routes or emergency credentials. This cannot happen for nursing or engineering among the undergraduate professions, nor for law or medicine among the postbaccalaureate professions. Therefore, there are really no ways to form comparison groups for studies that contrast those who are professionally prepared with those who are not in other professions.

Even more critical, it is quite unclear what would serve as the dependent variables in such studies. Would we use morbidity and mortality data for medicine or nursing? Bridge collapses and houses that fail inspection in engineering? Congregants who live pious lives versus those who backslide in the ministry? Although the use of changes in standardized achievement test scores has long been criticized in teacher effectiveness studies—in spite of the myriad forms of statistical correction for initial differences, unreliability, and noncomparability of experiences—educational researchers continue to employ such approaches in value-added studies of teacher effects.

Nevertheless, although not a single one of the professions that we at Carnegie have been studying over the past decade—law, engineering, the clergy, nursing, and medicine—has had the courage to take on the kind of predictive validity questions that we're wrestling with in teaching, it is laudable that we persevere. Are we having a hard time figuring out how to do that? You bet we are. But we're the only folks who are trying, and we ought to take pride in that.

Studies of Teacher Quality for National Board Certification and Beyond

It's important to recognize that serious work on the measurement and evaluation of teacher quality has been underway for many years. In the early 1980s, a group of us at Stanford University began the Teacher Assessment Project (L. S. Shulman, 1987), which led to the testing strategies now employed by the National Board for Professional Teaching Standards. The group that worked on that project is well represented in this volume, and its members are among the conference participants. Suzanne Wilson was the first project director of that study while still working on her PhD. Mary Kay Stein was a postdoc in mathematics education at the University of Pittsburgh with Gaea Leinhardt and collaborated on the original *wisdom of practice* studies and on designing the prototypes for the elementary mathematics exercises. Pam Grossman led the effort to organize our earlier studies of pedagogical content knowledge so that we could apply them intelligently to designing and making sense of the wisdom of practice studies of exemplary practitioners. Another graduate student, Deborah Ball, came from Michigan State University to evaluate how appropriately we had designed the mathematics tasks for teachers. A youthful reporter from a new periodical called *Education Week*, Lynn Olson, wrote a series of magnificent, detailed, and utterly accurate stories about the assessment development process that helped pave the way for its acceptance in the policy community. Gloria Ladson-Billings chaired a working group to help us examine the extent to which we were adequately addressing variations in context and background of teachers who would be the candidates. The policy board for the entire project was chaired by a researcher from RAND, Linda Darling-Hammond.

And Lee Cronbach came out of retirement. Yes, the Zeus of psychometrics agreed to work in tandem with Ed Haertel and the rest of our team on the psychometric quality of our assessments. He agreed to work with us on one condition, and I think Cronbach's principle is a powerful reminder of the priorities that should drive our current and future work in this field. He said, "I will work with this project on the condition that you first ask what kinds of assessments will be most faithful to your understandings of teaching and learning, and are likely to be of greatest value to the field. And then my job will be to figure out how to make them psychometrically viable. The moment I see you corrupting what you're doing to fit some psychometric principle or practice is the day I go back into retirement. We cannot permit the methodological tail to wag the dog of good pedagogical practice" (L. Cronbach, personal communication, 1985). And he never had to go back into retirement.

What we attempted to do in conjunction with the invention of the National Board isn't a bad model for thinking about some of the challenges we've been discussing at this conference. As Gloria Ladson-Billings pointed out, we didn't develop a one-size-fits-all model. We proposed to the then newborn Board that there not be one Board certificate but separate assessments by students' age level and by subject matter. Joan Baratz-Snowden was directing that aspect of the work from the Board perspective at that time. The first generation of assessments we developed involved four full days of performance simulations. We took over an entire school as our assessment center. We practically ran a day camp so that we could organize kids into simulated classes for teachers to teach. We worked out a lot of the psychometric problems on the fly with the guidance of Cronbach, Haertel, Bob Calfee, and others.

In the summer of 1987, when we finished the first complete field test of assessments in the teaching of elementary mathematics and secondary history, we felt we had invented the most comprehensive and highest-fidelity teaching assessment ever attempted. But we also concluded that this marvelous assessment was fatally flawed. Although it took account of students and subject matter, it ignored the critical role of context, and without context there can be no valid assessment of teacher quality.

So we started all over again and invented something called a portfolio-based assessment. Assessment "shells" could be extracted from the generic context of a simulated assessment center and rolled out in the specific setting of a teacher's actual classroom, documented and analyzed in a teaching portfolio, and submitted for peer review by teaching peers prepared to function as well-trained raters.

We purposely brought teachers from inner-city Philadelphia as well as Palo Alto, from rural areas as well as urban, because we were trying to adapt to the multiplicity of ways that teachers were employing informed professional judgment to adapt their teaching to the students and communities for whom they taught. The new generation of portfolio-based assessments, to be complemented by more traditional forms of examination, remained imperfect. Nevertheless, they moved us closer to our goal of creating assessments with as much respect for teaching's complexity and subtlety as was possible, while still preserving our capacity to rate and score those performances in a fair and reliable manner. Most important, we committed ourselves to the principle that this assessment would have *consequential validity*, that is, it would contribute to improving the quality of the performances and professional practitioners it was designed to assess.

Assessment *Of* and Assessment *For*

Our goal was not just to develop a great test. Our goal was not only—and this created some problems—an assessment *of* teaching quality. Our goal was also to create an assessment *for* teaching quality. The idea was to create a form of assessment in which the very experience of preparing to do the assessment—and our contrast case was a Stanley Kaplan approach to test coaching—the very act of preparing for and engaging in assessment would be a powerful form of professional development. Some measurement specialists had warned us that portfolios would never work because "teachers will cheat." I said, "What counts as cheating?" And they said, "They'll talk to each other and coach one another in preparing their portfolios." I responded, "Hallelujah. You are complaining that teachers are likely to learn from one another while preparing for the assessment."

Instead of trying to prevent that kind of teacher-to-teacher communication, we built in the expectation that teachers would form support groups and coach each other, watch each other's videotapes, and critique one another's entries. It created just the sorts of dilemmas that Cronbach had predicted. It created psychometric problems that were later addressed by Lloyd Bond, Dick Jaeger, and their colleagues in North Carolina who comprised the Board's technical advisory group (Jaeger, 1998). It created conceptual problems that were analyzed by Sam Wineburg (1997) in an essay comparing peer-coached portfolio development to T. S. Eliot's composition of *The Wasteland* with extensive coaching and editing from Ezra Pound. The approach created ethical problems of the sort that Judy Shulman and Mistilina Sato (2006) have captured in a new book, *Mentoring Teachers Toward Excellence,* because some folks just didn't understand the boundary between legitimate coaching and doing someone else's work for them. But that's a problem that every dissertation director has faced on countless occasions.

These are not insurmountable problems, only stimulating challenges and opportunities for new learning. I take great pride in the fact that, if you look at the world of teaching in the United States over the past twenty years, a large number of teacher preparation programs, both undergraduate and graduate, now use the National Board Standards as a curriculum framework, and those standards are much more enlightened than anything that we had then or would have had now. They have influenced accreditation by the National Council for Accreditation of Teacher Education, Interstate New Teacher Assessment and Support Consortium state licensure standards, and the almost universal use of teaching portfolios in teacher preparation and induction programs. The California PACT (Pecheone & Chung, 2006) assessment that Linda Darling-Hammond described, as well as ETS's own version of a similar assessment for California, shows the fingerprints and the DNA of the Teacher Assessment Project and the National Board. They are designed to serve not only as an assessment of but also an assessment for teacher quality.

With the splendid irony that so often accompanies such developments, ETS rapidly moved from its earlier role as the personification of everything teacher assessment had to escape—context-free multiple-choice tests of teaching such as the NTE—to serving as the prime contractor for the Board and contributing significantly to the refinement of the vision of portfolio-based assessment of professional competence under the leadership of Mari Pearlman and Drew Gitomer.

The Gordon Rule

I close with one final observation. Last June we had a conference on assessment, which my colleagues at ETS hosted in honor of the Carnegie Foundation's one hundredth anniversary. The Carnegie Foundation had been one of the three institutions that gave birth to ETS in 1948, contributing to the new institution a little housewarming gift called the Graduate Record Examination, which Carnegie scholar William Learned and colleagues had developed over the previous two decades. I was invited to close that conference (I'm beginning to feel typecast) and built my remarks around the notion of *a union of insufficiencies*. It was a concept that I had originally introduced when we were doing the teacher assessment work in 1987. The central idea was that all assessment instruments were inherently insufficient, flawed in principle. If an assessment were designed to be highly context specific, then it would be less valid in measuring the extent to which the candidate could generalize his or her performance to other settings. If it were too generic, it would have other limitations of the sort discussed earlier. Therefore, the ideal strategy of assessment for teacher quality was to construct a suite of assessments, each insufficient but approaching sufficiency in aggregate as the various instruments complemented one another's weaknesses. At the centennial conference I reiterated that principle and added new examples of its applicability to a number of problems.

Ed Gordon, my old and dear friend, responded to my remarks. His response was critical and persuasive. I now refer to the principle underlying his comments as the Gordon Rule. He asserted that the notion of a union of insufficiencies may be attractive, even seductive. But keep in mind, he warned, that if you simply add together a lot of insufficiencies, what you may well achieve is one great big insufficiency. Moreover, some kinds of tests do not merely measure imperfectly; they may actually do harm to the opportunities of some students in ways that are not likely to be compensated by other instruments. Why continue to believe that the existing building blocks, some of which are not only insufficient but even counterproductive, can magically be assembled into something worthwhile? That's the Gordon Rule. We heard versions of it from a number of the speakers at this meeting. We heard about the many faces of quality, among both teachers and assessments of teaching, and some of the dangers we confront when quality is absent. The message is quite simple: Identify different forms and approaches to the assessment of teacher quality that are individually excellent, even if not wholly comprehensive. Do no harm if it can possibly be avoided. Build assessments that will be educative for those who prepare for and undertake them. And if the approaches proposed employ assumptions that are simply untenable, don't remain quiet.

I'm reminded of one of my late mother's favorite Yiddish phrases. There are times, she would tell me, when you know something is the case but you shouldn't let on. These are occasions when it is best to pretend that you don't know that someone is seriously ill, or that their marriage is on the rocks, or that their business is failing, or that their hair has thinned considerably. Just pretend you don't know. In Yiddish, that phrase is *machen zich nisht visindig:* making yourself (as if) not knowing. But my mom also stressed that a wise person understands the difference between occasions when that rule held and others when feigned ignorance was unwarranted. With respect to the misuses of value-added and similar forms of quality assessment whose uses may be unwarranted and even misleading, we can no longer justify *machen zich nisht visindig.*

That's where I conclude. We have recognized during this conference, through combining both the insights and the caveats offered by our speakers, that a multifaceted and rich sense of what it would take to assess teaching quality in a responsible manner is within our grasp. In measurement, some simplifications are unavoidable, but finding a judicious blend of simple and complex is within our reach. We've got to allocate the necessary resources to mount a national effort to do this kind of work, an effort that will coordinate the enlightened measurement of learning with a sensible assessment of teaching. I think we're up to it.

References

Hill, H. C., & Schilling, S. G. (2007). *Evaluating value-added models: A measurement perspective.* Manuscript submitted for publication.

Jaeger, R. M. (1998). Evaluating the psychometric qualities of the National Board for Professional Teaching Standards. *Journal of Personnel Evaluation in Education, 12,* 189–210.

Pecheone, R. L., & Chung, R. R. (2006). Evidence in teacher education. *Journal of Teacher Education, 57,* 22–36.

Shulman, J. H., & Sato, M. (Eds.). (2006). *Mentoring teachers toward excellence: Supporting and developing highly qualified teachers.* San Francisco: Jossey-Bass.

Shulman, L. S. (1987). Assessment for teaching: An initiative for the profession. *Phi Delta Kappan, 69,* 38–44.

Shulman, L. S. (1989). The paradox of teacher assessment. In J. Pfleiderer (Ed.), *New directions for teacher assessment: Invitational conference proceedings* (pp. 13–27). Princeton, NJ: Educational Testing Service.

Wineburg, S. (1997). T. S. Eliot, collaboration, and the quandaries of assessment in a rapidly changing world. *Phi Delta Kappan, 79,* 59–65.

Author Index

Allen, M., 11, 19
Alonzo, A. A., 95
Anagnostopoulos, D., 185
Anderson, D. J., 84
Anthony, E., 112
Apple, M. W., 212
Arbaugh, F., 190
Aschbacher, P. R., 190

Bacolod, M., 80
Baker, E. L., 21
Balfanz, R., 31
Ball, D. B., 20
Ball, D. L., 15, 20, 80, 83, 90, 180, 184, 190
Barber, B., 176
Barth, P., 20
Bass, H., 15
Beals, M. P., 214
Beck, I. L., 191
Berk, R., 227
Berns, B. B., 180
Berry, B., 15
Bertenthal, M. W., 226
Bestor, A. E., 8
Betts, J. R., 115
Black, P., 190, 192
Blunk, M., 90
Boardman, A. E., 106
Bok, D., 53
Booher-Jennings, J., 100
Borko, H., 17, 95, 184
Borman, G., 86

Boston, M., 197
Boyd, D. J., 14, 24, 43–44
Bradshaw, D., 24
Bransford, J. D., 11, 16, 181
Braun, H. I., 230
Brewer, D. J., 15, 84, 100
Brown, A. L., 181
Brown, C., 190
Brown, J. S., 21, 184
Bryk, A. S., 190
Burant, T. J., 17
Burney, D., 49–50, 52
Burns, S., 30
Burstein, L., 183

Chiang, R., 85
Chubbuck, S. M., 17
Chung, R. R., 60, 242
Clare, L., 190–191
Clotfelter, C. T., 95, 112, 224
Cochran-Smith, M., 8, 11, 16, 175,
        218, 224
Cocking, R. R., 181
Cohen, D. K., 18–19, 58–59, 180, 184, 190
Coker, H., 114
Cole, M., 187
Coleman, J., 113, 116
Collins, A. M., 21, 184
Conant, J. B., 8
Corcoran, S. P., 80
Correnti, R., 84
Crenshaw, K., 214

Cronbach, L., 240
Cronin, J., 179

Danielson, C., 17, 185, 197
Darling-Hammond, L., 11, 15–16, 217
Day, T., 49, 52
Dean, C., 90
DeArmond, M., 80
Decker, P. T., 223
Delpit, L., 217
Desimone, L. M., 179
Dewey, J., 15
Diez, M. E., 71
Dolton, P., 80
Doyle, W., 192, 196
Duguid, P., 21, 184
Dunbar, S. B., 21

Edwards, V. B., 30
Eisner, E., 212
Elmore, R. F., 48, 58–59, 207
Evans, W. N., 80

Feinman-Nemser, S., 17, 80
Fenstermacher, G., 169
Ferguson, R. F., 80
Ferrini-Mundy, J., 11
Fetler, M., 15
Feuer, M., 226
Figlio, D., 100
Flexner, A., 53
Floden, R. F., 11, 15, 125n6
Freire, P., 164
Fries, M. K., 8
Fuhrman, S. H., 207
Fullilove, R. E., 217

Gagne, R. M., 181
Gallimore, R., 181, 184, 191, 197
Garcia, G. E., 180
Garvin, D. A., 49, 53
Glaser, D., 16
Glazerman, S., 223
Goffney, I. M., 90
Goldhaber, D. D., 15, 80, 84, 100, 112, 224
Goodlad, J., 169, 176
Gordon, R., 101, 124
Granier, H., 190

Gray, D., 31
Green, B. F., 226
Green, T. F., 160
Greeno, J. G., 184
Greenwald, R., 125n2
Grossman, P. L., 8, 15, 43
Grover, B. W., 189
Grymes, J., 207

Haberman, M., 175–176
Hamilton, L. S., 18, 95,
    179, 185, 199, 230
Hamilton, R. L., 191
Haney, W. M., 214
Hanushek, E. A., 31, 85, 100, 106, 113,
    163–164, 173–174, 218, 224
Harbison, R. W., 85
Hargreaves, A., 180
Harris, D. N., 99–101, 105–106,
    109–110, 112, 114, 116, 118,
    123–124, 127n14
Hauser, C., 179
Haycock, K., 31
Hedberg, B., 18
Hedges, L. V., 86, 125n2
Helsing, D., 21
Hemphill, F. C., 226
Henningsen, M. A., 189, 196
Herrington, C., 99
Hess, F. M., 179, 185
Hiebert, J., 52, 196
Hill, H. C., 15, 20, 80, 83–85, 90–91,
    95, 189, 237
Hoffman, L., 31
Holland, P. W., 226
Hong, G., 227, 230
Horn, S. P., 113, 225
Houang, R. T., 179
Houser, R., 179
Hu, S., 20
Hull, C. L., 181
Hume, D., 19

Ingersoll, R. M., 80, 210
Ingle, W., 100, 124, 127n14

Jackson, P., 21
Jacob, B. A., 114, 123

Jaeger, R. M., 241
Jones, K. E., 20
Joyce, B., 184

Kahlenberg, R. D., 53
Kain, J. F., 31, 113, 218
Kane, M. B., 21
Kane, T. J., 43, 84, 101, 115
Kimball, S. M., 86
Kingsbury, G. G., 179, 185
Knapp, M. S., 191
Knowles, K. T., 10
Koedel, C., 115
Koerner, J. S., 8
Konstantopoulos, S., 86
Koretz, D. M., 18, 95, 179, 185, 230
Kozol, J., 175, 211, 214
Kucan, L., 191
Kuh, G., 20
Kupermintz, H., 95

Labaree, D., 122
Ladd, H. F., 95, 112, 224
Ladson-Billings, G., 175–176,
    217, 220
Laine, R., 125n2
Lampert, M., 21
Lane, S., 196
Lanier, J., 183
Lankford, H., 43–44
Lave, J., 184, 187
Lefgren, L., 114, 123
Legters, N., 31
Levin, H., 119
Levin, J., 33
Levine, A., 100
Linn, R. L., 21, 179, 185
Lippman, L., 30
Liston, D., 17
Little, J. W., 183
Littlefield, V., 215
Liu, A., 80
Lockwood, J. R., 18, 95, 179, 230
Loeb, S., 43, 48, 80
Loewenberg Ball, D., 58
Lopez, G., 190
Lortie, D., 183–184
Lubienski, S., 15

Lynd, A., 8
Lyons, R., 214

Ma, L., 15
Madaus, G. R., 214
Matsumura, L. C., 189–191, 197
Mayer, D. P., 223
McArthur, E., 30
McCaffrey, D. F., 18, 95, 179, 230
McClam, S., 95
McEwan, P., 119
McGreal, T. L., 185, 197
McKeown, M. G., 191
McKnight, C. C., 179
McLaughlin, M., 185
McMannon, T. J., 176
McSpirit, S., 20
Medina, J., 43
Medley, D. M., 114
Meniketti, M., 15
Metzger, S., 11
Mewborn, D., 15
Midgley, M., 160, 173–174
Milanowski, A. T., 86, 114
Miller, L., 48
Miller, R. J., 84–85
Mitchell, K. J., 10
Mitchell, R., 20–21
Moncure, S., 95
Monk, D. H., 15
Mulhern, J., 33
Mullens, J. E., 85
Murnane, R. J., 85, 106, 114

Nagaoka, J. K., 190
Naum, J., 31
Nelson, B., 198
Newmann, F. M., 190–191
Noell, G. H., 24
Nye, B., 86

Ogbu, J. U., 114
Olson, A., 179

Pascal, J., 190
Pasley, J. D., 196
Patthey-Chavez, G. G., 191
Pecheone, R. L., 60, 242

Peck, R., 183
Peske, H. G., 31
Peterson, K. D., 114
Peterson, P. E., 179, 185
Plake, B. S., 10
Player, D., 80
Provasnik, S., 31
Putnam, R. T., 184

Quinn, M., 33

Raudenbush, S. W., 20, 58, 95, 227, 230
Reininger, M., 80
Resnick, L., 184
Richardson, V., 169, 181, 199
Rivkin, S. G., 31, 113, 218, 224
Robinson, D. Z., 10
Rockoff, J. E., 43, 84
Rogoff, B., 184, 187
Roosevelt, D., 181
Rose, M., 176
Rosenshine, B., 183
Rothstein, R., 206, 224
Rowan, B., 20, 80, 84–85, 90
Rubin, D. B., 228
Rutledge, S., 100, 112, 124, 127n14

Sable, J., 31
Sanders, W. L., 113, 225
Sandy, M. V., 55, 58, 61
Sarason, S. B., 169
Sass, T., 101, 105–106, 109–110, 112,
    114, 123, 127n14
Sato, M., 241
Saxton, A. M., 225
Schilling, S. G., 95, 237
Schmidt, W. H., 179
Schunck, J., 33
Schwab, R. M., 80
Sedlak, M., 16
Sentilles, S., 211
Shavelson, R. J., 183
Shepard, L., 179, 181
Shields, P. M., 191
Showers, B., 184
Shulman, J. H., 241
Shulman, L. S., 11, 15, 173, 183,
    185, 215, 218, 234, 239

Silver, E. A., 190, 196
Skinner, B. F., 181
Smith, M. S., 196
Smith, T. M., 80
Smith, T. S., 179
Snow, C., 180, 190
Spillane, J. P., 180
Staiger, D. O., 43, 84, 101, 115
Starbuck, W. H., 18
Stecher, B., 95
Stein, M. K., 189–190,
    196–198
Stevens, F. I., 207
Stevens, R., 183
Stigler, J. W., 52
Stipek, D., 52
Swanson, J., 180

Talbert, J., 185
Tamir, E., 8, 11
Tharp, R. G., 181, 184, 197
Thompson, C. L., 100,
    124, 127n14, 180
Thoreson, A., 15
Thorndike, E. L., 181
Todd, P. E., 106
Treisman, P. U., 217
Tucker, J., 183
Turnbull, B. J., 191

Ueno, K., 179

Valdés, R., 190
Vallance, E., 212
van der Klaauw, W., 80
Vigdor, J. L., 95, 112, 224

Walsh, K., 16
Wayne, A. J., 110
Webb, N. M., 183
Weiss, I. R., 196
Wenger, E., 184, 187
Whipp, J. L., 17
Whitcomb, J. A., 17
White, B., 86
Whitehurst, G. J., 11, 226
Wilcox, D. D., 16
Wiliam, D., 190, 192

Wilkerson, J. R., 17
Will, G., 17
Willett, J. B., 85
Wilson, S. M., 8, 10–12, 15, 19
Wineburg, S., 241
Wittrock, M. C.,
        183–184, 199
Wolf, M. K., 197

Wolpin, K. I., 106
Wu, M., 11
Wyckoff, J., 43

Youngs, P., 10–12, 110

Zeichner, K. M., 8, 11, 224
Zeuli, J. S., 180

Subject Index

Achievement measures, limits of, 225–227
Assessment
  blurred boundaries of, 13 (table)
  samples currently used, 12 (figure)
  See also Teacher effectiveness; Teacher quality
Astaire, Fred, 235

Ball, Deborah, 4, 150–151, 153–154, 156, 228, 230, 235, 239
Baratz-Snowden, Joan, 229, 231n, 240
Barber, Benjamin, 176
Berliner, David, 1
Bersin, Alan, 4, 71, 74–76
Bok, Derek, 53
Bond, Lloyd, 3, 229, 241
Borko, Hilda, 95
Brown v. Board of Education, 214
Bush, George H. W., 206

CA TPA. *See* California Teaching Performance Assessment
Calfee, Bob, 240
California Commission on Teacher Credentialing (CCTC), 54, 60
California teacher preparation and credentialing system, 57 (table)
California Teaching Performance Assessment (CA TPA), 60, 63 (table)
CCTC. *See* California Commission on Teacher Credentialing
Ceteris paribus, 236

Charlotte's Web (White), 211
Chester, Mitchell, 151–152, 154, 156
Classroom context, 170 (figure)
Clinton, William Jefferson, 206
Cochran-Smith, Marilyn, 175
Commission on Excellence in Education, 206, 211, 215
Content knowledge, and teacher quality, 152–154
Corruptibility, 122–123
Costs of experience, 128n20
Credentials, teacher, 138
Cronbach, Lee, 239–241
Curriculum, surveys of enacted, 142 (figure)

Daly, Timothy, 4, 72, 75, 76
Darling-Hammond, Linda, 1, 3, 71, 73, 239, 241–242
Death at an Early Age (Kozol), 175
Discipline-based art education (DBAE), 216
Dwyer, Carol, 229, 235

Early Language and Literacy Classroom Observation (ELLCO), 140–141, 141 (figure)
Education
  challenges to professionalism in, 51–54
  nature of research in, 52
  reinvention of schools of, 52–53
  systems approach to, 133 (figure)
  unionism in, 53–54

Education production functions (EPF), 104–106

Education Trust, 31

Education Week, 176, 239

Educational research, scale of, 52

Educational Testing Service (ETS), 1

Effective teachers, VAM-P research on credentials of, 109–113

Effectiveness, methodological limits for determining, 227–230

ELLCO. *See* Early Language and Literacy Classroom Observation

Enacted curriculum, surveys of, 142 (figure)

EPF (Education production functions), 104–106

Freire, Paulo, 164

Frontal teaching, 162

Gain score model, 105

Garvin, David, 49, 53

Gaston, Margaret, 3

General Educational Development (GED), 45n

General Secondary Credentials, 210

Gitomer, Drew, 242

Goals 2000, 206, 207

Goals statutes, 132

Goodland, John, 169, 176

Gordon, Ed, 242

Gordon Rule, 242–243

Grading criteria, example, 193 (figure)

Green, Thomas, 160

Grist, exhibited in texts, 191

Grossman, Pam, 237, 239

Haberman, Martin, 175

Haertel, Ed, 239, 240

Hakuta, Kenji, 229

Harris, Douglas, 150, 152–155, 235–236

Harvard Educational Review, 215

Highly Qualified Teacher Provision, 2

Hill, Heather, 4, 150–151, 153–154, 156, 228, 235, 237

How to Succeed in School without Really Learning (Labaree), 122

Human capital management, elements of, in K-12, 134 (figure)

Instruction, measuring for teacher learning, 179–200

Instructional core, focus on, 58–59

Instructional Quality Assessment (IQA), 190, 192

Jaeger, Dick, 241

Johnson, Henry, 72

Julie of the Wolves (George), 192, 195

Kahlenberg, Richard, 53

Kaplan, Stanley, 241

Keeling, David, 4, 72, 75–76

Kelly, Jim, 1

Kennedy, John, 161

Klein, Joel, 44

Knowledge, teacher, 138–140

Kozol, Jonathan, 175

Ladson-Billings, Gloria, 5, 175, 228, 235–236, 240

Landgraf, Kurt, vii

Langemann, Ellen, 52

Lanier, Judith, 1

Learned, William, 242

Learning environment, 211–212

Learning system, professional, 198

Leinhardt, Gaea, 239

Littlefield, Val, 215

Loeb, Susanna, 237

Madeline Hunter Model, 183

Maniac Magee (Spinelli), 192, 193

Math Content Specialty Test, average scores, 42 (table)

Mathematical knowledge for teaching (MKT), 88–89, 91

Mathematical quality of instruction (MQI), 91, 94

Mathematics Academy Program, 139

Mathews, Jay, 71

Matsumura, Clare, 5, 228

Measurement
  context and, 223–231
  issues, 1–5
  See also Teacher effectiveness;
    Teacher quality
Measures, multiple, 104. *See also* Teacher
  quality measures
Mentoring Teachers Toward Excellence (Sato
  and Shulman), 241
Midgley, Mary, 160
Missed Opportunities (Levin and Quinn), 33, 34
MKT. *See* Mathematical knowledge for teaching
MQI. *See* Mathematical quality of instruction

Nation at Risk, A (Commission on
  Excellence in Education), 206, 211, 215
National Board for Professional Teaching
  Standards (NBPTS), 1–2, 112, 139, 145,
  162, 173, 216, 218
National Council for Accreditation of
  Teacher Education, 17
National Education Goals, 206
National Education Standards and
  Improvement Council, 206
National Evaluation Systems (NES), 10
National Mathematics Panel, 20
National Reading Panel, 16
National Research Council (NRC), 47
National Teacher Corps, 176
NBPTS. *See* National Board for Professional
  Teaching Standards
NCLB. *See* No Child Left Behind
New York City Teaching Fellows Program,
  33, 36, 41
New York Times, 43
No Child Left Behind (NCLB), 2, 10, 55,
  68n2, 100, 116, 138, 147, 152, 163, 176,
  207, 213

Olson, Lynn, 239
Opportunity to learn, 207
Opportunity to teach, 207, 209–214, 228

Pacheco, Arturo, 5, 228, 230, 235
PACT. *See* Performance Assessment for
  California Teachers
"Paradox of Teacher Assessment, The"
  (Shulman), 234

Pearlman, Mari, 75, 242
Pedagogy of poverty, 175
Pelton, Claire, 1
Performance Assessment for California
  Teachers (PACT), 60, 62 (table)
Philadelphia Teaching Fellows Program, 36
Policy validity
  conclusions about, 123–124
  evidence interpretation, 117–123
  introduction, 101–104
Policy variables, 172 (figure)
Pound, Ezra, 241
Poverty, school-level, relationship to value-
  added achievement, 144 (figure)
Practice-based professional development, 184
Praxis II tests, 10, 139
  sample questions, 140 (figure)
Praxis III, 140
Process-product paradigm, 200n2
Profession, hallmarks of, 48–51
Professional entry, 71–72
  measurement issues for, 74–76
Proxies, samples currently used, 12 (figure)

QUASAR research, 196

Reagan, Ronald, 206
Reductionism, 173
Response-to-literature assignment, example,
  193 (figure)
Rogers, Ginger, 235
Rose, Mike, 176
Rules statutes, 132

Sandy, Mary, 4, 71, 74, 76
Sarason, Seymour, 169
Sass, Tim, 105
Sato, Mistilina, 241
Scalability, multiple measures and, 156
Schilling, Steve, 237
Sentilles, Sarah, 211
Shanker, Albert, 53–54
Shepard, Lorrie, 179
Shulman, Judy, 241
Shulman, Lee, 1, 3, 5, 173
Siegfried, Karen, 17
Stable-unit-treatment-value assumption
  (SUTVA), 227–230

Stecher, Brian, 95
Stein, Mary Kay, 5, 228, 239
Stipek, Deborah, 52
Student achievement, and teacher education and experience, 111 (table)
Student learning, change in, 143–144
Student outcomes, and teacher qualities, 224–225
Student work
  expectations for quality of, 192–193
  sample of high quality, 194 (figure)
Students, contributions to teaching and learning, 166

Task, intellectual demands of, 191–192
TE (Teaching Event), 60
Teach for America (TFA), 9, 43
Teach, opportunity to, 206–221
Teacher Assessment Project, 239
Teacher certification, teacher quality and, 84
Teacher Corps program, 176
Teacher credentials, 138
Teacher education programs, outcomes, 19 (figure)
Teacher effectiveness
  approximations of, 131–148, 137 (figure)
  assessing, Ohio's approach, 138–147
  improving, 103
  measuring, levels of approximation, 135–137
  predicting, 102–103
  value-added modeling for accountability (VAM-A) research on, 113–117
  See also Teacher quality
Teacher Incentive Fund, 100
Teacher knowledge, 138–140
Teacher learning
  historical perspectives on, 181–187
  measures of instruction for, 187
  measuring instruction for, 179–200, 190–197
Teacher licensure tests, states using, 10 (table)
Teacher practice, 140–143
  measuring, 187–189
Teacher quality, 72–74
  alternative views of, 218–221
  approximations of, 131–148
  assessing, 138–147, 214–218
  California credentialing system and, 54–58
  challenges of assessing at entry, 15–22

conceptual challenges in assessment, 15–20
content knowledge and, 152–154
contextual complexity, examples of, 161–164
defining, 151–152
examining, 84–86
hiring for, at the district level, 30–45
improving assessment system for entry, 22–24
institutional challenges in assessment, 21–22
mapping the terrain of, 160–177
measures See Teacher quality measures
outcomes and, 18 (figure)
problem identification, 33–40
state context, 173
studies of, 239–241
variables that impact, 166–173
See also Teacher effectiveness
Teacher quality measures, 150–157
  challenges in assessment of, 20–21
  complexity of, 173–177
  costs of, 118–119
  current, 9–14
  for professional entry, 8–25
  functions of, 117–118, 118 (table)
  in practice, 80–96
  methodology, 198–200
  policy uses of, 99–124
  policy validity of, 99–124
  weight given to, 121 (table)
Teacher-student interactions, 164–166, 165 (figure), 167 (figure), 171 (figure)
Teachers
  contributions to teaching and learning, 165–166
  effective, VAM-P research on credentials of, 109–113
Teaching
  assessment, 1–5, 234–243
  curriculum and, 212–213
  evaluation, coherent system of, 65
  examining quality of, 86–95
  misaligned relationships, 186 (figure)
  suggested realignment of relationships, 188 (figure)
  of unfamiliar subject matter, 210–211
  views of, 182 (figure)
  See also Frontal teaching

Teaching Event (TE), 60
Teaching Fellows Program, 9
Teaching Performance Assessment (TPA), California, 59–65
Teaching Performance Expectations (TPE), 61
Testing, standardized, 213–214
TFA. *See* Teach for America
The New Teacher Project (TNTP), 31–33, 35–36, 40–44, 72, 75–76
Timpane, Michael, 2
TIMSS 1999 Video Study, 196
TNTP. *See* The New Teacher Project
Treisman, Uri, 217

Unintended Consequences (Levin, Mulhern, and Schunck), 33
Union of insufficiencies, 242, 243
Urbanski, Adam, 1

Validity, statistical and costs, 120 (table)
Value-added achievement gains, relationship to school-level poverty, 144 (figure)

Value-added modeling for accountability (VAM-A), 108–109
Value-added modeling for program evaluation (VAM-P), 108–109
Value-added modeling (VAM), 101, 154–156
Value-added models, 104–109, 237. *See also* Teacher quality measures
VAM. *See* Value-added modeling
VAM-A. *See* Value-added modeling for accountability
VAM-P. *See* Value-added modeling for program evaluation

Wasteland, The (Eliot), 241
White, E. B., 211
Williams v. State of California, 208
Wilson, Suzanne, 73, 74, 75, 77, 235, 239
Wineburg, Sam, 241
Wisdom of practice studies, 239

Zelman, Susan Tave, 151, 152, 154, 156

About the Contributors

Deborah Loewenberg Ball is dean of the School of Education and the William H. Payne Collegiate Professor of mathematics education and teacher education at the University of Michigan. Her work as a researcher and teacher educator is rooted in practice, drawing directly and indirectly on her experience as a classroom teacher. Her work focuses on studies of instruction and of the processes of learning to teach, efforts to improve teaching through policy reform initiatives, and teacher education.

Alan D. Bersin is chairman of the San Diego County Regional Airport Authority. He is also a member of the California State Board of Education. From July 2005 to December 2006, he served as California's secretary of education following a seven-year term as superintendent of public education in San Diego. Between 2000 and 2004, he also served as a member and then chairman of the California Commission on Teacher Credentialing. Bersin has also served as the U.S. Attorney for the Southern District of California and the U.S. Attorney General's Southwest Border Representative. He received his bachelor's degree from Harvard College in 1968 and his law degree from the Yale Law School in 1974. Bersin also attended Oxford University as a Rhodes Scholar.

Mitchell D. Chester began his tenure as Massachusetts Commissioner of Elementary and Secondary Education in May 2008. From 2001 through 2008, he worked for the Ohio Department of Education, where he was the second ranking educator. He served as the executive director for accountability and assessment for the School District of Philadelphia from 1997 through 2001. Prior to working in Philadelphia, he was chief of the Bureau of Curriculum and Instructional Programs of the Connecticut State Department of Education. He holds a doctorate in education from the Harvard Graduate School of Education.

Timothy Daly, president of The New Teacher Project (TNTP), manages its efforts to engage the wider educational community in the organization's work to close the achievement gap by increasing teacher quality. He previously served as TNTP's managing partner for multiple contracts, including the New York City Teaching Fellows program, the largest of TNTP's alternate certification programs, with approximately 8,000 active teachers in over 1,000 schools across New York City. Daly began his career in education as a middle school teacher in Baltimore. He holds a bachelor's degree in American studies from Northwestern University and a master's degree in teaching from Johns Hopkins University.

Drew H. Gitomer is a distinguished researcher and senior director of the Center for the Study of Teacher Assessment at Educational Testing Service (ETS). He is also coeditor of *Educational Evaluation and Policy Analysis*. His research interests include policy and evaluation issues related to teacher education, licensure, induction, and professional development. His recent studies have focused on enhancing the validity base for teacher licensure assessments as well as advanced certification of teacher assessments. Gitomer's research has also focused on the design of assessments, particularly those that support the improvement of instruction. He received his doctorate in cognitive psychology from the University of Pittsburgh.

Douglas N. Harris is an economist and assistant professor of educational policy studies at the University of Wisconsin at Madison. His research interests include teacher labor markets, cost-benefit analysis, accountability, achievement gaps, and college financial aid. He recently led a multidisciplinary group of scholars to organize the National Conference on Value-Added Modeling. Currently, he is leading a team of researchers in a $1 million project funded by the U.S. Department of Education to use value-added and other research methods to investigate various approaches to preparing and selecting teachers. In addition to his academic research, Harris is a consultant and advisor to policymakers and educational organizations such as the National Academy of Sciences, the National Council of State Legislatures, RAND, the U.S. Department of Education, and state education agencies.

Heather C. Hill is an associate professor at the Harvard Graduate School of Education. Her primary work focuses on developing measures of mathematical knowledge for teaching and using these measures to evaluate public policies and programs intended to improve teachers' understanding of mathematics. Her other interests include the measurement of instruction more broadly, instructional improvement efforts in mathematics, and the role that language plays in the implementation of public policy.

David Keeling is The New Teacher Project's (TNTP) director of communications. At TNTP he has overseen communications strategy and operations for the New York City Teaching Fellows program and advised TNTP sites and urban school districts on communicating teacher quality–related policies and initiatives. With Timothy Daly, he is coauthor of the organization's spring 2008 policy brief, *Mutual Benefits: New York City's Shift to Mutual Consent in Teacher Hiring.*

Gloria Ladson-Billings is the Kellner Family Professor of Urban Education in the Department of Curriculum and Instruction, and the faculty affiliate in the Department of Educational Policy Studies at the University of Wisconsin–Madison. She is a former president of the American Educational Research Association and a member of the National Academy of Education. Her research examines the pedagogical practices of teachers who are successful with African American students. She also investigates critical race theory applications to education.

Ida M. Lawrence is senior vice president of Educational Testing Service's (ETS) Research and Development Division and is responsible for the research, statistical analysis, and assessment development organizations of ETS. She began her career at ETS in the Statistical Analysis Division, where she designed and directed measurement work for the Preliminary Scholastic Aptitude Test/National Merit Scholarship Qualifying Test and the Scholastic Aptitude Test. Lawrence received a bachelor's degree in psychology from Barnard College and a master's and doctorate in educational psychology from New York University. Her areas of technical expertise include test equating and scaling, test design, and validity research.

Stephen Lazer, as vice president of assessment development at ETS, is responsible for managing almost 500 individuals who develop assessments and related materials. Before taking on this assignment, he served as executive director of the National Assessment of Educational Progress, also known as *The Nation's Report Card.* Lazer has served as a test developer as well as a program director at ETS. He has written about the results of national and international education surveys, and with John Mazzeo and Michael Zieky of ETS, he recently cowrote a chapter in the fourth edition of *Educational Measurement.*

Lindsay Clare Matsumura is an assistant professor in the University of Pittsburgh's newly created Learning Policy Center. Previously, she was a senior researcher at the National Center for Research on Education, Standards, and Student Testing at the University of California, Los Angeles (UCLA). She received a doctorate in psychological studies in education, with a concentration in psychocultural studies, from UCLA. Her research focuses on the implementation of urban school reform policies, professional learning, the relation of task quality and student learning, and developing measures of instructional quality. Matsumura is the principal investigator on the Institute of Education Sciences–funded study "Content-Focused Coaching for High Quality Reading Instruction."

Arturo Pacheco is El Paso Electric Professor of Educational Research at the University of Texas at El Paso (UTEP) and served as the dean of the College of Education from 1992 to 2002. Prior to that, he held positions at the University of California at Santa Cruz and Stanford University. As dean of the UTEP College of Education, he led his college in a complete restructuring of its teacher education program into a clinical field-based model. His coauthored book, *Centers of Pedagogy*, describes that work. In 2003, Pacheco was awarded the Pomeroy Award for Outstanding Contributions to Teacher Education by the American Association of Colleges for Teacher Education. He received his master's degree from San Francisco State University and his doctorate from Stanford University.

Mary Vixie Sandy is executive director of the Cooperative Research and Extension Services for Schools (CRESS) Center in the School of Education at the University of California, Davis. CRESS sponsors professional development, research, and evaluation services for teachers and schools, and fosters collaboration between university faculty and K–12 educators that is designed to support teacher development and student success. She has served as a policy consultant and manager with the California Department of Education, the California Postsecondary Education Commission, and the California Commission on Teacher Credentialing, and as the associate director of teacher education and public school programs for the California State University system.

Lee S. Shulman is the eighth president of the Carnegie Foundation for the Advancement of Teaching. He was the Charles E. Ducommun Professor of Education at Stanford University after being professor of educational psychology and medical education at Michigan State University. He is a past president of the American Educational Research Association and the National Academy of Education, a Guggenheim fellow, and a fellow of the American Academy of Arts and Sciences. Shulman's research investigates teaching and teacher education, assessment, the scholarship of teaching, and signature pedagogies in the professions. His Stanford University research team developed the National Board for Professional Teaching Standards assessment prototypes. He received the 2006 Grawemeyer Prize in Education for his book *The Wisdom of Practice*.

Mary Kay Stein holds a joint appointment as professor in the School of Education and senior scientist at the Learning Research and Development Center, both at the University of Pittsburgh. Over the past decade, her research has transitioned from focusing exclusively on classroom-based mathematics teaching and learning to seeking to understand how institutional, interpersonal, and policy contexts shape teachers' learning and practice. Her work has been published in the *Journal for Research in Mathematics Education, American Educational Research Journal, Teachers College Record, Urban Education,* and *Harvard Educational Review.* Stein is the lead author of a widely used casebook for mathematics professional development, *Implementing Standards-Based Mathematics Instruction,* and coauthor of a book on educational reform in San Diego, *Reform as Learning.*

Suzanne M. Wilson is currently chair of and professor in the Department of Teacher Education at Michigan State University. She was the first director of the Teacher Assessment Project, which developed prototype assessments for the National Board for Professional Teaching Standards. She collaborated on several large-scale projects, including the National Center for Research on Teacher Education and the Educational Policy and Practice Study. Wilson's current work concerns the development of measures of teaching and teachers' knowledge for teacher education and education research, as well as a study of jurisdictional battles over who should control teacher education and licensure.

Susan Tave Zelman has been superintendent of public instruction with the Ohio Department of Education since 1999. During those years, she has advanced Ohio's educational system from the middle of the pack in state rankings to seventh in 2008 in *Education Week*'s annual Quality Counts Report. Previously, she served as deputy commissioner of the Missouri Department of Elementary and Secondary Education, served as associate commissioner of the Department of Education Personnel in the Massachusetts Department of Education, and chaired the Department of Education at Emmanuel College in Boston. Gannett Newspapers named Zelman as one of the ten most powerful and influential women in Ohio state government. She holds a doctorate in education from the University of Michigan.